Identification and Price Guide

QUILTS

Other **CONFIDENT COLLECTOR** *Titles*
of Interest

FINE ART
IDENTIFICATION AND PRICE GUIDE
(2nd edition)
by Susan Theran

Avon Books are available at special quantity discounts for bulk purchases for sales promotions, premiums, fund raising or educational use. Special books, or book excerpts, can also be created to fit specific needs.

For details write or telephone the office of the Director of Special Markets, Avon Books, Dept. FP, 1350 Avenue of the Americas, New York, New York 10019, 1-800-238-0658.

Identification and Price Guide

QUILTS

FIRST EDITION

LIZ GREENBACKER & KATHLEEN BARACH

The CONFIDENT COLLECTOR™

AVON BOOKS · NEW YORK

If you purchased this book without a cover, you should be aware that this book is stolen property. It was reported as "unsold and destroyed" to the publisher, and neither the author nor the publisher has received any payment for this "stripped book."

THE CONFIDENT COLLECTOR: QUILTS IDENTIFICATION AND PRICE GUIDE (1st edition) is an original publication of Avon Books. This work has never before appeared in book form.

AVON BOOKS
A division of
The Hearst Corporation
1350 Avenue of the Americas
New York, New York 10019

Copyright © 1992 by Liz Greenbacker
Cover art courtesy of Telephoto
The Confident Collector and its logo are trademarked properties of Avon Books.
Interior design by Robin Arzt
Published by arrangement with the author
Library of Congress Catalog Card Number: 92-23814
ISBN: 0-380-76930-1

All rights reserved, which includes the right to reproduce this book or portions thereof in any form whatsoever except as provided by the U.S. Copyright Law. For information address Avon Books.

Library of Congress Cataloging in Publication Data:

Greenbacker, Liz.
    Quilts: Identification and price guide / Liz Greenbacker and Kathleen Barach.—1st ed.
        p. cm.—(The Confident Collector)
    Includes index.
    1. Quilts—Collectors and collecting—United States—Catalogs. I. Barach, Kathleen.
II. Title. III. Series.
NK9104.G74   1992   92-23814
746.9'7'0973075—dc20   CIP

First Avon Books Trade Printing: November 1992

AVON TRADEMARK REG. U.S. PAT. OFF. AND IN OTHER COUNTRIES, MARCA REGISTRADA, HECHO EN U.S.A.

Printed in the U.S.A.

OPM   10   9   8   7   6   5   4   3   2

For
Lynn, who should have had time to see all these quilts.
Jan, who should have had Time to see all these quilts.
Liz, who gave me the time to see them all.

—*Kathleen Barach*

To
Great-grandmother Campbell, whom I never met,
but still know because she stitched together
my beautiful Dresden Plate quilt,
and, to Kathy for keeping *me* stitched together.

—*Liz Greenbacker*

ACKNOWLEDGMENTS

Although many people helped with the information in this book, and many supported us in other ways, we are especially grateful for the time and efforts of these special people:

Connie Sprong, of the Quilt Loft, who arranged for us to see more quilts, at shows and elsewhere, and provided more photo opportunities than we could have imagined.

James Carroll and Diane Reese, also of the Quilt Loft, whose information was invaluable.

Margaret Cavigga, of the Margaret Cavigga Quilt Collection

Ginnie Christie, of Ginnie Christie Quilts

Laura Fisher, of Laura Fisher/Antique Quilts & Americana

Susan Parrish, of Susan Parrish Antiques

Gloria White, of Rocky Mountain Quilts

Larry Zingale, of Warwick Valley Antiques

Ann Spagnola Argenio, quilt artist

Michael James, quilt artist

Special thanks to Dorothy Harris, our creative, insightful and, most of all, kind editor whose support and encouragement was invaluable.

And Karen Shapiro: efficient, professional, and fun—who turned editing a manuscript into pure enjoyment. Also, everyone else at Avon Books, the best, brightest, and most efficient staff any writer could want.

Finally, our thanks to the "Duchess" for the use of the hall!

CONTENTS

❖

Collecting
Quilts

INTRODUCTION:
WHY COLLECT QUILTS?

❖

There are as many reasons to collect quilts as there are quilts. Each quilt is unique and each one that survives today was once someone's treasure. Tactile and visual, the charm of quilt collecting is that these treasures of the past are also today's treasures. A collection begins the first time you fall in love with a quilt.

You'll probably buy your first quilt for decorative or emotional reasons. There, hanging in an antiques store, at a flea market, or in a quilt shop, is *the* quilt in just the right colors to match your bedroom, living room, or den. Using quilts for decoration is as old as quilting itself and as new as the most recent issue of *Better Homes and Gardens* or *Architectural Digest*. Quilts, with their bold or soft colors, geometric or curved patchwork, complement any decor from Colonial to Victorian to Modern, and any setting from farmhouse to mansion to corporate office.

Even if it isn't the right color scheme, something about a quilt may speak to your heart. Whether it's the pattern or pattern name; exquisite workmanship; the history of the quilt; or the story of the woman who made it, something makes it impossible for you *not* to buy it. The first quilts in most collections were purchased simply because the buyer fell in love with them—which, according to some collectors, is still the only reason to buy a quilt.

Falling in love may explain the first quilt purchased, but what compels collectors to keep buying? Quilt collecting, like most collecting, can be termed a compulsion. The first acquisition leads to many others, and the search for the best and the brightest demands delving into history, technology, technique, and art so that the collector gains an extensive knowledge of quilt lore that is as valuable as the quilts themselves. The first quilt might match your living room, but the second, third, fourth, or hundredth is bought for other reasons. Two collectors told us they bought quilts because they love everything about textiles: the history of cloth, clothing, and decorative textiles; the history of dyes and dyeing; everything about how textiles were, and are, used. Another collector narrowed down her selections by buying only quilts, tops, or blocks signed or dated by the maker.

After you're hooked on quilt collecting, one reason to continue collecting is that quilts tell us stories of our country, our families, and the women who made them. Quilts, as we know them today, are uniquely American. Quilting is far older than our country, and undoubtedly the women who crossed the Atlantic brought quilting skills and techniques with them, but it was the American quiltmaker who improved quilt design, created intricate and deceptively simple designs of geometric piecing or appliqué. It was here that quilts were raised to art. While they improved, created, and elevated them, American quiltmakers documented much of our history.

There were quilts made to commemorate the Centennial of our nation's birth, to re-create in fabric the Lincoln-Douglas debates, and to honor First Ladies. There is even one that was created for the Nixon resignation. An an-

The pinwheels on the Flying Dutchman variation quilt are shades of blue stripes, gray prints, yellow prints, and gold solids. The border and sets are orange. A very graphic look. The quilt, made in the 1940s, shows excellent assembly and straight-line quilting.
Quilt courtesy of Brian Comstock

tique quilt show held in 1992 at the New England Quilt Museum consisted solely of quilts focusing on presidents, presidential candidates, and campaign issues, with one quilt dating from the late 1700s. There is a quilt block for the Women's Christian Temperance Union and a quilt using the initials and symbol of the National Recovery Act. The California Heritage Quilt Project found a quilt that had been pieced in a wagon train bound for California.

Historic quilts are not confined to the telling of our nation's past. There are many quilts, unsigned, undated, that commemorate family events. Weddings, births, even deaths, were occasions to create quilts from the fabrics used in the bridal gowns, the christening outfits and baby clothes, and the clothes of the deceased.

Quilts have always been prized possessions—at least those known as "best quilts." Few, if any, functional quilts survive today because their very functionality wore them out. The quilts that survive are those that were special then as well as now. Friendship quilts, given to families moving westward, were highly prized by the recipients. They knew they'd never see their friends and family in the old hometown again. To reminisce, to return if only for a few moments, the recipient had only to unpack the lovingly made souvenir, read the blocks, caress the cloth, and she was home again. To the pioneer, making quilts was a special challenge. The lack of material, time, light, and energy point out that these quilts must have been of great importance to the people who made them. During the Civil War quilts were looted from homes. The soldier with a quilt had a blanket, a cushion, a raincoat—and a knapsack for other, more breakable, loot. Soldiers also knew to slit the fabrics and search for money, which was sometimes stuffed inside a quilt because quilts were supposedly safe from marauders. Families of the westward migration also stuffed their money inside a quilt for safety.

"Quilts are, in sum, incomparable documentary artifacts that reflect the time during which they were made as well as revealing much about the makers themselves," wrote Jean Ray Laury in *Ho for California!* Quilts as historical documents, revealing both our history and the inner sense of beauty of the makers, may be the oldest form of American memorabilia; older even than Paul Revere's silver and pewter, older than the Hitchcock chair. (See chapter 2 for a discussion of the long history of quilting.)

Unraveling the history of a quilt is another reason to collect. At a quilt show held at Center Congregational Church in Meriden, Connecticut, several old hexagonal blocks pieced of triangles were brought in for identification. Even some of the individual triangles in the blocks, from fabric of warm brown prints indicative of the late 1800s, were carefully pieced; the prints matched so well that the seams were almost invisible. The owner didn't know the pattern. Neither did anyone else. But we unraveled this mystery! Through our research we discovered that those elongated hexagons were the basic block pattern for an Ocean Waves quilt. It was a thrill to solve that puzzle!

Even more exciting, and something most quilt collectors dream of, is the search of Jenny Spees of Illinois. In a recent issue of *Quilt* (Fall 1991), Jenny wrote the Quilt Detective about a set of twelve blocks she purchased at a flea market in Missouri. The blocks were intended for a friendship quilt as each was made and signed by a different woman. The dealer Jenny bought the blocks from remembered buying them from an estate sale. To start her search, Jenny listed the blockmakers' names in her letter. She also sent a letter listing the names to the *St. Louis Post-Dispatch*. Although she hasn't gotten any answers, Jenny isn't giving up her search. She'd hoped to find descendants of the original quiltmakers to offer back the squares. For now, Jenny plans to go ahead and have the blocks set together and finish the quilt. What a great start to a collection!

Historical documentation isn't the only reason to collect quilts. Sheer admiration for the textiles, workmanship, pattern, and color balance are also strong draws toward quilts. We can only marvel at the time, care, and sacrifice that went into each and every antique quilt on the market today. What better way to collect samples of the history of textile design and quality than to do it with quilts? Some workmanship is excellent, whether it was done by women with no formal training in design, drafting, or geometry who nevertheless produced geometrically precise piecing for such complicated designs as stars or Compass Rose quilts, or by women who used predesigned, even precut, quilt kits to make their creations.

Patterns and assembly styles have histories of their own, from the simple one-patch designs such as the hexagon to the ornately decorated stitching of a crazy quilt to the complex appliqué of a Baltimore Album quilt. The use of color over the four centuries we've been making quilts is astounding. With no art training, using an eye developed only by instinct and emotional response, and, at times throughout our history, little choice as to color because of the unavailability of manufactured dyes or materials for homemade dyes, quilt-makers startle, amuse, awe, and amaze us with their color sense.

"Handicrafts represent a particularly rewarding area of investigation, for the needle became the most common means of creating the ornamentation that reconciled utility and art," wrote Jean Ray Laury in *Ho for California!* "No craft achieved this union more successfully than the uniquely indigenous American art form, the quilt."

These Ocean Waves blocks were made in the 1880s and are true scrap bag pieces incorporating numerous colors and printed fabrics. They will make a stunning quilt when assembled.
Quilt courtesy of Miriam Zimmer

Some quilts were made by men. But the fact that most were made by women leads us to another reason to collect quilts: they are one of the few, if not the only, antique collectible made predominantly by women. In an article for *Architectural Digest* (June 1990) Meryl Gordon quotes Kay Kopp, owner of America Hurrah!, a quilt shop in Manhattan:

"You begin to read the lives of the women by looking at their work. There's a soul to the quilts." The soul of every quilt is the woman who made it, whether she signed it, dated it, or left its origin a mystery by doing neither. In fact, most women didn't sign or date their quilts, leaving us to marvel at what we can see: their innate design sense, use of color, selection and assembly of pattern, and workmanship. These ancestors put into their quilts what they

This Pine Tree variation is done in a lovely green-and-gold paisley fabric on a white ground. Made in North Carolina in the early 1900s, its simple border and classic block arrangement create an elegant look.
Quilt courtesy of Cindie Freeman

were too shy or reserved to speak aloud: memories, aspirations, ambitions, love. Included in every quilt, if we look for it, are clues to the maker's past. Those clues can be as obvious as the lambs, pansies, shooting stars, or feather and blanket stitching of a silk or velvet crazy quilt. Those are clues that tell us what was important in her life and that she had more leisure, and probably more money, than other women. A two-color quilt can be a clue to a more prosperous family or it can mean that only those two fabrics were available to a pioneer woman. Even workmanship, both bad and good, gives us clues to a quiltmaker. Was she trying out a fad, therefore inexperienced with the technique? Is the workmanship inferior because it was her first quilt? We can only imagine the hours that went into an elaborately pieced or appliquéd quilt, with its thousands of tiny, closely placed stitches. Was that superior workmanship accomplished because the quilt's creator had more time to devote to it than other quiltmakers? Or was it simply due to perseverance and the pursuit of perfection? To our modern eyes a quilt is either well done or inferior, pretty or ugly.

But to the now anonymous maker, each quilt represented her best attempt to create something beautiful out of something useful. A quiltmaker's sense of pride is evident in the few photos that survive of pioneer women sitting proudly in their small rooms with a quilt either finished or in progress on their laps. The fact that a woman chose her quilt to be the single prized possession to be photographed with her tells us a great deal about her pride in that quilt.

Whether a quilt is exceptional or, to our eyes, average, there's a warming of the soul that occurs when we view the work of a woman and know that the quilt, whatever its quality by today's standards, was designed and made for a special purpose in her life—even if that purpose was known only to her and is now buried with her. Though she may be gone, her quilt remains. There, in our hands, on our bed, on our wall, is a connection to that unknown woman that affirms and confirms her existence perhaps more than all the biographies, awards, and commendations that adorn the history of women. For quilts are not only documents of history, they were first documents of love: love of country, love of family, and even love of self. No stronger link with feminine past can be made than to own the anonymous outpouring of love a quilt represents. Thus, with a quilt, we warm ourselves twice. Once with the physical radiance, touch, and feel of the quilt around us, and then again caught in the romance of all the maker's mysteries.

Quilts, unlike other art, are tactile. They invite and allow us to touch them. We can wrap up in them, sleep under them, hang them on a wall, and touch them to our heart's content. Who would carefully caress between their fingers a Rembrandt or snuggle with a marble statue? But, because quilts were made by women to be touched, caressed, viewed, each is a tactile work of art both beautiful and functional.

We can collect quilts because they are art. Even if art is defined, as Jonathan Holstein states in *The Pieced Quilt: An American Design Tradition* (Galahad Books, 1973), as art only when the maker *knows* she's making art, quilts fit the definition. Even if we have a looser definition of art, one that defines it as anything of impact, beauty, uniqueness, and soul, then quilts are art. We disagree, wholeheartedly, with this statement from Holstein: "The women who made pieced quilts were not 'artists,' that is, they did not intend to make art. . . ." We maintain that any antique quilt that survives to this day is art because it was knowingly made to commemorate, to add beauty, and to last. Why else would the generations after the maker have saved them so carefully? The quilts that survive today are art and that was their function when they were made. Otherwise, they would have been worn out—used for a saddle blanket, as a door for a chicken coop, in a dog's bed, for privacy across the outhouse

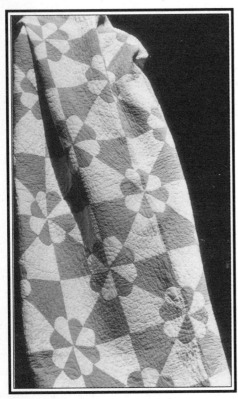

Beautiful concentric circle, feathered wreath, and grid quilting set off the Borrow and Return pattern of this 1928 quilt, which was made by a nineteen-year-old woman. The colors are bright pink and white, which have lost little with minimal use.

door, or to replace a shutter in a barn—like the myriad of functional quilts made over the centuries. The quilts that survive today are art because they were made to be handed down from family to family, made to be treasured with painstaking care. Whatever we think of their design and color choices today, quiltmakers made best quilts their art. Hence, both our definitions of art are satisfied: the antique quilts we collect today were consciously made to be beautiful, not just functional.

Quilts are also one of the few collectibles that include contemporary work as well as antique. Such quilt artists as Michael James, Faith Ringgold, and Jean Ray Laury transform traditional quilting forms into art that does match Holstein's definition and make contemporary quilts as collectible as antiques. Contemporary quiltmakers adding their own personalities to traditional quilt styles and patterns, such as Judy Wasserman Hearst, Jinny Beyer, and Barbara Moll, are also highly collectible.

The final reason to collect quilts is the same as the first. Putting all historical, intellectual, and artistic implications aside, ultimately you will collect your quilts because of their unique emotional impact, because something in them touches your eye, heart, and mind.

"I look for quilts that make me laugh," said James Carroll, quilt collector and maker. "Never buy a quilt for an investment. Quilts were made to enjoy and use. A quilt is worth any price if you love it!"

We researched over forty books and as many articles, and we interviewed collectors, dealers, and quiltmakers from all over the country to write this book. Although no single book can give you all the information you need to find your way in the world of quilt collecting and history, this one is guaranteed to get you started. Browse through the price listings, read the chapters, and use the bibliography and source listings in the back to start your own quilt-collecting journey.

Enjoy!

Identification and Price Guide

QUILTS

CHAPTER ONE
HOW TO START A COLLECTION

◆

Quilts are so closely connected to family life and lore that your relatives are your best contacts if you want to start a quilt collection. There is probably at least one quilt already in your family, even if it's the one owned by your aged second cousin twice removed and was made two or three generations ago. Even if no one has quilted since, if your childhood memories include images of Grandmother, Great-aunt, even Grandfather, stitching one square to another or appliquéing scraps on a ground fabric to form a flower or an animal, you know there's a quilt or two somewhere in the family. Let your whole family know you're interested in owning those quilts.

The problem in this approach is that other members of your family may also want them. Work out an equitable division if you can— one that doesn't include ripping the quilt down the middle! (We heard one story about two sisters who couldn't agree who should own their grandmother's sampler quilt, made in the early 1800s. In desperation—and, one assumes, sheer frustration— one sister finally cut the quilt, kept half, and sent the other half to her sister. Quilt collectors all over the world are still shuddering over the loss of that quilt.) Relinquish your claim to the family quilt before you allow it to be cut into pieces.

All too often, as the scores of quilts in the hands of dealers testify, no one in the family really wants that antique quilt. We heard many stories about quilts found in old trunks in attics, barns, and garages, the owners unaware of their value, their history, even their existence. As tastes changed, or opinions of Grandmother's workmanship changed, quilts were relegated to storage chests. No one wanted them, but no one was willing to throw them out either. This cavalier treatment of family history has created the supply of quilts available to us today. Don't let that happen in your family. Ask if anyone has a quilt that isn't wanted. Ask your relatives to search through those unopened-for-decades trunks, boxes, and barrels.

The California Quilt Heritage Project documented 3,300 antique quilts in California alone, all in the hands of descendants of the makers or private collectors. More than half of the states completed their own Quilt Projects, and the number of quilts retained as family heirlooms is astounding. But as the

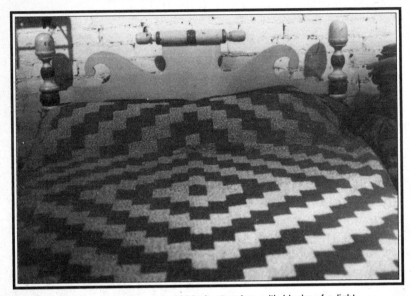

This Zigzag pattern from the early 1900s is stunning, with blocks of a light blue on white print alternating with red blocks. A very country look.

number of generations increases between the original maker and the current owner, these quilts become candidates for sale. The story of the quilt may be lost. The current generation may have no interest in keeping a quilt it doesn't view as particularly pretty or well done. A family line may simply die out because there are no heirs and the quilt goes to the highest bidder at an estate auction. By telling everyone in your family that you're interested, you can reap the benefits of their disinterest and become the proud owner of an antique quilt with real meaning—a blood tie. Despite its orange-and-purple color combination, despite its mismatched points or long quilting stitches, the family quilt will be the most prized of your collection.

Don't confine yourself to completed family quilts. Works in progress which you can finish yourself or commission a quilter to finish, are also gratifying because of the familial tie. If your relatives are relieved to empty that trunk of its old quilts, imagine how happy they'll be to get rid of that box filled with miscellaneous odds and ends of fabric they couldn't bring themselves to throw away. Unfinished tops and squares made by an ancestor are glorious finds because you become part of a multigenerational quilt project. Liz Greenbacker, one of the authors of this book, has already completed and quilted three tops found in two different attics. One, a basket quilt, was probably started by her grandmother-in-law. The sashings were added by her mother-in-law and Liz completed the borders and quilting. The other two were both tumbler quilt tops owned by Greenbacker cousins, made by their grandmother, and found during renovations of the ancestral farmhouse. All three are now prized possessions of the makers' daughters and granddaughters.

Don't pass up that box of old clothes or fabrics either! You may need it to authentically complete the top you found in a trunk or purchased from a dealer (see chapter 6). Greenbacker's scrap bag includes family fabrics that date from the late 1940s. She uses them to repair and complete quilts and make new family heirlooms.

Once you own that family quilt, you'll want to document it as best you can. Ask the current owners to tell you anything they know about the quilt, including the maker's full name, when the quilt was made, the pattern name, and any stories connected with it. If it's a quilt you remember, write down your memories. If there are any family Bibles, histories, or letters, check through them to get more information about the maker or her descendants and ancestors. If all you have is a name, try to find the cemetery where the maker is buried and copy the information on the tombstone. Or check with the church the maker belonged to; its pastor may be able to supply you with dates of birth and death or even anecdotes.

With the dates in hand, you can check newspaper morgues to find the maker's obituary and maybe even the birth announcement. In those articles you'll find either names of descendants or parents' names, more information to help you track the maker down through family Bibles and histories. Researching a family quilt also starts you on your family's genealogy!

Next, carefully check the quilt and note the colors, print patterns, and type of fabric; the pattern; the style of assembly; and the quality of the workmanship. These are clues to the age of the quilt, as we'll see in chapter 3. Also note the condition of the quilt. Are there any worn spots? Is the binding frayed? Are there any stains or color loss? Has it been washed or do the quilting lines still show on the fabric? Keep a careful record of this information. You'll need it to document the age of the quilt, to properly repair and clean it, and to satisfy your own curiosity. Each quilt you add to your collection, whether it's a family heirloom or purchased, should be documented the same way. Keep a notebook, file, or scrapbook solely for your quilts. Pictured on page 5 is a modified version of the form we used to find the over eight hundred quilts and prices listed in this book. It lists all the important information you need, or want, about each quilt in your collection.

Even while you're notifying family members that you'd like to own now or inherit the family quilts, you're probably attending quilt shows, going to shops and dealers, and watching for quilts at fairs, flea markets, and tag sales. As you do this, notice if your eye gravitates to a certain type of quilt. Once you've exhausted the quilt sources in your family, you'll have to start buying to add to your collection, and at some point that means you'll specialize. You'll find that you prefer piecework over appliqué, or Victorian-era crazy quilts over the simpler, less elaborate crazy quilts of the early 1900s. Maybe you prefer to collect only Log Cabin quilts, or only Sunbonnet Sues. You might even pick a certain time period, say the miniatures period of the late 1800s through the 1940s, during which some quilts were made with tens of thousands of tiny pieces. Maybe you'll specialize in exquisite workmanship, preferring only those quilts with stitches ten or more to the inch or without a single point mismatched. You might even specialize by collecting quilts of predominantly one color. One collection, owned by collectors Paul Pilgrim and Gerald Roy, shown at the Museum of the American Quilter's Society in Paducah, Kentucky, featured forty antique quilts using orange fabric. You might decide to collect only signed and dated quilts or quilts whose maker and history are known. Or you might specialize in commemorative, political, or social statement quilts. The possibilities for specialization are endless. Only by seeing what's available in the marketplace can you decide which quilts you want. Deciding on a specialization may take years, but the hunt is so enjoyable you shouldn't mind waiting to make up your mind.

One way to enjoy the hunt is to attend as many quilt shows and fairs as you can. Even shows of contemporary quilts can help you decide what you want to collect while increasing your store of knowledge about quilts and quilt history. Quilt shows abound, and experts are always eager to talk about their specialty. Show quilts are usually better documented because they're loaned by the owners. Because many of these loaned quilts are family heirlooms, the owners know when they were made. Take notes on these quilts. We'll talk later about using those notes to do your own dating.

So far we've talked about being your own quilt picker. Pickers are the folks who scour the countryside looking for quilts to sell to dealers who, in turn, sell to you. The only other step a picker takes to find quilts that we haven't discussed is knocking on doors to ask families if they have quilts they want to sell. Sandy Mitchell, a quilt picker in the Midwest, estimates that in the 1970s she purchased a thousand quilts a year to sell to dealers in Houston, Paris, New York City, and California. She made the rounds of flea markets, antiques shows, and door-to-door appointments with families to find each of those quilts.

```
                                          Quilt Code/Number: _____ _____

                    QUILT INFORMATION FORM

TECHNIQUE:  Patchwork _____  Appliqué _____  Trapunto _____  Reverse Appliqué _____
PATTERN: _____ PRICE: _____
PREDOMINANT COLOR: _____ SIZE: _____
STYLE:  Scrap bag _____    Coordinated _____    Number of Fabric Patterns _____
FEATURES:  (Border, flowers in basket, appliqué on patchwork, etc.)_____
_____
_____

AGE: _____  HISTORY/MAKER: _____
QUILTED HOW:  Hand _____   Tide _____    Machine _____
CONDITION:  (per source) Excellent _____   Good _____  Fair _____  Poor _____
   Torn/worn top _____   Torn/worn back _____   Torn/worn binding _____
   Repairs _____  Faded _____  Stains _____  Other _____
_____

WORKMANSHIP: (per source)  Excellent _____   Good _____  Fair _____  Poor _____
   Small even stitches _____  Stitches per inch _____  Uniform length _____
   Can't see appliqué stitches _____  Points/junctions match _____
   Other _____
GENERAL COMMENTS: _____
_____
_____

PHOTO AVAILABLE: _____
★★★★★★★★★★★★★★★★★★★★★★★★★★★★★★★★★★★★★★★★★★★★★★★★★★★★★★★★★★★

SOURCE NAME: _____  DATE: _____
LOCATION: _____
```

Sample quilt documentation form.

You can be your own picker if you have the nerve and the time. Many pickers also started as collectors. Picking means a lot of traveling. If the thought of thirty phone calls or visits to find one quilt doesn't bother you, try it. But pickers are professionals at what they do. They know patterns, workmanship, quality, condition, and price. Until you're well educated on those aspects of quilt collecting, don't rush into the job. It is one way to educate yourself about quilts, but the education could be costly if you don't acquire the quilts the dealers and collectors want. Most quilt pickers work part-time. Relatively few do it full-time, year-round.

After finding quilts yourself from either your family or friends, your next step toward building a collection is to establish a relationship with a reputable quilt dealer. Quilt dealers should not be confused with quilt shops. Shops usually offer supplies and fabrics for contemporary quiltmakers, or new quilts either commissioned by the shop or taken in to sell on consignment. Quilt dealers specialize in antique quilts, tops, blocks, fabrics, and sometimes quilting ephemera: tools, sewing cases, machines, books. You should find a quilt dealer with a good reputation who is knowledgeable about quilts and has been involved as either a dealer or collector for more than five years. We've listed dozens of these dealers in Sources and Resources, starting on page 291.

You need to trust your quilt dealer, and that requires asking questions. You should ask how the dealer acquires quilts. You want a dealer with a wide network of pickers, or other dealers, so you know there is possible contact with a large supply of quilts. Does this dealer do, or have contact with someone who does, quilt repair? What's the dealer's policy on letting the customer know that a quilt has been repaired?

"You can do anything you want to a quilt," said Connie Sprong, part owner of the Quilt Loft, an antique quilt store in Groton, Massachusetts, "as long as you tell the customer you did it." On most quilts, the binding is the first spot to wear because, when in use on a bed, it may drag or rest on the floor. Ideally, quilts should be in original condition, but a badly worn binding may devalue a quilt more than putting on a new binding. The important point to remember is whether your dealer will admit to repairing a quilt. A dealer who passes off a repaired quilt as an original would be, in our opinion, untrustworthy.

A relationship with a dealer becomes more important as you start to specialize your collection, and it's essential if you are not confident of your own ability to recognize and date an antique quilt. Because they have a wider area, and greater number, of contacts across the country, quilt dealers are more likely to find you the quilt you want faster and cheaper than you can yourself. Along with their knowledge of quilts, quilting, and quilt history, dealers know the marketplace for price and availability of quilts better than the nonspecialized antique dealer, who might have just a few quilts in stock along with a myriad of other Americana memorabilia. As a specialist, focused on quilts, the quilt dealer can be your best source for additions to your collection.

For the price guide portion of this book, we assembled a list of quilts with descriptions and prices. Many of these were beautiful, excellently made, and in great condition. But the quilts on hand in the quilt dealers' inventories were not the best quilts they found for sale. Just stopping in a quilt dealer's store isn't enough. Not every quilt on the market ends up in a showroom. In fact, the really good ones are scoffed up before they get to the store.

"Quilts sell the most in the spring," said James Carroll of The Quilt Loft. "What's left in the store is not the best of the bunch. We're constantly looking for quilts for our best customers. They tell us what they're looking for and if we find it, we send it directly to them."

"We know our customers very well," said Sprong. "If I see a quilt I know someone will like, I'm more apt to buy it on speculation because I'm pretty sure a customer I trust will buy it." Therefore, building a relationship with a quilt dealer means you'll get first pick on the type of quilts you want.

Once you've established a relationship with a quilt dealer you'll want to arrange a method of viewing the quilts. It isn't necessary to have a quilt dealer close by because most dealers are happy to send you a photograph of the quilt along with its story. If you've established with the dealer that you are very serious about quilts, and have good credit (which you'll probably have to establish by paying before delivery several times), dealers will send you quilts to view in your home or office. Usually they're mailed, sometimes shipped, always insured, and not a single dealer we spoke to complained of losing one. Of course, seeing and holding the quilt in your hands is a much better way to evaluate the quilt than looking at a photograph.

Be specific with your quilt dealer. List your preferences for size, condition, workmanship, or pattern name. Also list your exceptions. A truly magnificent crazy quilt not in the best condition might be acceptable to you. If you don't tell the dealer that, you might miss the one quilt you really want because the dealer stuck to your list of ideal specifications.

It might appear that a quilt dealer is the last place you should contact looking for quilts. Wouldn't flea markets, antiques shows, and auctions be better? They might be, if—and it's a big if—YOU know everything you need to know about quilts to spot a fake or confirm the date of a quilt. Dating a quilt, as we'll see, is tricky. The history of textiles, dyes and dyeing, styles of quilting, and patterns is complex. When did cotton quilts become the norm? When was a lavender dye perfected? Which is older: the Victorian crazy quilt or the miniaturized Postage Stamp quilt? Can you tell the difference between silk and satin? Is the batting cotton, wool, or polyester? Is that really old fabric or has it been tea-dyed to look old? Can you tell if that funny brown fabric was originally brown or was it a green that faded to that color with age?

"Determining the age of a quilt is a matter of finding enough reliable clues in the quilt to build a case for a date," wrote Barbara Brackman in her book *Clues in the Calico* (EPM Publications, Inc., 1989). "Even knowing something as specific as the date a pattern was published or a scrap of fabric printed cannot tell you exactly when the quilt was made." In the past, just as today, many quilts were made from scrap bag fabrics. Bits and pieces of cloth left after making clothing, still-good pieces of fabric cut from old clothing, fabric from the last quilt made, all went into the quiltmaker's scrap bag then as they do now. A scrap bag like Liz's, dating from the 1940s, can contain fabric from many generations accumulated over many decades. One piece of 1960s fabric in a quilt dates it to that time period unless you know the piece was used only to repair the quilt and isn't part of the original work.

You have to be a combination detective and scholar to learn how to date quilts. Before you can go off completely on your own to the nonspecialized antique quilt sources, you need to know as much as you can about the history of quilts and textiles. To start your education, read the next two chapters. We've included a brief history of quilting and the strongest dating clues we found in our research. At the back of the book is a bibliography, and that list can get you well on your way to being quilt-literate.

We suggest that as you attend shows and fairs you jot down notes on quilts that have been dated. Of course, the only time we can be absolutely certain of a quilt's date is when the quilt was signed and dated by the maker. Take down all the information and clues on those quilts. These notes should include colors used, types of fabric, pattern names, quilting patterns, the backing fabric, and the batting material if known.

Carry graph paper to jot down a block pattern you never saw before. Quilt block names number in the thousands, and the same block can have many different names. When you come across one you don't recognize, graph it out and add it to your files.

Start a fabric file by collecting fabrics, often offered by quilt dealers, that are dyed in the same colors but are of different ages. Eventually you'll have samples that graphically show how the color red, or green, or brown, has changed over the years. These samples will also show how fabric ages. As we'll see in the chapter on dating, some dyes made certain fabric deteriorate faster than other fabrics in the same quilt. Some dyes faded quickly and some lasted, as vibrant as new, for decades.

Don't limit yourself to quilt shows and fairs. Go to museums, too. Museums go to great lengths to date their acquisitions as closely as possible. Take the same notes, paying special attention to any exceptional features of the quilt noted in program books or on signs. These notes, from shows and museums, along with your reading, form a reference file you can refer to when dating quilts you want to purchase or when checking the accuracy of a quilt already assigned a date.

Complete your quilt education by attending more shows and going to more museums. This time, however, appraise the date, workmanship, and condition of the quilt before you read any signs, program books, or ask the owner. Once you've settled on a date, check your results with the program book or owner. If your date agrees with the assigned date, all your work and study has paid off! Your education isn't complete, it never will be, but at least you know you're on the right track.

"Trust your judgment," wrote Brackman. "There are many mistakes in print and more than a few exaggerations in family stories. An appraiser has good visual discrimination skills and good visual memories."

If it all seems like a lot of work it's only because you've just begun. The quilt quest is fascinating, and as you journey along you won't notice that you're working—it'll all seem like fun! Educating yourself also insures that you won't get stuck with a quilt that's been misrepresented, which is why we suggest that in your search for quilts to add to your collection you go first to a dealer—until you know what to look for in evaluating a quilt yourself. Now you're ready to be a quilt picker and scour the nonspecialized antiques shops, flea markets, and auctions on your own. Because these suppliers are antiques generalists, not quilt specialists, they're more easily misled about the real age and condition of a quilt. You have to be the expert, the picker, to find the bargain.

Find flea markets, tag sales, and antiques shows by reading your local papers or by reading a regional newsletter, newspaper, or magazine that lists them. Get familiar with the antiques magazines available. Many list upcoming shows and events. Find quilt dealers by checking the yellow pages in phone books. Most libraries have phone books for at least the capital cities of each state. When checking the yellow pages, be careful. Names listed under "Quilts" may often be general antiques stores that happen to carry a few quilts. Call first so you don't waste a trip.

Go to these sources with some idea of what you want or just to look, to add to your store of knowledge. When you find a quilt that you want, always ask the dealer if there's any story behind it or anything else known about that quilt. It's up to you, and the dealer, whether you'll haggle over the price. Some dealers simply won't negotiate on price, while others enjoy dickering so much you're almost cheating them out of half their fun if you simply hand over the money. In either case, it never hurts to ask if the price is firm or if you can negotiate.

There are slews of stories about quilts found at tag and garage sales for paltry sums like five dollars. This probably doesn't happen as much as the folklore implies, but it does happen. One tip on attending tag sales is to read the ads closely. Those that say they're emptying a house or an estate should probably be first on your list. You're more likely to find a quilt no one wants at a sale of that type than you are at one where a family merely cleaned out its closets and is taking a chance on getting some money for the detritus. Here you can dicker on the price if you want. People expect to negotiate prices at these owner-run clearinghouse sales.

It's at a flea market, antiques show, tag sale, or garage sale that you, as your own picker, may discover the quilt mother lode, as Jenny Spees did when she bought her twelve friendship quilt squares. Instead of seeing twelve unfinished blocks and the prospect of more work, Jenny saw the opportunity to own a piece of history, to become an amateur detective on the trail of the twelve women who made the blocks, and to possibly restore the blocks to descendants of one of the original makers. Jenny saw possibilities because she knew the value of the squares when she saw them. Like Jenny, this is where your quilt education reaps benefits.

The place where you'll really need all your education is at an auction or estate sale. An auction can be exciting and stimulating, also overwhelming and intimidating. Unless you're an expert and can set a realistic price for a particular quilt and stick to it, you're better off saving auctions for entertainment only and buying your quilts elsewhere. Should you decide to venture into this arena, however, there are some things you should know.

Quilts are sold at various types of auctions, from those exclusively for quilts, to auctions that include a variety of related and unrelated items, to estate auctions where a quilt just happens to be part of the household merchandise. There are many large and small auction houses around the country that, during the year, present auctions that may offer a few, or dozens, of quilts at one time. These are often called "Americana" auctions and may include textiles, furniture, tools, home or cooking implements, and antique decorative pieces along with the quilts.

Christy's and Sotheby's are two of the biggest and best-known national auction houses. Regional or local auction houses can be found in the yellow pages or listed in local newspapers. You can find out what's offered and when by calling the auction house directly. Request to be added to the house's mailing list, so you will receive notice of future auctions. Many auction houses charge for this—catalogs from the bigger auction houses cost anywhere from $5 and up; they may be thick glossy volumes complete with pictures and extensive descriptions. Smaller auction houses may have glossy brochures or simple type-written listings.

The prime rule, if you decide to chance a purchase at auction, is to look over the merchandise extremely carefully. There's always preview time before any auction, sometimes even days before, to see the offered merchandise. Previewing doesn't mean standing a few feet away and admiring the pattern or colors. It means taking the quilt out of its box, down from its rack, or off the table and really looking at it. Unfold the quilt and look at the back as carefully as the front.

"At an auction, never buy a quilt that you haven't previewed," said Connie Sprong of the Quilt Loft. "All quilts look good from a distance. You want to know how they look close up before you bid."

Spread the quilt out and look at it all: squares, borders, and other features. Do the colors balance? Does the quilt look like something you want to own or to give as a gift? There may be one square that is badly torn or that is of completely different colors that change the whole look of the quilt. If you hadn't unfolded it you would have missed the flaw. Check every inch of the quilt for the quality of workmanship (see chapter 5) and its condition (see chapter 4).

At auctions it is always buyer beware, for items are sold exactly as you see them. If you get your treasure home and discover flaws, you have no one but yourself to blame for not looking more carefully. There are no returns at auctions.

The final decision to make before you bid is how much you think the quilt is worth and how much you're willing to pay for it. Many of the larger auction houses will note an "expected price" in the catalog and this can be helpful. This price, however, is often higher (or lower) than what the item finally sells for; price depends on who is at the auction and willing to buy.

When you've made the decision to bid on a quilt, there are a few other steps to take before the bidding starts.

All auctions have a standard procedure they expect you to follow should you be the successful bidder. You must make arrangements for payment before you even start bidding. If you're not familiar with the requirements of the particular auction to which you're going, *ask*. A few auction houses may take a credit card, most will not. Unless you're prepared to pay cash, all auction houses require that you establish credit before they accept your check. This is not really credit, per se, but verifying that your check will be good. This step may be as easy as showing a major credit card and photo ID, or as complicated as direct contact with your financial institution. Be sure you arrive at the auction early enough to establish your credit. Ask if the auction house will take a personal check or if it requires a bank check. Find out if it will hold items for you until you can get the proper check. Most will not—or if they do, will hold items for only a very short time.

If you plan to pay cash, the auction house may require a certain amount before they allow you to bid. This may seem paranoid, but if you are the successful bidder and then can't pay for the item, the auction house has lost the sale and may not be able to recoup.

After you're approved as a buyer, you'll usually be given a bidder number. At the bigger houses, this may be a plastic number that you hold up for the auctioneer to see. It may also be a number scrawled on a piece of cardboard or a slip of paper. At some auctions, you may not get a number at all. You might be asked for a refundable deposit on the number to be sure you return it at the end of the auction. In any case, once you have done the preliminaries, you may then find a place, either standing or seated, from which you make your bids. Sit down and relax, and wait for the auction to begin.

If you are not familiar with the bidding procedure, ask. You may feel foolish, and the auction staff may look at you as if you have two heads, but this will be nothing compared to what you'll feel when someone else walks out with your treasure because you didn't know how to make your bid. It's wise to go to a few auctions before you become involved in active bidding, just to see how it goes and to determine if you can stand the pressure and the pace.

The bidding process is just as hectic and confusing as it seems in parodies on TV sitcoms. The auction house needs to sell the maximum amount of merchandise in the shortest possible time, and the bidding process usually goes fairly quickly if not at a lightning pace. The auctioneer will announce the item to be bid on, usually with the catalog number, if there is one. He may or may not describe the item, giving you time to recognize it as the quilt you want. He will then offer a price at which he wants the bidding to start.

If this price seems too high to you, don't bid. If no one starts the bidding, the auctioneer may drop the beginning price. Don't let this fool you into thinking that the quilt is necessarily going to sell lower than the price the auctioneer first mentions. Once people start bidding on an item, the hope of the auction house is that desire and excitement will override sensibility and thoughtfulness, pushing the price higher and higher.

If others start bidding at the first price the auctioneer mentions, and that price is higher than you are willing to pay, you may have to rethink your top price or, more wisely, let the quilt go. Unless you have unlimited funds, you should set a reasonable price for the quilt you want and not go over it—unless, of course, this is the quilt you cannot live without and you want to break the bank for it.

During the bidding, pay close and careful attention. Raise your hand or your number when the next price is offered if you are willing to pay it. If the auctioneer goes from $200 to $300 and no one takes $300, and you are willing to go to $225, say so. The auction house would prefer you to go up in the increments it offers, but it will usually take other bids.

If the auctioneer doesn't acknowledge that you waved your number on the offered bid, be more aggressive next time. Auctioneers are very good at reading the most subtle signs, but if you sit like a bump on a log, barely moving, he will think you are asleep and not bidding. Usually, once you have joined in the active bidding, the auctioneer will keep an eye on you in order to offer you other opportunities to bid. Just remember that if someone else is willing to go higher, he is not going to look to you for long.

Remember, too, that the decision of the auctioneer is final. If you feel that he didn't see you wave your hand or hear you shout your bid and he gave the sale to someone else, whining about his lack of awareness won't change his mind. Next time, pay closer attention or make yourself heard.

If you are the highest bidder when the auctioneer says "Sold!" hold up your hand or your number so that the auction staff can make note of it. If there are no other items on which you wish to bid, you may then leave the floor and pay for your quilt. Be aware that most auctions will add what is called a buyer's premium onto the price of your quilt. This can be a flat fee or a percentage, and it is almost the standard in the auction industry. It pays the auction house's bills, leaving the actual price of the item to give the seller. You should figure this premium into your pre-auction calculations of what the quilt is worth and how much you're willing to spend.

If reading about auctions has your heart pounding in anticipation, you are an adventurous soul and ready to take wallet in hand and head for the nearest auction house. If it has your heart pounding in fear, scurry back to your ever faithful quilt dealer and find your treasures there. Auctions can be great places to find and buy quilts. They can also be great places to spend too much and get stuck with overpriced merchandise.

So, as we head into the chapters on history and dating, welcome to the exciting world of quilt collecting. Your journey has begun!

CHAPTER TWO

THE HISTORY OF QUILTS AND QUILTING

Americans didn't invent quilting. They didn't even invent the art of quilting. There is evidence that quilting was done in ancient Greece, India, and China before the birth of Christ. Persians used quilting to make prayer rugs, carpets, and draperies from linen, silk, and satin. Portuguese traders brought quilting to Europe, as did the returning survivors of the Crusades. The Crusaders used appliqué and piecework to make their banners and flags. Middle Ages folk of all means quilted coats and hoods, and soldiers wore quilted items to cushion their heavy armor. By the eleventh century, quilting had spread throughout Europe and was especially used for bed clothing.

One quilt historian mentioned a great freeze that took place across Europe in the fourteenth century and that led to even more quilting. It was during this period that the first quilt frame was used and that the Italian style of trapunto, or stuffed, quilting began. By the 1600s, quilting was used to add warmth, weight, and beauty to all kinds of outer and under clothing as well as bed-spreads and bed furnishings. When the settlers arrived in the New World, they brought along not only quilts but quilting techniques.

"It is quite certain that quilts were among the household furnishings given precious space on the first small ships to the New World," wrote Jonathan Holstein in *The Pieced Quilt: An American Design Tradition*, a 1973 book published by Gallahad in New York City. "And it is likely there were some fine quilts carefully tucked into chests with other treasured household items." That these quilts were brought with the Colonial settlers out of necessity there is no doubt. We'd also argue that they were brought for their family heirloom and sentimental value as well, just as the pioneer family carried its quilts to the West.

That quilting was well known in the Old World is evidenced by the fact that the oldest whole quilt in existence dates from 1708 and is an appliqué in the Broderie-Perse style using India chintz. Although completed in the eighteenth century, this oldest surviving quilt contains fabric from the 1600s.

Broderie-Perse is the method of using large printed designs cut from imported chintz or calico. The cut pieces were placed on a ground fabric of white cotton or linen and their edges were turned under and sewed down. This method of cutting out preprinted forms is the earliest known appliqué technique. The fabric used for Broderie-Perse came primarily from India, imported to Europe as early as the mid-1600s. This seventeenth-century quilt, now in Levens Hall in England, is typical of the English-style quilt with its large central motif. It is this central-medallion style that Colonial needleworkers revised and adapted to create a uniquely American style of quilting.

The first quilts made in America were probably simple designs made of whole cloth, created more out of necessity than for beauty. Whole-cloth quilts were simply that: two pieces of cloth stitched together with a batting in the middle. There are at least fifteen date-inscribed quilts made by American needleworkers that exist today from the eighteenth century and four of these are whole-cloth quilts, according to Barbara Brackman in *Clues in the Calico*. The balance of these fifteen eighteenth-century quilts are pieced and appliqué dated after 1770. The oldest quilt in America is a McCord quilt dated 1726.

No form of needlework achieved hobby status until the mid to late eighteenth century. Even then, needlework was never just a creative outlet, it was a woman's occupation.

"To create with brain and fingers, with needle and thread, goods of admittedly economic value, was perforce a part of a woman's job," wrote Ruth E. Finley in 1929 in her book *Old Patchwork Quilts*. Quilts were considered so economically valuable, in fact, that they were listed along with other assets in personal and wedding inventories. Their disposition was noted in wills. Purchases of quilting materials were listed in account books. Advertisements for quilt materials were placed in Colonial newspapers as early as 1721.

Quilting, and attendant services such as printing homespun cloth, was a cottage industry in Colonial days. Homes had looms to make their own cloth, which was then taken to professional dyers who decorated the homespun by hand painting or hand printing using wood blocks or copperplate. Once a quilt was pieced, the Colonial housewife who could afford it would hire someone else to quilt it. Schools were formed to teach the finer techniques of needlework. Bridget Suckling ran a needlework school in Boston in 1751, but only the wealthy could afford it.

Even if they had the means to hire the work out, all women were expected to do some needlework. For the wealthy woman, quilting was a way of keeping herself busy, for the poor it was a necessity. Quilting was within the means of everyone in Colonial America.

Girls started their needlework training at an early age. Most learned by doing, guided by their mothers. The wealthy attended special schools such as the one run by Bridget Suckling. Needlework education often began at the age of four or five. At anywhere between six and eight, a Colonial girl started her first quilt, laboriously working, matching, ripping out clumsy stitches and replacing them with small, even ones. When they married, tradition dictated that each bride take with her, as part of her dowry, a baker's dozen of quilts. The thirteenth quilt was her bridal quilt, made after she was betrothed. If a bridal quilt was started before a girl was betrothed, it was said she'd never marry. Another superstition about a bride's quilt stipulated that these were the only quilts that could include hearts in the pattern or quilting design. To place a heart in one of the other twelve quilts was to invite spinsterhood.

It was only in needlework that a woman held full control. Her dowry, income, and home were controlled by her husband. Finley states, emphatically, that women didn't even have control over their own clothing. She notes that the men ordered the material for their wives' and daughters' gowns when they ordered their own clothing. Although Finley implies that women had no choice in the matter, it seems improbable that the Colonial husband came home with fabric for his wife's gowns that she had never seen or approved. While technically the husband did control important aspects of her life, it would take a rare man, totally devoid of common sense, to not let his wife pick out her own dress fabric from whatever small choice was available.

Whether she chose it or not, a woman certainly held full sway in how fabric was used in the home. As life became easier in Colonial America, with the increased availability of quality imported goods, Colonial women stamped their mark on the art of quilting and created works of beauty as well as utility. Women who could afford it cut cloth and experimented with appliqué techniques. The poor turned to piecing patterns, using up the leftovers from other needlework.

Politics also entered into the creation of quilts. From the very beginning, England attempted to discourage the development of manufactured textiles in the American colonies. However, Massachusetts and Connecticut had laws stating that every family must plant and raise flax to turn into homespun. If they made their own, there was no need to demand manufactured fabric or to rely on England for imports—and imported cloth was one of the highly taxed items that led to one of the most familiar of our country's slogans: "No taxation without representation." The importation of cotton into the colonies cut into England's wool and linen business, so purchasing these fabrics was pronounced illegal. When the colonists bought the banned cotton anyway, England imposed a double tax on the goods.

It seems ludicrous that the scarcity and high cost of fabric, so easily accessible today, would have helped foment a revolution. But cloth, and what can be made from it, is so essential to daily life that that is exactly what happened. The taxation of calico and the discouragement of a textile industry in America helped fuel the American Revolution, although this factor is not as dramatically remembered as the Boston Tea Party. Even after the Revolution, England outlawed the exportation of clothmaking technology, going so far as to search passengers going to America for machine blueprints. It wasn't until the 1790s that Slater's Cotton Mill opened in Pawtucket, Rhode Island. Samuel Slater, an engineer, memorized the plans and specifications of mass-producing cotton cloth machines, took his knowledge to the Colonies, and opened the first mill. Alexander Hamilton started the Society of Useful Manufacturers to produce cotton cloth, but England flooded the new country with cheap imports and the venture failed. By 1810, however, 87 cotton and printing mills were healthy, successful businesses.

The oldest quilting pieced pattern is the crazy quilt style. It was out of necessity that American quiltmakers first started experimenting with new patterns. Leftover scraps of fabric were sewed together, haphazardly, to create an assembled whole cloth that could be quilted into a bed covering. Until this time, quilts were primarily made of whole cloth. Even the expensive Broderie-Perse-style quilt required a piece of whole cloth as a ground for the appliqué. The high price of imported fabric coupled with the English-imposed tax on calicoes turned cloth into an expensive commodity. Scraps were saved to be used, somehow, later. Even worn clothing was cut of its good spots, salvaging fabric that could be used elsewhere. Every inch of cloth was saved. It had to be.

". . . the family quilt was like the turkey soup made from the left-overs of the Christmas feast," wrote Finley. "A positively last appearance." This last appearance of the household fabric resulted in what we regard as the single most significant American contribution to quilting: blocks.

Blocks were already an element of quilts. Adelaide Hechtinger wrote in *American Quilts, Quilting, and Patchwork* that early eighteenth-century quilts were made of four blocks, each 36 inches square. When these were assembled, an 18-inch border was added, making the completed quilt 108 inches square. Beds were large in those days, states Hechtinger, and high off the ground to accommodate a trundle bed beneath. Quilts were made large enough to cover the bed as well as to cover several, sometimes many, occupants sleeping together.

Block-style quilting as we know it today is the result of a gradually increasing quality of life as much as economics or necessity. Imports arrived more frequently to America and goods were cheaper, at least for those living along the eastern seaboard. Yankee peddlers went inland carrying printed textiles in specially designed wagons with flaps on the sides to protect and display the bolts of cloth. More of the necessities of life were provided for and quiltmakers tired of the functional whole-cloth or four-square quilts. They decided to make their bed coverings beautiful as well. Quiltmakers experimented with smaller blocks, cutting fabric pieces into precise geometric forms and assembling those together. Once enough blocks were pieced, they were assembled into a quilt top.

"Precious as the material might have been, quiltmakers preferred to trim them into geometric shapes rather than piece them as they came as in the crazy quilt . . . " wrote Holstein. These cut geometric forms were more pleasing, more challenging. An increased lifestyle and less expensive goods made block-style quilting affordable and creative expression possible.

". . . the block style furnished a work method and a geometrically based aesthetic which was endlessly variable and could be manipulated for the most diverse results," continued Holstein. "No two quilts are ever alike."

With the advent of the block style, quiltmakers were able to plan a quilt rather than letting the fabric dictate its design. Even Broderie-Perse dictated the form of the central-medallion-style quilt because of its use of preprinted designs on chintz fabric. Simply rotating a pieced block a quarter turn could result in a very different, very dramatic change in the overall pattern of a quilt top. Variety was indeed endless with the pieced block when quiltmakers added their own color and fabric choices to the basic block design. Reversing placement of light and dark fabrics within a pieced block was enough to create what looked like a completely different pattern.

Block-style quilting made the whole job easier. Instead of working with a bulky piece of cloth the same size as the finished quilt, blocks were small and portable. They could be worked on in short periods of time whenever that time was available. They could be carried with the quiltmaker so that her hands were never idle, even when visiting. Suddenly piecing could be done anywhere. And just as suddenly, geometric quilts of great beauty were produced and a woman could express, through her quilts, her innate creativity. And, blessing of all blessings, it was still economical! Thrifty, even, because now the quiltmaker could use up all the scraps of fabric left over from her other needlework and still produce something of value. Block-style patchwork flourished from its beginnings in the mid-1700s.

The most important aspect of the advent of block-style quilting is that it spawned hundreds of geometric patterns (still used today) and also led to the creation of album, autograph, signature, friendship, bride, presentation, and sampler quilts. These quilts are among the most collectible today.

Quilting bees date from Colonial days and are another purely American

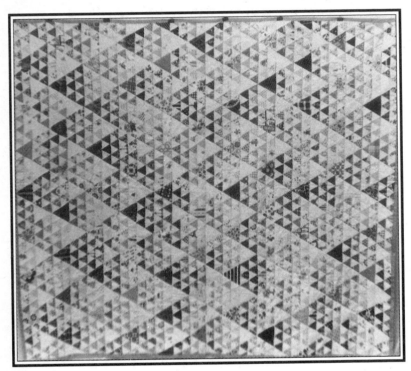

The overall effect of this diamond center Ocean Waves quilt is quite dramatic. Made of 1930s fabrics in multiple prints and colors, the quilt was left as a top until about ten years ago, when it was completed by an enterprising quilter.
Quilt courtesy of Sally Zemke

addition to the art of quilting that continues to the present. Today's quilt guilds and clubs are the natural evolution of the Colonial quilting bee. And they're held for the same reasons: to further the education of the individual on quilting technique; to share patterns and fabrics; to talk, laugh, and, yes, to gossip; and to gather together in a social context. Today's quilt groups work in a different format. Rarely does the group meet to finish another member's quilt unless it's a fund-raising project.

Bees were different in Colonial and pioneer days. Then, quilting bees were family and community events involving women, men, boys, and girls. Guests arrived early, admired the quilt top, and set to work attaching it to the quilt frame. They spent the rest of the day talking and quilting. Husbands and

A closer look at this quilt reveals the wonderful prints and excellent assembly. The woman who finished the quilt wisely went with just minimal straight-line quilting, as more extensive quilting would have been overshadowed by the effect of the whole quilt itself. *Quilt courtesy of Sally Zemke*

sweethearts were invited to supper and they arrived wearing their Sunday-best clothes. After supper, all stayed for talk, games, and dancing. One of our sources noted that a 1752 quilting bee was held in Narragansett that lasted ten days!

Bees were also part of courtship. One superstition practiced at bees was for the young men and women to hold the completed quilt while a cat was placed in the center. Whoever the cat jumped over to get off the quilt would be the next of the group to get married. Sometimes a betrothed man might design a quilt for his bride-to-be to make for their new home.

Usually a quilting bee consisted of eight women: seven guests and the hostess. To work comfortably and efficiently, this meant two women on each side of the quilt, their heads bent over the job, talking and sharing details of their lives. In rural areas, where a neighbor traveled a long distance to attend, the quiltmaker might wait until she had two tops to quilt and would invite fifteen women. They would work in shifts, alternating between quilting and preparing the evening meal until the stitching was completed.

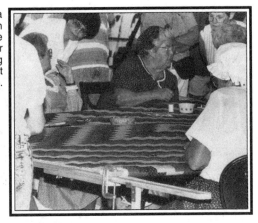

At the Kutztown Pennsylvania Folk Festival, modern quiltmakers gather around the quilting frame just as their ancestors did, sharing patterns, techniques, and not a little gossip.

Although the tradition of a bride bringing thirteen quilts to her marriage meant that girls started piecing and appliquéing their tops early in life, they rarely finished the quilts until they were betrothed. The expensive part of finishing a quilt is adding the batting and backing. Since this wasn't necessary until the girl needed to furnish a new home, the tops were stored. Any girl who invited her friends over for a quilting party to work on her tops was actually announcing her approaching marriage. In some areas it was considered bad luck for the bride to make her own bridal, or the thirteenth, quilt. At the bee to complete this quilt she could help mark the quilting lines, but she wasn't allowed to stitch on it.

Girls not old enough to be married held friendship bees. Each girl brought enough scraps from her own clothing to make a block. When the blocks were finished, they were set and the completed top was given to one of the guests. The girl who received the quilt then gave a friendship bee of her own at which another girl was given a quilt. The round continued until each of the guests received a completed quilt top.

Around the 1840s bees became exclusively female gatherings. The men weren't invited and the dinner, dancing, and games ended. Gone too was the courtship aspect of the quilting bee. But for the pioneer women who joined their husbands and families in the westward migration, bees continued to be eagerly sought social events. Alone they pieced, but together they quilted. Often there was only one quilt frame in the area, another reason for continuing the tradition of quilting bees. And on the frontier there was usually a rifle propped up against the quilt frame—a startling contrast to the simple thread, needle, and scissors the quilters used but, when needed, as much a necessity in the face of attack from wild animals as the quilt was to ward off the cold.

In urban areas, album parties were held to make quilts for revered members of the community or a soon-to-be-moving-away, much-beloved minister's wife. Bees were also held to raise money for churches by either raffling off the finished quilt or by working for hire to quilt someone else's patchwork top.

Bees became quite exclusive and political, too. The inexpert, or disliked, women of the community weren't invited to join in the work. Any woman who wanted to get ahead, or fit in, was wise to sharpen her needlework skills. And bees could have been the starting point for the feminist movement. We found two references that stated that Susan B. Anthony, to further her cause of giving women the vote, gave her speeches where the women were—in church basements at quilting bees!

The first half of the nineteenth century saw quiltmaking flourish. Advances in technology and a lifestyle with more leisure time had their effect on the art of quilts. In 1814 the Lowell Cotton Factory opened in Waltham, Massachusetts. It was the first factory in the world to combine, under one roof, all the operations of producing cloth, from ginning raw cotton to producing finished yardage. Imported materials were available in great variety and at cheap prices. In fact, even after the War of 1812, England did its best to discourage the growth of textile manufacturing in America by flooding the United States with cheap cotton fabric. So strongly did the British want to preserve their import position that they actually sold the fabric at a loss to cut into domestic sales. Because of this importation of reasonably, even cheaply, priced goods, American quiltmakers incorporated much English-made cloth into their quilts well past the 1850s. It's possible to find quilts with English fabrics in the tops and homespun for the back.

The period from 1775 to approximately 1840 was a boom period for quiltmaking.

"The decline in fabric prices and increasingly available fabric, plus a rising middle class with money to spend on fabric, made the quilt a more universal bed covering," wrote Barbara Brackman in *Clues in the Calico*. In the early 1800s, quilting patterns were available that could be traced on fabric using a wheel. In 1810, the first agricultural fair was held in Pittsfield, Massachusetts, and soon regional fairs were held all over the United States; they continue today. Prize categories for needlework, quilts in particular, were included at the fairs. The competition among quiltmakers was friendly but intense. Quilts were judged by the quality of the work, beauty, or originality in the use of a regional pattern. These show quilts exhibited the woman's thrift, work, and reflected her expertise as a homemaker. Winning first prize at the county fair made a quiltmaker famous throughout her area, and gaining a reputation for expert needlework was sometimes more valued than the dictionaries, encyclopedias, newspaper subscriptions, and cash given as prizes.

It was at these fairs that regional patterns were disseminated. Quiltmakers copied the winning designs to re-create and adapt them on their own. Like bees, fairs added to a woman's quilt knowledge and pattern pool because they exposed her to a greater number of quiltmakers. Women's fairs first appeared in 1833, when the Philadelphia and Boston branches of the Female Anti-Slavery Society started selling the needlework of their members to raise money for their cause.

Also during this period, 1775 to 1840, quilting remained a source of income for women who needed to work. In Philadelphia women with no means of support were hired by the Female Society for the Relief and Employment of the Poor to do knitting, spinning, and quilting. In 1831, the average daily pay for these professional quilters, if they were expert, was fifteen cents. Stitching of less quality earned the women twelve and a half cents per day.

In 1830 the first edition of *Godey's Lady's Book* appeared, and starting in 1835, the magazine often included quilt block patterns. Magazines would not become a major source of quilt patterns until 1875 and after. Except for *Godey's,* which was actually aimed at urban, middle-class women, the sources of new patterns for most quiltmakers continued to be trading between themselves and copying them from quilts entered in fairs.

Economic changes in the 1840s caused further changes in the making of quilts. From this time on, except for the pioneers, the popularity of quiltmaking alternately waned and peaked, influenced by depressions, economic booms, and wars. There was a general pattern to these peaks and valleys. As a general rule, during periods of prosperity quiltmaking declines. During recessions and depressions, quiltmaking increases. It also appears that quiltmaking increases during periods of national unity such as the Civil War, the Centennial held in Philadelphia in 1876, both World Wars, and the Bicentennial period.

Starting in the 1840s it was more common to see urban women working outside the home. Domestic textile production increased and cloth was still inexpensive and plentiful. Quilting was one of the forms of needlework included in the category of "fancy" handwork, skills even the working urban woman retained. Although she no longer had to make quilts out of necessity, she had both the money and the materials to create quilts of beauty. It was during this period, from the 1840s through the Civil War, that geometric pieced quilts saw the most development and innovation.

"The most extraordinary examples of optical illusion quilts began to develop from the mid-nineteenth century onward, as block-work quilts became the preferred American system for construction," wrote Laura Fisher in her book *Quilts of Illusion*.

Not everyone in the country was enjoying the fruits of a growing economy. While eastern seaboard quiltmakers reaped the benefits of a plentiful supply of cheap fabric by returning to the more fabric-intensive appliqué-style quilts, pioneer families began their trek west in search of more land to farm and lured by the prospect of gold. For the pioneer quiltmaker, cloth was scarce and, when she could get it, expensive. Many quilts were taken along during the westward expansion. They were used for more than warmth while sleeping. Wagon train travel was dirty, gritty, exposed to the elements. Quilts were used to warm and comfort the ill, injured, and newly born. They were even used to wrap the dead before burial. All this took its toll on the family quilt. Given these circumstances, it's amazing that any survived at all. Yet, the California Heritage Quilt Project located 3,300 antique quilts that settled in California, originating from forty-six states, five foreign countries, and three territories. Some of these quilts arrived in California via ship while others survived the torturous Panama route, carried by donkey across the isthmus.

Triangles Make Diamonds on this visually pleasing quilt that is made of wools and wool twills. Made in the early 1800s, this quilt is in very good condition and is tied, with no quilting. It has some very lovely black feather topstitching in the block junctions. *Quilt courtesy of Betty Wilson*

Pioneer quiltmakers, by necessity, returned to old methods. They grew their own flax, raised sheep. They carded, spun, and wove their own wool on their own spinning wheels and looms. They saved every scrap of fabric left over from other projects and used the last remnants of the calico dresses brought with them from the East. They collected natural dye recipes from neighbors and the folks back home to create their own colored fabrics. When fabric was available, they bought it and then shared scraps with their equally isolated neighbors. It's not unusual to find antique quilts from the same area that were made by different quiltmakers but containing the same swatches of fabric.

Not all pioneer women made quilts. Settling the wilderness was a time-consuming and backbreaking job. Many didn't have the time, money, or materials for quilting. But those who did created beautiful geometric quilts of bright shades of red, green, purple, blue, pink, and yellow. Even for these isolated pioneer women, civilization arrived, and it wasn't long, relatively, before they too were creating quilts as much for their own enjoyment as out of necessity.

It was in the mid-1840s that the sewing machine was invented. Quiltmakers grasped the new technology quickly, and Holstein estimates that fully half of all the quilts made after 1860 were machine pieced, a time-saving technique still used by most quiltmakers.

In the middle of this important period in the evolution of quilt design, the country went to war—with itself. Old traditions of thrift and economy returned as cloth manufacturers turned their machines to the production of uniforms and blankets. Women's groups of both the North and the South turned their quiltmaking talents to providing quilts for soldiers. In *Quilts: A Window to the Past*, Victoria Hoffman notes that an astounding 250,000 quilts were made for Civil War soldiers! Most of these were used in hospitals. Since sterilizing a quilt was impossible, when a soldier died his quilt was burned. In a 1987 article for *Quilting* magazine, Joseph Harriss told about a quilt made by the women of Westport, New York, for the town's militia, Company A. Westport's Company A fought at Antietam, Gettysburg, and Richmond. The quilt was returned to Westport, brought back by Company A's survivors—the last three men. Many quilts were lost in the burning of the South and many were stolen and used so thoroughly their remnants were thrown away. Fabric was again scarce, especially in the South. Northern embargoes on both domestic and imported cloth to the South increased prices to a high of $100 per yard. Once again every scrap of fabric was saved to be used again, including militia uniforms, flannel sheets, old coats and cloak linings, and even petticoats.

Many commemorative quilts were made during this period depicting heroes, generals and leaders of both sides. Northern appliqué quilts included eagle designs and flags with all thirty-four stars, obvious statements of their makers' Union sentiments.

After the Civil War, cloth was once again plentiful and inexpensive. In fact, as the country was converted from wartime to consumer production, manufactured goods of all kinds became readily available. Although it was in this time period that the first mass-produced, ready-made blankets appeared, quiltmakers stuck to their needles to produce bed coverings. Quiltmaking was still the most economical method of providing nighttime warmth. (In the late 1860s six yards of cotton for a quilt top cost only 36 cents. Three yards of backing fabric sold for 75 cents, and batting prices ranged, according to quality, from 28 to 77 cents. The manufactured blanket cost anywhere from $2.25 to $8. When an entire quilt could be made with materials costing less than $1.50, why buy blankets? To save time and labor, of course.) But eventually mass-produced blankets ate into hand quilt production. Increased technology produced copies of previously high-priced curtains, hangings, and Oriental rugs. Women turned to other forms of fancywork, such as needlepoint, to satisfy their creativity.

The last quarter of the nineteenth century saw quiltmaking reach an epiphany. The Centennial celebration held in Philadelphia in 1876 revived interest in all forms of needlework, including quilting. The fad was for Colonial-style furnishings and this produced a quilting frenzy.

"Women whose families had left them quiltless were forced either to collect or make quilts in order to be in fashion," wrote Penny McMorris and Michael Kile in *The Art Quilt*. What we know as typical of Amish quilting began in the last quarter of the nineteenth century. This same period brought a revival of the crazy quilt style. Once the lowliest of quilt designs, a purely functional use of leftover fabrics, the crazy quilt reached its high point in the late 1800s and became the "best quilt" of choice. The crazies were exquisite, elaborate, and expensive. Material of silk, satin, brocade, and velvet was bought expressly to make these quilts—no leftovers for these family status symbols! The album quilt also developed during this period. In its short, two-decade-long appearance, the Baltimore Album quilt, the most elaborate, most exquisitely worked of all album quilts, made an indelible mark on quiltmaking history. Such quilts were highly valued as gifts then and are equally valued by collectors today.

But eventually the frenzy died out. By the late 1800s, quilting was a rare pastime. There were still some clubs, the occasional article in a woman's magazine, and prize categories at regional fairs, but quiltmaking took a back seat to the technology of mass production. In the 1890s, ready-made comforters were

This wool crazy quilt has the usual scattered assembly of pieces and yellow topstitching. Made in 1916, the quilt also features fans in the corners, a nice touch.
Quilt courtesy of Helen Warner

available in dry-goods stores. Although available since before the Civil War, factory-made blankets were not in general use until the late 1800s and early 1900s.

Finally, the fashion trend toward manufactured bedspreads further reduced the amount of quiltmaking. In 1903 *Cutter's Red Book of Ready Reference* was published. In it, the use of quilts on beds was discouraged as being out of fashion. To replace them, the book recommended the current fad for all-white manufactured spreads. The convincing argument was that once a quiltmaker's labor was added in, a manufactured spread was actually cheaper than a quilt. Many quilt owners turned their pieced and appliquéd masterpieces over, showing the plain white side decorated with quilting instead of the patchwork top.

But quilting never disappeared. In 1915 the first full-length work on quilting, *Quilts: Their Story and How to Make Them*, written by Marie D. Webster and published by Doubleday, Page, and Co., appeared just in time to be used by a new wave of quiltmakers. Not only advice was available. In the quilting revival that occurred "between the wars" (as Carter Houck described it in an article for *Quilt Craft* magazine), new dyes and new print technology produced inexpensive cottons in many colors and prints.

Even through the Great Depression, quilts were made from these fabrics. Depression-era quilts are among the most endearing of all quilts ever made. This was the era of Sunbonnet Sue, Scotty Dogs, Airplanes, Scrap Bag, Trip

The Flying Geese pattern in this late-1800s crib quilt is made of pale prints of stripes and windowpane plaids. Although they look like they go vertically, the quilt is actually assembled in horizontal strips, which are then attached to each other to form the vertical look.

Around the World, Double Wedding Ring, Grandmother's Flower Garden, and Dresden Plate. In the late 1920s fabric stores carried not only reproductions of old glazed chintz and upholstery fabrics but also cloth printed with old quilt designs. Called cheater cloth, the preprinted design eliminated the need to piece a block—the fabric came printed with it! Cheater fabrics are still available today. The Great Depression also saw many a quilt made from the printed cloth of feed bags. Sometimes Depression-era quilts were used to pay debts in lieu of cash, and some were even used to meet tithing pledges at church.

To meet the demand of the quilting revival, the years 1927 through 1939 saw the most quilting brochures ever published. Patterns were developed by specialized businesses such as the Home Art Studios, Colonial Pattern Company, McKim Studios, and Ladies Art, to name a few. Quiltmaking supply houses, such as Mountain Mist, also created patterns and supplied them free inside their packaging. Newspapers ran their own quiltmaking and pattern columns or bought syndicated columns. In 1934 over four hundred newspapers ran regular quilting columns.

In 1933, Sears, Roebuck and Company sponsored a quilt contest in conjunction with the Chicago World's Fair, named the Century of Progress Exposition. Although the Depression was far from over, and perhaps because it *wasn't* over, 24,878 quilts were entered in the contest competing for a $1,000 first prize. Many of these were pictorial, all were beautiful, and they fueled the raging interest in quiltmaking.

Also contributing to the quilt revival of the 1920s and 1930s was Eleanor Roosevelt's active promotion of American arts and crafts, which gave all women's arts new status. The WPA even funded some quilt projects. The social, political, economic, and patriotic events of these decades even revived the practice of using a quilt to make a statement. Political and commemorative quilts were made again, and many quilts were made with the Scotty Dog pattern, which originated with Roosevelt's little dog, Fala. Following a tradition almost as old as our country itself, quilts as fund-raisers helped to buy at least one bomber for use in World War II.

It was toward the end of World War II that quilt kits abounded. These kits contained everything needed for an entire quilt—with color, size, and design already chosen, and, in some cases, the fabric already cut into pattern pieces—and were readily available. According to authors Penny McMorris and Michael Kile, the proliferation of these kits, which eliminated color and design decisions, led to the decline in quiltmaking that followed the war. Opportunities for creativity and individuality were starkly reduced using the kit method.

It's more likely that the postwar decline in quiltmaking should be attributed to rapid changes in the lives of women. Many kept their war-production jobs and started careers, leaving little time to devote to needlework of any kind. The 1950s were a prosperous and optimistic period. Quilts were a reminder of the Depression. In the 1950s, scrimping was over. Machine-made quilts were available in department stores, the result of the quilting revival of the previous three decades, which had spurred manufacturers to produce cheap reproductions of antique quilts. The 1940s, 1950s, and early 1960s passed with much fewer quilts made and little added to quilt design or innovation. The Baby Boom sent women back to their sewing machines, but it was to produce needed clothing, not quilts.

Then the beginning of a new revival occurred when *Vogue* magazine included photographs of interior home design that included patchwork quilts. Soon all the magazines followed suit, using quilts in their photo spreads depicting the perfectly decorated home. The late 1960s also saw a renewed interest in the arts and crafts of the late 1800s. According to McMorris and Kile, both the use of quilts for interior decoration and the crafts revival were reactions against the increased technology of the time. People were turning away from what they perceived to be the evils of industrialization and were surrounding themselves with examples of a simpler time and lifestyle—and prime among these examples were quilts.

Inflation, unemployment, and the gas crises all contributed to a return to quiltmaking. Making and using a quilt as a wall hanging was cheaper than throwing out what you had and buying new furniture. Quilts were also viewed as valuable gifts. The same amount of money one would spend for a much smaller gift could produce a stunning quilt. By the end of the 1960s quiltmaking was once again established as the darling of all needlework.

From 1965 to 1974 sales of all hobby supplies doubled. For the first time in many years, companies selling how-to books and quilting supplies saw profits rise. Magazines and newspapers were once again carrying, on a regular basis, columns and articles about quilting. The 1970s, with the Bicentennial looming ever closer, began a nostalgia craze that increased the value and status of antique quilts and quiltmaking in general.

". . . for it is only recently that quilts have been acknowledged as the visual precursors of many of the design innovations and color systems that were later employed in practitioners of Op Art and other contemporary painting," wrote Laura Fisher in her book *Quilts of Illusion*. Museums exhibited collections of antique quilts, showing them hung on walls rather than spread on beds, and the quilt began its slow yet unswerving journey toward achieving art status.

The Bicentennial fueled this latest quiltmaking revival. *Good Housekeeping* sponsored a national quilt contest. Quilts from kits were not eligible. The quilts had to be traditional or innovative designs. It estimated 3,500 entries and received over 10,000.

The 1970s produced the next evolution in quilt design: the art quilt. Quilt shows were held in halls, schools, and churches all over the country in tribute to the two-hundredth anniversary of our country's birth. Quiltmakers went back to work or entered the hobby for the first time.

Art quilts aside, the Bicentennial quilt revival will be remembered for its plethora of sampler quilts and the use of coordinated fabrics. The sampler quilt, with each block a different pattern, was still the best way to learn quiltmaking quickly. By completing twenty, twenty-four, or thirty different blocks, the beginning quiltmaker learned most of the piecing and appliquéing techniques she needed to "graduate" to more difficult designs or to create her own. These sampler quilts, which we think will be the most collectible quilts of the Bicentennial period, were made with coordinating fabrics—the 1970s were not a scrimping time any more than the 1950s had been. Fabric was bought expressly, exclusively, and sometimes expensively, for quilts. The scrap bag quilt, though some were made, was mostly ignored. This trend toward complementary fabrics in a quilt continues today. Personally, we hope that contemporary quiltmakers will eventually return to their scrap bags and innovate with them.

There are those historians who believe that, along with the nostalgia craze started by the Bicentennial, the feminist movement also fueled the current quilt revival. The interest of contemporary women in their female ancestors necessitated the study of quilts. As women became more and more aware of the contributions of their grandmothers and great-grandmothers, quilts were recognized as valuable records of their ancestors' lives. With this recognition came the realization that quiltmaking was one way to preserve their own history as well.

By 1986 there were 600,000 subscribers to quilt magazines. Over 1,200 quilt shops supplied books, fabric, thread, batting, and tools for quiltmaking, and over 4,000 quilt guilds worked together and shared their knowledge of quiltmaking technique, history, and lore.

Following another time-honored tradition, contemporary quiltmakers continue to combine political statements with their stitching. The Boise Peace Quilt Project, started in 1981, gave its first completed quilt in 1982 to the Soviet cultural affairs attaché in Washington, D.C., who, in turn, sent it to the Soviet Women's Committee in Moscow. Still making quilts, the Boise Peace Quilt Project sends completed quilts to powerful leaders in foreign countries to promote peace. It has even made a quilt that is circulating among the members of the U.S. Congress, each congressman who volunteers sleeps under it for one night.

One outgrowth of the renewed interest in quilts from the Bicentennial period is the many quilt discovery projects that occurred across the country. Usually organized by state, these committees of knowledgeable quiltmakers and historians advertise special days and locations where residents can bring their prized family heirloom quilts, or collections, to be photographed, dated, and appraised. In this way, thousands and thousands of quilts are now recorded, with pictures, including the details of their pattern, maker, and history. Estimates are that the hundreds of hours of work by these groups have uncovered only about 10 percent of the antique quilts that exist today.

Another vital contribution from the documentation of existing antique quilts is the increased information available to quilt historians. Because the quilts were closely studied and their histories recorded, several myths about quiltmaking history are being challenged. Perhaps quilts were not quite as common in Colonial days as was previously thought. Certainly quilts were not only made when fabric was in short supply. In several periods of our history when fabric was plentiful quiltmaking flourished.

Finally, the myth that all quilts were created solely from necessity is being refuted. It seems that if only we could let go of legend and let our common sense prevail, we'd be able to see in our antique quilts that they were always works of art. Quilting was, and is, time-consuming, and homemakers have always been thrifty and efficient. To spend the countless hours it takes to make a quilt of striking beauty when it was only necessary to ties three layers together would have been ridiculous—an endeavor scorned by the practical, frugal homemaker. Logic dictates that the creation of quilts had to be a work of love and art. If for nothing else, we owe a debt of thanks to the quilt-recording projects for dispelling the myth that quilts were made only out of necessity. The women who made these treasures from the past knew they were creating beauty not solely function.

At the height of the 1970s quilt revival, quilts from the previous century were considered the most valuable. Because they were "of our own time," twentieth-century quilts were overlooked as collectibles.

"The '20s and '30s were still too close to have great appeal," wrote Carter Houck in *Quilt Craft* magazine. "Collectors looked to the 19th century for pieces 'worth having' and the owners of 'Depression Quilts' that had come down in their families used them at best in the kids' rooms and at worst in the driveway when they had to get down to inspect the nether regions of a car."

Fortunately, that attitude no longer prevails in the 1990s. Starting in the 1980s, with the advent of the quilt documentation projects, many people realized the importance of quilts from the first half of this century. As we became more interested in the history and significance of quilts, we realized that we had a pool of quiltmakers from those years who were not anonymous. Here were quiltmakers we could actually talk to, with their own quilts that we could see and feel. From these twentieth-century quiltmakers we gained a firsthand knowledge of the period and the quilts they produced, complete with memories, anecdotes, and experiences we could share. Our longing to know the intimate details of a quilt could be satisfied. Written records are readily available. It's possible, sometimes relatively easy, to trace a family's path of migration, to locate descendants, and to verify the clues, suggestions, sentiments, and opinions included in a quilt. We realized that we should preserve our own books, papers, letters, and memories so that future generations would know the reasons for our choices rather than be left answerless, wondering and imagining.

Quiltmaking survives today because it is as beautiful and versatile an art as it ever was and because it continues to make and reflect history. Though interest in it may wane and peak over long periods of time, we're sure this art will continue for many more centuries. Certainly the collection and preservation of quilts will continue. Very soon, those coordinated-fabric sampler quilts made during the Bicentennial will join their precursors as valuable collectibles. After all, in less than eight years we'll enter the twenty-first century. Then, even the quilts being made now will be from the previous century!

No, Americans didn't invent quilting and they didn't invent the use of quilting technique or its result as decoration. But they did challenge their creativity and expand quiltmaking beyond what it was to discover what it could be: art.

CHAPTER THREE

DATING A QUILT

Approximating the date a quilt was completed is important in determining its value. Age isn't the only standard for value. A truly stunning, but newer, quilt is sometimes far more valuable than a dull older one. But the age of a quilt is important. Unless the maker dated it, determining the age of a quilt is an exacting, sometimes instinctive, job.

The easiest way to date a quilt, of course, is if the maker thought to include the day and year she completed her quilt. Marilyn Lithgow wrote of finding a crazy quilt with two dates: 1894 and 1896. This quiltmaker started her crazy in 1894 and took two years to complete it, finishing in 1896. We're very grateful to this quiltmaker because she has added immeasurably to our study of antique quilts simply by adding those two dates. She left us a record of what fabrics were available during those years, what style of quilt was popular, and the quality and diversity of stitching patterns used by quilters in the last years of the nineteenth century.

There were fads and fashions in the way a quilt was signed just as different patterns were popular at different times. We cover them later in this chapter. Easily located dates on quilts are those that were written in pen or indelible marker or those that were appliquéd. Dates and signatures quilted on are the most difficult to find because they tend to blend in with the rest of the quilting stitches. Check both the back and the front of a quilt, especially the borders, if the quilt has them, inch by inch, looking for a date or signature worked in quilting stitches.

Most quiltmakers didn't sign or date their quilts, so if you don't find a date, don't despair. Dating without notation on a quilt is tricky. All aspects of the quilt must be taken into consideration: the fabric, colors, patterns, quilting style, batting, thread, and techniques used can all point to a quilt's age. Since the specifics of dating follow in this chapter, we'll give you one example now:

A quilt's age is determined by the date it was finished, not started. Many quilts are multigenerational, sometimes skipping a generation in between the original maker and the finisher. For whatever reasons—death, illness, lack of time, or boredom—someone started a quilt, never finished it, and stored it away. Along comes a descendant, a daughter or granddaughter, who discovers

In an unusual assembly, nine of these 1940s dated Grandmother's Flower Garden blocks are appliquéd onto a yellow ground fabric with yellow sashing embroidered with children's names. The color balance in each block is good, as is the stitching and assembly; and the overall look is interesting.
Quilt courtesy of Lois Belden

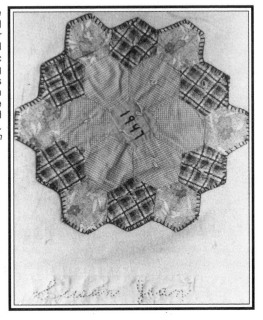

the uncompleted quilt in a drawer or trunk. She scoffs it up, delighted over her find, and finishes the quilt using fabrics from her own time period. Although the original fabrics may be much older, the addition of new fabric and the completion process dates the quilt to the time when it was finished. The older fabrics can be, and should be, noted in the documentation on the quilt, but it is still dated to the time period it was finished. If the finisher knew when the quilt was started and included that date along with the finish date, this would add to the value of a quilt. Most multigenerational quilts are not signed or dated either. The moral of this tale is that a quilt should be dated by finding the newest, youngest fabric in it.

Even when a quilt was completed by only one quiltmaker, the newest fabric is still the most accurate judge of when it was made. Scrap bag quilts are still in style and have been for centuries. A woman's scrap bag can include some very old fabrics. Just because they're used in a new quilt doesn't make that quilt an antique.

"My own scrap bag contains fabric fifty years old," said author Liz Green-backer. "It's full of remnants from my grandmother, my mother, and myself. I'm still making quilts from these scraps in the nineties and I'll keep making them well into the twenty-first century."

The arrangement of the strips in this quilt, with the same color diagonally across each block, gives the look of narrow sashing—an interesting way to get this effect. This 1947 strip quilt has scrap bag fabrics and straight-line quilting.
Quilt courtesy of Brian Comstock

Other considerations for dating a quilt include checking the batting and thread, noting a popular color or fabric print style specific to a period in textile history, and the waning and peaking of quilting techniques and styles. And that's when dating gets tricky.

If you're going to pursue this hobby, or invest your money in quilts, you'll have to educate yourself to the fads and fashions of four centuries of quiltmaking. Although that sounds like a daunting task, don't despair. It's fun! We'll get you started in this chapter to increase your knowledge and hone your instincts. We certainly can't cover the dating of quilts in the detail you'll require in a book this size. But we hope we'll pique your interest, sending you to the bibliography at the back to begin your journey to quilt historian status.

Your education should include, along with the books listed in our bibliography, any you can find on your own. You'll want to attend museums, both quilt and textile, and add their papers, exhibit catalogs, and specially published books to your collection. You'll want to scour through old textile manufacturers' catalogs and advertisements in old newspapers for dry goods, read and study the tips for home decoration found in old magazines, and make notes and compile your own date-specific list of quilt attributes.

Most important, you'll need to look at quilts. Go to as many quilt shows as you can. Find all the dealers in your area and visit them. Watch for quilt dealers and shops everywhere you go. Make notes of these visits, too, recording the exceptions you find, always adding to your growing pile of quilt lore and fact. At some point you'll find yourself questioning the date a museum or dealer has on a quilt and you'll know then that you're well on your way to being an expert.

We strongly recommend you start your own historical quest with the following: Barbara Brackman's *Clues in the Calico*, Ruth Finley's *Old Patchwork Quilts*, and Larry Zingale's video *How to Buy Antique Quilts*.

To accurately date a quilt, you should know something about the material it's made from.

Fabric

Until the 1900s, there were only four sources from which to make fabric, and these were all natural. The two animal sources were silk and wool; the two plant sources were linen and cotton. Quilts were often made incorporating different types of fabric as well as different weaves and textures. It wasn't too long, however, before quiltmakers realized that using the same type of fabric throughout was both easier and more pleasing when finished.

You'll need to know about these four types of natural fabrics. Silk is cloth woven from cocoon wrappings, primarily those of the silkworm. Silk was always a high-cost, luxury fabric, yet a wide variety of imported raw silks and silk goods were available. Bombazene (or bombazeen) was introduced after the sixteenth century. It had two distinctive features. First, it was woven with a silk warp and a worsted weft. Second, it was dyed after it was woven instead of before. The sheen of silk was imitated in other fabrics, most notably in chintz, by using a glaze and in worsteds by pressing.

Wool is cloth made of carded, short-staple wool fibers. It was the English wool broadcloth industry that the British tried to protect by discouraging a textile industry in the American colonies. Once the wool was woven, it was shrunk to tighten the weave. The finished fabric was dense, heavy, and warm. Calendered wool was finely woven and shiny. (When a wool was "calendered," it was pressed between two heated rollers that produced a sheen on the fabric.) It was a popular fabric from 1750 to the 1840s, so a quilt with this fabric strongly points to those dates.

Linen is made from fibers from the flax plant in an arduous process. In Colonial days it took over a year to grow the flax; remove the seeds; rot the plant; separate the fiber from the chaff; separate the fine, weavable fibers from the tow; spin it; and weave it. That any linen was made at all seems a superhuman feat to us.

Before we go on to cotton, let's discuss linsey-woolsey. Linsey-woolsey is a fabric with a linen warp and a woolen weft. It's a coarse fabric used more for utility than "best quilts." What is commonly referred to today as linsey-woolsey is a top layer of woolen or glazed worsted dyed a single color, usually dark but sometimes a light blue, raspberry, or pink. The backs of these quilts were made from a coarser woolen fabric in its natural color or dyed yellow or gold. This was layered with carded wool and intricately quilted with floral, feather, heart, cornucopia, interlocking circle, or crossed diagonal designs. These quilts are also noted for their notched-out corners, so that they would lie flat on the bed, their edges hanging around the bedposts. These quilts are huge and heavy. Some of these linsey-woolsey quilts were probably imported. Even those made here used imported fabric for the tops and either homespun or old fabric for the backing. There is also a linsey-woolsey made from a top layer of linen and a backing of wool.

The weaving of woolens and linens and the combination linsey-woolsey was common in Colonial households. The weaving of cotton was not—until after the Revolution and the development of the spinning jenny, fly shuttle, spinning frame, and power loom.

From the time of the Revolutionary War until the present day, quilt-makers preferred cotton, especially calico. Today we know calico as a cotton printed with small figures, but in the past it meant any cotton, plain, printed, or white, and included chintz and muslin. Even the spelling of the word has changed over the centuries from "callicoe" in 1700 to 1775, to "calicoe" in 1775 to 1825, and finally "calico" as we know it today. Calico was the most popular fabric for gowns, hence it was also popular for quilts. Half of the textiles made in the world today are cotton!

It's important to know something about the various weaves of cloth. There are three main weaving patterns: plain, satin, and twill. From these all other variations are derived. In the plain weave, warp and weft threads are equal. The filling yarns, or wefts, pass under and over the warps in alternating rows. This is also called taffeta or tabbyweave. Plain weave is so common among all fibers that it's not reliable for dating.

In the satin weave, the weft threads, those that run side to side on the fabric, don't go over and under each of the warp threads, those that run the

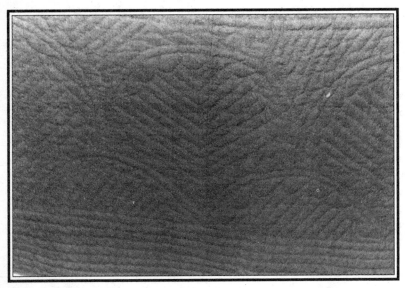

Beautiful feather and line quilting adorn this Whole-cloth Woolsey-woolsey quilt from the 1830s. The fabric is a soft brown that looks like a walnut dye, and as one would expect in a quilt this old and well used, much of it has deteriorated and been lost.

length of the fabric, as they do on the plain weave. These "loose" thread lengths on the surface of the cloth produce the high sheen. Although the same process of weaving is used to make both satin and sateen, there's a difference: satin is usually made from silk or silky threads, while sateen is made from cotton.

The twill pattern is similar to the satin in that the weft doesn't go over and under each warp thread but may go under one and over two. Unlike the satin weave, however, the pattern is alternated so that it produces diagonal lines over the fabric instead of the smooth surface sheen of satin weave. A short trip to the fabric store will get you enough samples of each weave so you'll be able to recognize them when you see them.

The compactness of the weaving is measured by the number of warp and weft threads to the square inch. The more compact a weave, the more durable is the fabric. Tightly woven fabric is of higher quality. To give you some idea of the numbers, tobacco cloth is a very loose weave, with a count of twenty threads. Fine percale sheeting, on the other hand, is a tight weave, averaging two hundred threads to the square inch. The cotton most typical in quilts is a standard weave of fifty to seventy-five threads per square inch.

The style of weaving is rarely used to date a quilt but it does help in distinguishing quality fabrics from cheap ones.

Glazes are used on fabrics to make them stiffer and give them sheen. As was noted before, glazes were used to make cotton competitive with silk. Glazes made from wax, egg whites, or resins were applied to plain and twill weaves. Another style of glazing was to calender, to force the fabric between two heated cylinders. The combination of heat and pressure creates a surface glaze on the fabric.

No discussion of quilting fabric is complete without mentioning homespun. Homespun fabric is one way to date a quilt. By the second quarter of the nineteenth century, homespun was a thing of the past in all but the most remote areas of the country. Settled communities had ready access to cotton. Any quilt containing homespun should be dated before the 1830s. But it's not as easy to identify homespun fabric as you might think.

Homespun fabric is defined by irregular sized threads. The thickness of the thread varies randomly throughout the fabric and the weave is loose, supposedly as a result of the inferior expertise of the Colonial spinner and weaver. However, some home spinners created homespun of very high quality with even threads and a tight weave. Some textile manufacturers produced a cheap backing cloth that could be described the same way as the traditional homespun. In fact, fabric that looks like homespun is still available in stores today. So just looking at the fabric and noting thread irregularities and loose weaving isn't sufficient to call a cloth homespun.

There are ways to tell, however. Most homespun is from wool or linen. The quilts called linsey-woolseys, which we discussed earlier, could have homespun backing fabric. The first thing to check on homespun wool is the number of piles in the thread. If the cloth was woven from single-ply thread, chances are it's homespun. If a double ply of threads was used, then the piece was probably manufactured.

A fabric claimed to be cotton homespun should be tested by determining if the quilt was made in a cotton-producing region and whether the quiltmaker was so isolated from civilization that she simply had to invest her time in hand spinning. Even if the answer is yes to both these tests, it still doesn't guarantee that the cloth is homespun. Home-produced wool and linen were used in quilts, and pioneer families, isolated from dry goods stores, did make their own fabrics, but finding homespun in a quilt is much rarer than was once believed.

There are other difficulties in dating a quilt by determining its fabric content. Fabric names and styles have changed over the four centuries of quilting. A fabric we recognize today may have had a different name a hundred years ago. Some fabrics have disappeared and new ones have been created, and even the names that existed two hundred years ago have come to mean something else.

As we move closer to our own time, there were some fabric styles that are good indicators of the date of a quilt. For most of the nineteenth century, ending in approximately 1875, a fabric called sarsenet cambric was popular. This was an opaque cotton of fine weave with a smoothness that approached silk. From 1875 to 1925 cotton flannels in plaids and stripes were used to back wool quilts. You can safely place such a quilt within those years. In that same period pile weaves became popular for quilting. Pile weaves (velvets and corduroy) add an extra yarn, loosely woven, into the fabric. These "loose" yarns actually stick up from the fabric and are evenly cut to produce the soft, fuzzy texture of their surface. These fabrics were combined with the brocades, taffetas, and satins in crazy quilts.

Another distinctive fabric popular from about 1880 to 1920 was cretonne, an unglazed twill weave with large prints. It was used for curtains and upholstery and found its way into scrap bags and then into quilts. In the 1890s, feed sack prints were introduced, and many of these found their way into quilts and were used until the 1940s. These were loosely woven cotton printed in bright patterns. Quilts of Sunbonnet Sue, Dresden Plate, and Double Wedding Ring patterns made from feed sack cloth can still be found.

The first quarter of the twentieth century saw the quality of fabrics deteriorate. Weaves were less compact, the result of trying to keep prices down, and dyes weren't colorfast. There was a chintz produced that was so cheap it lost its sizing in the first wash. "Chintzy" became a popular word for anything cheap, and what was once the highest quality cotton used in quilts now became the most ignored. Inexpensive but quality cottons were available in limited plain colors such as blue, gray, black, and maroon.

Cotton sateens were popular in the second quarter of the twentieth century, making them a good indicator of the age of a quilt. Synthetic satin was also popular for whole-cloth quilts and tied comforters. Coverlets of satin, in the puff style, were popular during the period of 1925 to 1950. So popular were they, in fact, that manufacturers mass-produced them.

We've included some specific fabric names, descriptions, and definitions in our glossary.

Color

Throughout history people have searched for better, brighter, more colorfast dyes. They turned to plants, the soil, rocks, even animals. As technology and science advanced, they turned to synthetic compounds as well.

Rarely does a single color give us many clues as to the date of a quilt. Luckily, quiltmakers have chosen print fabrics for their quilts from the very beginning. These printed fabrics, and their use at different periods over the history of quilting, combined with what we know were fashionable combinations of colors, do provide us with evidence to date a quilt.

Different fabric fibers need different methods of dyeing. Some natural dyes don't fix to animal fibers and a mordant must be added to the dye mix to make the fabric absorb the dye. *Mordant* comes from the Latin *mordere*, which means to bite. That's basically what a mordant does. It allows the dye to "bite" the fabric, or become fast. Mordants are metallic oxides or minerals such as alum, cream of tartar, ammonia, chrome, tin, iron, copper sulfate, tannin, vinegar, baking soda, or oxalic acid. Some metallic salts that worked on both animal- and vegetable-based fabrics were used as mordants because they improved colorfastness. To place several different colors on the same fabric a mordant is used so that the dye used with it "bites" or bonds only where the mordant lies on the fabric.

The resist method of dyeing is the opposite of mordanting. In this method the portions of cloth that are not to be printed are treated with a resisting chemical. When the fabric is dyed, the dye will not take to the fabric treated with the resist and in these areas the background color shows through. In half resist, the areas where dye is not wanted are only partially protected from the dye. This produces a blend of colors, or in the case of white, a lighter shade of the background color.

Until 1856 the only dyes available for either manufacturers or individuals were derived from vegetable, mineral, or animal sources. Among these were blue from indigo, browns and Turkey red from the roots of the madder plant, black from logwood, and yellow from the wood of the fustic tree in the West Indies. Madder was grown in the American colonies in small amounts. Most was imported. Indigo was the only commercial dye crop grown in America, and Southern ports exported many tons of it to the world.

Quiltmakers joined in the quest for colorfast dyes. It just didn't make sense to put all that work into a best quilt, one that you wanted to give as a gift or hand down to your children, only to find that the colors bled, faded, or crocked and ruined it. Over the centuries they tried the new dyes brought on the market, rejected those that were inferior, and returned to those that were colorfast.

Dye recipes, like quilt patterns, were handed down over generations. *Godey's Lady's Book* regularly printed dye recipes. Fabric was dyed at home commonly up to 1860, and women knew their recipes so well that they manipulated them, as they did their favorite family food recipes, to produce shades and tones of color they wanted. Often they dyed entire bolts of cloth—as much as twenty yards at a time. Piece dyeing continued in the home through the 1950s and actually continues today. In 1863 the first packaged dyes, of natural sources, were marketed. In 1880 the first synthetic dyes became available. Up until World War I, Germany was the source for good synthetic dyes. Now the United States is the number-one exporter of dyestuffs.

Just as it's hard to determine if a fabric is homespun or manufactured, it's also difficult to recognize a home dye job from a manufactured one. Homemakers and manufacturers used the same commercial dyes and both did good and bad jobs using them. Don't assume that a low-quality dye job was done in the home.

"Most of the blotchy, fading fabrics we see in old quilts were probably factory fabric," wrote Barbara Brackman in *Clues in the Calico*.

Gingham fabrics are weak indicators for dating fabric. In these fabrics, the yarns were dyed first and then woven together to produce the checks and stripes. Ginghams derive their color scheme from weaving, not printing, and were so widely used over the centuries that they are not a good indicator for dating the quilts that incorporate them.

Like the quiltmakers before her, Susan Parrish, of Susan Parrish Antiques in New York, believes that color loss on a quilt contributes more to a loss in value than stains. Sometimes, as we'll see when we get to specific colors, loss is indicative of a time period. In this case it can increase the value of a quilt simply because we know more about that quilt's history.

We'd like to point out some general trends in the use of color before we get down to specifics. For reasons we'll soon cover, the colors most preferred in Colonial days, if the ads from the period are read, were blue, crimson, and green. It's not too surprising, actually, since these dyes resulted in the most colorfast fabrics of the time. Red and white, and blue and white, were, and continue to be, traditional color choices for such patterns as Drunkard's Path and Irish Chain.

New dyes for brown, based on manganese, were introduced in 1825. These browns were brighter, less dull than the browns achieved from vegetable sources. They worked particularly well as backgrounds because they didn't overpower other colors printed on them. The Civil War, with its attendant low supply and high prices, brought the cheaper browns back into use. But even these new browns took a back seat, for a time, to the lavender and gray colors popular in the 1850s. Madder-brown dyes were still used until the end of the 1800s. Some of the "new" brown dyes didn't stand the test of time. They corroded the cotton where the dye had fixed. You'll find quilts with holes in the tops that correspond to the figure or print on the fabric. Those holes were probably created by the corrosive effect of the dyes.

Aniline dyes were introduced after the middle of the nineteenth century. The discovery of aniline for use with dyes added colorfast mauves, alizarin red, greens, and other browns to a quiltmaker's range of colors.

More quiltmakers purchased fabric specifically for quilts starting about 1840. From then until the turn of the century, there was a fashion for quilts of only one color combined with white. Turkey red and green, with a white background fabric, were the most often chosen. Navy, red, or green was chosen to go with white in two-color quilts. One quilt historian surmised that so many of these quilts survived to our time because their basic colors made them difficult to decorate with. One-color and two-color quilts are valued by collectors.

There was a tan period in quiltmaking history dating from the 1860s through the 1880s. There's an odd blue, described as a dark blue with green-turquoise overtones, that can date a quilt to the 1870s and 1880s. Rusts were popular in quilts from 1885 to 1910. A cotton print with a black background was a popular fabric for quilts starting in 1890 and continuing through the first quarter of this century.

The early 1900s saw a revival of the use of tan in quilts, and popular color schemes in the 1920s were blues and green, with lavender making a brief comeback in the 1930s. This was also the period of the pastels, those brightly colored, often thought gaudy, calicoes so popular in Dresden Plate and Double Wedding Ring quilts. The 1920s and 1930s were also the period of the feed sack cottons with their bright prints.

Let's get specific.

White

White, as an indicator, isn't very date-specific. It's been used in quilts during all periods. To get natural fibers white, they had to be bleached. Sun bleaching fabrics was common as early as 1774, until the discovery of chlorine in 1807. Chlorine shortened and simplified the bleaching process but it also damaged the fibers and made the cloth wear out sooner. Grass bleaching, to remove the lettering from flour and sugar sacks so they could be used in quilts, became popular again in the 1930s and 1940s. The only white that can point to a date for a quilt is actually print on white. From 1870 to 1925, quilters used white background shirting fabrics distinctive for their small figured prints. After 1925, use of these shirting fabrics died out and quilters returned to plain white fabric.

Blue

This is another color that has had so much use over the centuries that it isn't a good indicator for dating. Indigo was the only blue dyestuff available until 1856, and it was still used as late as 1880. Although it was highly valued for its colorfastness, indigo was difficult to work with. It required an alkaline agent because it was insoluble in water—the very feature that made it colorfast. Once the fabric was dyed and dried, the dye stayed through many, many washings. When aniline dyes were invented in the middle 1850s, they gradually took indigo's place as the favored blue dyestuff because, also colorfast, they were easier to work with.

Prussian blue was a dye used in Colonial America but it's a dating clue to the period from 1830 to 1860. Prussiate of potash combined with iron salt produces a white solution that turns blue as it dries and oxidizes. Prussian blue was first used in a broadcloth made in Philadelphia in 1832 named "Lafayette" blue. This vibrant blue was used in plain cottons and prints. It was common in florals, chintz-scale pillar prints, and as a background for rainbow prints. It was often used with a dull tan. Fabrics containing Lafayette blue indicate a middle 1800s date.

Light blues have also been heavily used by quiltmakers over the centuries and don't generally indicate a date. But one light blue, with a violet tone, was popular with checks, florals, and geometrics in shirting fabrics from approximately the 1870s through the 1890s. Watch for this violet-tinged light blue as an indicator of the late 1800s.

A grayish blue, called cadet blue, appeared as a background color around 1890. It was usually printed with a small figure, a stripe, or a dot. Used for everyday clothes and aprons, this colored fabric found its way into the quiltmaker's scrap bag.

Red

Madder, a red dye derived from the plant *Rubia tinctorum*, originally from Asia Minor, is one of the oldest of dyestuffs. Madder produced a red that became known as Turkey red, and it took thirteen to twenty different steps to produce a fabric colored Turkey red. The process was never attempted on a commercial level in the United States but Turkey red was the most important of red dyes used through the 1800s. The synthetic alizarin, using a much faster, easier process to achieve the vibrant red, was introduced in 1868.

You need to be very familiar with Turkey red to distinguish it from later red dyes. Usually a red that has stayed vibrant in a quilt that has other date indicators can be classified as true Turkey red and dated sometime after the 1830s or 1840s. Since Turkey red was used for over a hundred years, printed fabric with the red as the background is a more reliable indicator of the date. Calicoes with Turkey red as the background for tiny cones, flowers, or geometric prints are good indicators to the early 1800s.

You can also determine a Turkey red from its distinctive wear pattern. As Turkey red wears, the color comes off of individual yarns rather than changing color or fading in patches. When this happens, the fabric appears to have white streaks running through it. The process used to achieve Turkey red was quite hard on fabrics. If only the red patchwork on a quilt seems lighter in the loft parts of the quilt, that's an indication of Turkey red fabric. At one point, home dyers could get a synthetic dye labeled Turkey red. Since Turkey red is a process, not really a dye, these dyes didn't live up to their name. They turned color, fading to either brown or pink. The quilt pictured on page 48 is a red-and-white Drunkard's Path. It wasn't made to look the way it does. The white areas of the quilt show a faint pink tinge, and it's believed that, running out of Turkey red, this quiltmaker might have dyed her own from the falsely advertised synthetic dye or bought fabric that used it. Over time, the Turkey red stayed red and the inferior dye faded to white. It leaves a striking quilt, but not in the way the maker intended. The presence of faded red fabric in a quilt is a good indicator to a date between 1875 and 1925.

There were other red dyes available. Cochineal dyes were used more for fine cloth than were the cheaper madder dyes and along with red, produced pink, crimson, and scarlet. It was a prominent dyestuff after 1793. Annatto dye, derived from the seeds of a tropical plant, produced pink, reddish-orange, and blues for cotton and silk. Brazilwood was used in Colonial America in the early 1800s but its use declined as Turkey red became more popular.

During the last quarter of the nineteenth century and the first quarter of this century, American textile manufacturers produced a very popular, very cheap, red background fabric with various black figures printed on it. Called robe prints or Garibaldi prints, the most common figures were anchors, horseshoes, tennis rackets, paisley cone-shaped feathers, and florals. A dull burgundy, actually a purplish-red that didn't fade was manufactured from about 1890

No, the maker did not leave out some of the patches on this red-and-white Drunkard's Path; rather she used two different materials, one with a stable dye and one with an unstable dye, which, when it faded to an almost white pale pink, left this unusual look. Unstable red dyes are a help in dating, and the look that is left does show off the straight-line quilting on this 1890s quilt.

through 1925. There was also a red tinged with cinnamon used in the last half of the nineteenth century that is referred to as "madder-style." It was used on all cloth from cotton to silk. It's distinctive for its orange tinge and was used to produce colors ranging from red to red-brown. Prints with this background used light purple and light blue as accent colors.

Most pinks are not good date indicators because they, too, had a long period of popularity in both early quilts and those made as recently as between 1925 and 1950. Double pinks, a dark pink print on a light pink background, were very popular from 1875 to 1900, so these bright pinks are an indicator of that period. A plain pink, sometimes found in sateen weave, was very popular as a dominant color theme in quilts made in the second quarter of this century.

Brown

Brown is a difficult color to use to verify the date of a quilt. Brown was the easiest color to produce from natural dyes. Clay-pot browns were made in the

South using distinctive red dirt. Mud dyeing was simple. Cloth was literally buried in mud, producing a terra-cotta shade. Butternut and black walnut shells were used as brown dyes. There were, of course, many recipes and synthetic dyes developed as well. Shades of brown can narrow down a date, but it takes time to train yourself to distinguish them.

A light tan, with a green tinge, is the tan used with the Lafayette of Prussian blue dyed fabric we discussed earlier. Popular from 1830 to 1860, a tan with this blue is a valid date indicator. There was also a Manganese bronze–style tan, almost khaki, with red and white figures that was printed from 1850 through 1910, and was especially popular toward the end of that time frame.

Another reason browns are difficult to identify and date is that they may not have been browns originally. Many fabrics faded to brown with use, washing, and age. Appliquéd fabrics that are obviously stems and leaves but are done in tans or browns were probably green when they were made. Brown grapes and roses are not the results of a weird color scheme chosen by the quiltmaker. They are the results of inferior dyes. Fabrics used from the end of the nineteenth century, from the start of synthetic dyes, just didn't hold their original colors. Green, purple, blue, and red all faded to shades of brown. Some reds faded to a salmon-tinged tan, while blues and purples faded to khaki. Don't assume the browns and tans you see in a quilt are as they were intended. Clues that a fabric has faded to brown can be found by inspecting the pattern. Roses are not brown and most stems and leaves aren't either. Since quiltmakers copied nature, there's no reason to assume that any of them decided to appliqué a brown rose by choice.

Quilts with a predominantly brown color theme, not that way because of fading, can be assumed to be from before the twentieth century. In the early 1900s, quiltmakers turned to blacks, grays, and blues as dominant color themes. The brown color scheme made a short revival in the 1970s and 1980s.

Browns are among the first fabrics to deteriorate because of the iron mordant used to fix the dye. The mordant weakens, or tenders, the fabric. You'll often see fabric with rotted holes in the shapes of the prints that originally adorned it.

Green

There was no single vegetable dye to create green. A method to dye fabrics green in one application wasn't discovered until 1778. Until that time, a combination of yellow and blue was used, one color placed on top of the other, to create green. This process worked fine for plain fabrics, but green in a printed calico was difficult. The overlay color, whether it was yellow or blue, had to be overprinted. If the hand or stencil printing didn't line up perfectly with the first color, the printed figure had an edge of yellow on one side while the other side of the print showed a strip of blue. The process always delivered a green that was tinged either with yellow or blue, depending on which dye was stronger. The colors could also fade differently. If the blue faded from a quilt's flower stems it left them yellow. Blue stems and leaves is an indication that the yellow faded out of an overdyed fabric. How else can we explain blue leaves and stems? Surely no quiltmaker would depict flowers with blue stems when they don't exist in nature. Overdying to obtain green continued until the last quarter of the nineteenth century.

Mineral green dyes were not as bright or true as the vegetable dye combinations. They still used overprinting, and some were colorfast, but they lacked the vibrancy of their vegetable dye counterparts. If you find a lifeless green, it's a good indicator to a date in the first half of the nineteenth century.

Single-step application of green dyes didn't become common until 1875, after synthetic dyes were developed. Overprinting blue on yellow or yellow on blue was still being done during this time. If the overprinting was done expertly and the prints lined up perfectly, it's difficult to tell if a green is a single application or an overprint.

The synthetic green dyes didn't hold up well. They have faded to a tan, slightly khaki, slightly mustard, color that indicates the period from 1875 to 1900. If your quilt has some tan in it, try lifting or pulling it up slightly so that you can see the seam allowance. More protected from the effects of use and washing, the seam fabric may be the original shade of green. A tan or brown fabric quilted with green thread is also an indication it was originally green since quiltmakers tended to match their thread color to the fabric color. Some historians believe that those red, white, and tan quilts dated from the end of the nineteenth century originally were red, white, and green. As quiltmakers noticed their greens fading to tan, they stopped using green fabrics in their quilts. From 1890 to 1925, green was not a common color in quilts. If you've bought a quilt with an attributed date between 1875 and 1900 and it has green in it, determine how the green was achieved. If you don't and you hang or wash the quilt, you may find your lovely green quilt turning tan. The inferior synthetic dyes of the late 1800s and early 1900s could even fade completely to white.

There is a colorfast dark green that appears in quilts from the last half of the nineteenth century. This was an indigo or Prussian blue overdyed with chrome yellow that has kept its color very well. A nile green was manufactured in the 1920s and 1930s. It is one of the colors reproduced in contemporary fabrics, making repairs to the Depression-era quilts that contained it a little easier.

As you look at quilts, you'll notice that there's a lot of green background fabric printed with tiny figures. These fabrics were common in three periods of quiltmaking: the 1870s, the 1930s, and the 1970s. You'll probably have to see a lot of these fabrics to tell the difference in their ages. Watch for quilts that have valid dates from other dating clues to learn which is which.

Yellow

There were many yellow dyes, both domestic and imported, that American quiltmakers used, but the three most popular dyes were fustic, quercitron, and chrome yellow.

Fustic was an economical dye in use in the Colonies. There are records of its use dated 1661. The fustic yellow was colorfast but dull. Fustic was also used to produce other colors.

Quercitron was derived from oak tree bark and made in America. Quercitron produced a bright, colorfast yellow. It was used mostly to dye woolen fabrics but was used on cottons and silks as well. Combined with other dyes, quercitron was an important ingredient in making olive, oranges, red-yellows, and cinnamons.

Chrome yellow was introduced in the mid-1800s. This was a mineral dye that, although fast on cottons, didn't fix well on wool. It first appeared in the United States in the 1830s.

Yellows are good clues to dating a quilt to the mid- to late 1800s. There's a burnt orange, popularly used in charm quilts and Log Cabins, that you can rely on as an indication to a date in the last half of the nineteenth century. Butterscotch-colored cloth is also a good indicator for that period. Cottons of plain yellow and calicoes with yellow background color can date a quilt to the late 1800s, as can a plain cotton with a true orange color.

For all of the 1800s and into the first ten years of the twentieth century, there was a long-standing popular fabric with a navy background printed with bright yellow figures. Tangerine, melon, and peach are indicative of the period 1925 to about 1950.

Two yellows, both popular, tend to crock over time. (Crocking is the loss of surface color on a piece of fabric.) These two were the plain chrome orange and a loud, gaudy yellow-orange that one historian called safety yellow because it reminded her of the lines painted down the middle of our streets and highways. The safety yellow is a good clue to the mid-1800s or after. If you have a quilt with one of these colors, the chrome orange or safety yellow, always store it layered and wrapped with acid-free tissue paper (see chapter 7 on care). If you don't, the color will crock off the yellow or orange and onto other fabrics in the quilt, creating permanent, unsightly spots and blotches.

Black

Early black dyes came from logwood. Black was a hard dye to use but it was in use in England from about 1580. The logwood black was combined with other dyes to produce navy and green and was in use until the beginning of World War II. Black dyeing was done mordant style and silks and cottons were especially affected by the harsh dyeing process. Black is another color that tended to eat away the cloth where it was applied, leaving distinctive, pattern-shaped holes behind. It wasn't until the 1890s, just in time for the crazy quilt period with its high use of black fabric, that a reliable dye was created. Then black colorfast cottons became readily available.

Black provides us with several clues helpful to dating quilts. In cotton quilts, black was used from approximately 1890, when the new dye became available, until 1925. For silk, black was a predominant color from 1860 to 1910. Wool quilts incorporate black from about 1880 to 1925. With the advent of the pastel period, starting in the 1920s, black went out of favor except among Amish quiltmakers, who still use it as a design element today.

Prior to the Civil War, black was used primarily for designs and figures printed on Turkey red cloth. It wasn't used as a color on its own until after the 1860s. In the last half of the eighteenth century, black was a required fabric for the fashionable quilts of the day: Log Cabins, crazies, and fan quilts.

Black background prints indicate the 1890s through 1925. These multi-colored, bright prints used magenta, purple, yellow-green, pink, and gold as their accent colors. The designs look very modern.

Black figures were closely printed on white backgrounds to produce the shirting fabrics so popular from 1890 to 1925. The designs were so small and so closely packed that, from a distance, the fabric appears gray.

Fabric with a gray background, or plain gray, was used after the 1940s. The prints are easy to spot because they are especially whimsical. While visiting dealers and shops, we saw several examples of this fabric with gypsy dancers in brightly colored clothes, figures busily at work, and farm animals.

Purple

We include this color because there are at least two specific periods in quiltmaking history when it was popular. Purple provides valuable, reliable clues to dating a quilt.

There were two purple periods in quiltmaking history. The first was around the time of the Civil War. Before synthetic dyes, purples were a lifeless lavender that tended to fade to brown or pink. Be careful dating a purple or lavender fabric in a quilt. This color was available, in varying qualities of tone, during all of the nineteenth century. Don't assume that a fairly bright, unfaded purple is necessarily a synthetic. Perhaps the quilt was properly stored and unaffected by light.

The second purple period came during the 1920s to the 1950s, when dyes that produced a stronger purple and a true lavender became available. Plain and print purples as well as lilac, raspberry, orchid, and lavender are strong indicators to the second quarter of the twentieth century.

Dating a quilt by color is tricky. Use, washing, and exposure to light may have caused bleeding, fading, and migrating of the colors. Improper storage could cause crocking fabrics to stain the fabrics placed on top of them. Harsh dyes, mordants, and resists also took their toll on quilts and quilt colors. Investigate thoroughly, look at lots of quilts, and hone your instincts for recognizing colors as they are and interpreting what they were.

Printed Fabric

The prints on fabric have their own tale to tell about the age of a quilt. Creating fabric decorated with figures, geometric shapes, or designs is accomplished by one of four methods: direct, discharge, mordant, or resist.

In direct printing, a color, or several colors, are applied to a solid-colored fabric or a plain white, or a white design can be applied to a colored background fabric.

The discharge method used a previously dyed background fabric and then bleached out the design, turning the figured area to white. After the discovery of chlorine as a bleaching agent in 1807, fabrics that incorporated the discharge method will show wear in the bleached areas before the background sections do.

The mordant method meant that up to four colors could be applied to the same background cloth. Since different dyes required different mordants to make them fix to the cloth and stay there, the use of four mordants meant that when the cloth was dyed only those areas treated with a mordant that attracted a specific dye would result in that color. The area not treated with the right mordant remained either the background color or the color attracted by a different mordant.

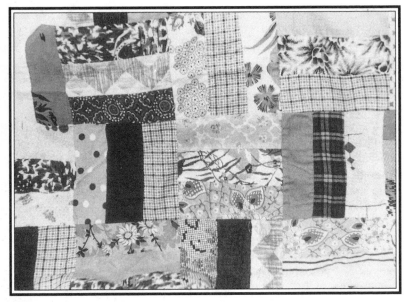

This 1940s scrap bag Rail Fence quilt top shows a multitude of fabrics and just how busy a quilt can look.

In the resist method, wax or a chemical paste is applied to the fabric in the shape of the design wanted. When the dye is applied, it won't fix to the treated areas so they stay the same color as the background. After dyeing, the resist substance is removed and the fabric shows the design intended.

Printers can combine these methods, using the mordant and discharge operations together, or the resist and mordant methods to produce multicolored printed fabrics.

The most frequently used methods of applying dye were hand-painting, wooden block, copperplate, and roller printing. Wood-block and copperplate printing are clues to dates before 1850. Roller prints were not used before 1800. Ikat prints, like ginghams and plaids, are actually the result of a weaving method, not a result of printing. In this method, the yarns are dyed before weaving and the pattern results from the way the yarns were woven. Tie-dying was also used.

Wood-block printing used the mordant method. A different mordant, or strengths of the same mordant, and a separate wood block were used for each design element in a print.

By the end of the 1700s, factories were using the copperplate method. Copper sheets, with the design cut into them, were pressed onto the cloth to print fabric up to a yard square. This vastly reduced the time it took to print fabric.

The next labor-saving, and cost-reducing, advance in printing technique was the advent of cylinder printing; it was similar to copperplate, but the advantage was that the process was continuous. It was first used for upholstery and curtain fabrics and usually printed only one color. Other colors were added later by plate methods. By 1835, multiple cylinders were used, each adding a different color. Cylinder printing was improved when pantograph methods etched several series of a design to the same cylinder, further reducing production costs.

There are ways to recognize the different printing methods. Copperplate printing is highly detailed, usually depicting a scene such as a landscape, fair, or cityscape. Intricate florals and trees were popular patterns. These prints were usually one color. The fabric ranged anywhere from 33 to 45 inches square. You might find a fine white line running through some copperplate prints. This is probably not a design element but the result of poor registration caused by inexpert application. (Registration is the matching, perfectly, of the design elements so that it's impossible to tell where the plate ended. If the registration is off, the design doesn't match and the fine white line appears.) Some of the prints from copperplate soak through the fabric to the back in a fainter shade than the original. Unless you have an unfinished quilt, you won't be able to see this, but you can look for it if you find uncut fabric you think was printed with copperplate.

Early cylinder printing used a roller only 16 inches in circumference. Look for where the design repeats on a piece of fabric. If you measure from repeat to repeat, you'll get the length of the original design. If this length is greater than 16 inches, and you have other clues to an early date for the quilt, then it was probably pressed with a plate rather than rolled.

Different styles of printed fabrics were used differently over the course of quiltmaking history. Chintz, over the centuries, has consistently meant a cotton with a large-scale design that was glazed. We still recognize a chintz by its large print. But the size of the print today and the size of the print in the late eighteenth century are drastically different. Today a chintz print is a larger design than our calicoes. But in the past, a chintz pattern was the size of a bed top. It was these chintzes that quiltmakers prized for Broderie-Perse. This type of appliqué required cutting out that large-scale design and stitching it down on a whole-cloth background. It was difficult work because of the size of the piece. The large Tree of Life pattern, done in this medallion style, is indicative of a date before 1850. Eventually, quiltmakers made work easier for themselves and began cutting smaller design elements out of fabric to appliqué in a design of their own choice. Palm trees and game birds were popular in the first half of the 1800s, while floral wreaths and baskets were made from approximately 1790 until the late 1840s.

So popular was the fashion for cutting out design elements from printed fabric that, in the early 1800s, chintz fabric was designed in Europe in patterns sized to be cut and used specifically for the corners and centers of quilts.

There is one other fabric print that dates from the eighteenth century. Paisley originated in Kashmir, India, but by the end of the eighteenth century, Scotland was producing a quality copy. Paisley fell so out of fashion in the 1870s that the mills in Paisley, Scotland, stopped producing it in 1886.

By the 1820s and 1830s, the American textile industry had found its footing. It produced calicoes with small floral prints for the design. In the 1830s and 1840s, American factories designed geometric chintzes based on quilt patterns. Beautiful printed cottons were made. The most popular were red and green backgrounds with small yellow or black figures. Geometric designs on cloth were popular from 1840 through 1900.

In the 1850s the first cheater cloth came on the market. Since the fabric was already printed in blocks resembling pieced work, all the quiltmaker had to do was cut out the squares and sew them together. In the 1850s these were imitation chintz patches. Log Cabin and charm quilt cheaters colored with madder dyes appeared in the early 1900s. In 1933, Sears offered Grandmother's Flower Garden, Dresden Plate, and Double Wedding Ring patterns in cheater cloth style.

Plaids are poor age indicators because they were used often in quilts. They fell out of fashion after the Civil War but revived briefly in the late 1800s and early 1900s.

The 1880s were a boom period for print fabrics. During this time there were many notable and beautiful prints produced: small floral sprigs on dark backgrounds; checks, stars, small bouquets, and black-and-white designs. This was the period of the shirting fabrics, those white backgrounds covered with tiny black dots, swirls, leaves, tennis racquets, oars, horseshoes, anchors, sailboats, and baseballs, as well as geometrics. Large geometric designs, startling, were produced in the 1880s through 1890s. Many of these designs stayed in production for many years. The Ely Manufacturing Company still produces eighteen designs dating from 1878.

This cheater cloth, printed in shades of red, pink, gold, and brown, could have been quickly quilted into a finished piece with the piecework look without the piecework work.

The invention of copperplate printing created the commemorative print. These were available as early as the end of the 1700s. Europe imported a commemorative depicting George Washington in 1785. The last half of the nineteenth century produced many commemorative fabrics that appeared as both yardage for quilts and as handkerchiefs that could be incorporated into a quilt. There was a "The Union Forever" commemorative with a star and clasped hands, several depicting Ulysses S. Grant, at least one for Horace Greeley, and many for the American Centennial and for Queen Victoria's Jubilee. Presidential campaigns produced many pieces of commemorative cloth.

There are two other date indicators for printed fabric. As a general rule, the higher the number of different colors in a single fabric piece the better it indicates a date either before 1875 or after 1925. In between, it was much cheaper to print a single color on a ground fabric.

The second date indicator deals with registration, or design matching. Printing several colors on a cloth makes it difficult for each color to line up in the proper place on the design. To counteract this, and to cover up any mis-

An unusual combination, this quilt from 1920 has blocks stenciled with yellow, peach, and pale green flowers and flower bowls. The simple Nine-patch color blocks, in a shade of soft brown, almost get lost in the overall lines and look of the quilt.
Photograph courtesy of Susan Parrish

takes, a solid black outline was added to character prints in some fabrics before 1850. White halos around figures also indicate a pre-1850 or 1925-to-1950 date. Multicolored, perfectly registered printed fabric was at its peak from 1840 to 1890.

Technique

How a quiltmaker worked, the type of quilt made, how stems and leaves are represented, and the quality of the work all give us general dating clues.

"Although exceptions occurred, especially in the category of silk Show Quilts, late nineteenth-century cotton quilts generally show lower levels of hand workmanship," wrote Brackman in *Clues in the Calico*. Brackman attributes this decline in work quality to the increase in popularity of the sewing machine. The new machine, and the availability of ready-made clothing and furnishings, freed women from the yoke of needlework. It was no longer necessary to teach young girls the uses of the needle. Without all that practice, needlework skills declined.

Stems, animal eyes, and faces were commonly hand-painted on quilts made before the 1850s. Hand-painting returned during the crazy quilt period, when flowers and animals were added to the heavily embroidered blocks. The 1920s brought a minor fashion, revived in the 1960s, of drawing on cloth with crayon. When the wax was washed out, the dye stayed. Liquid embroidery pens and markers were used to create some quilts in the 1950s.

Embroidery was used extensively in quilting for several periods. Embroidered quilts of the 1880s and after depict designs in outline embroidery only and usually in a single color. These were sentimental, simple designs of flowers, children, pets, fans, cattails, and crosses. Embroidery was essential to the crazy quilt of the Victorian era. Herringbone, feather, and buttonhole stitches, as well as other fancy embroidery, covered the seam lines of the crazy quilt patches. Embroidery decorated the blocks, too, showing the quiltmaker's favorite things. After World War I, floral baskets, state birds, nursery rhymes, and the alphabet were popular designs for outline embroidery quilts. Signature quilts were often single-color embroidery designs.

One trend that might explain the number of unfinished early twentieth-century quilt tops available today was the custom of quilting "on shares." A client purchased enough fabric for two quilts. The quilter made one quilt for the client and kept the remaining fabric to make a quilt for herself or to sell.

There are two appliqué formats. The medallion style was popular before 1840 and used the very large-scale chintz patterns that were cut out of the cloth and appliquéd to a whole-cloth ground fabric. The block style became popular after 1840 because it was easier to work with the smaller piece of cloth.

There are three types of appliqué. The conventional style is Broderie-Perse, common in the eighteenth and early nineteenth centuries. To make the work simpler, smaller pieces of fabric were used. A piece of cloth is cut in the desired shape, its edges are folded under, and it is then stitched to a ground fabric. Conventional appliqué was used in both the body of the quilt and in the borders. The album quilts of the later 1800s are all done in appliqué. Conventional appliqué fell out of favor for a while at the turn of the century but reappeared in the 1920s and 1930s.

Reverse appliqué is also an old technique with examples appearing from the last three centuries. In reverse appliqué, the top layer of fabric is cut away to reveal the backing fabric. The inside edges of the cut design are folded under and stitched down. This is a tricky, time-consuming method of quiltmaking, and examples are rare.

There are appliqué patterns such as Sunbonnet Sue, Whig Rose, and Rose of Sharon that many quiltmakers copied and used. But appliqué quickly became an individually designed form. Designs were sketched on paper and then cut out of fabric. Some pieces were cut freehand, and many an appliqué has been designed around the shape of a cookie cutter, teacup, or other household item.

Appliqué stitches should be invisible with only a few exceptions. The most popular stitches were the blind and overcast. Embroidery stitches were sometimes used to represent flower stems and leaves. One strong date clue is the use of the sewing machine to appliqué. These stitches were not invisible and they weren't meant to be. Machine owners purposely stitched their appliqué by machine to show off the new technology. There are examples of this from the 1860s. A black buttonhole stitch was used around the outside edge of appliquéd designs in the years between 1925 and 1950, and this is another appliqué stitching date indicator.

There are several methods of assembling pieced blocks. One is called the English style. A paper pattern is cut out, the fabric is wrapped around it, pressed, and then whipstitched to another piece formed the same way. The last step is to remove the paper backing. This method was used primarily in the

The "logs" on this Courthouse Steps Log Cabin are very narrow, about 1/2 inch. The quilt is all silks, with some wear and fabric deterioration, but for an 1890s quilt it looks just fine. A good example of the foundation method of assembly.

nineteenth century. If you can find a top with the paper inserts still intact, check for a date. It's an excellent way to accurately place a quilt in its proper period.

The foundation method, or pressed piecing, was popular in the last quarter of the nineteenth century, particularly to make Log Cabins, crazy quilts, and string quilts. In this method, the quiltmaker started by cutting enough large squares to get the dimensions she wanted. To these foundation squares, she stitched the pieces of her pattern until she had covered the original squares. Sometimes newspapers were used as foundation squares. We saw one Log Cabin quilt top that still had the newspaper on the back. You can sometimes see a foundation fabric in a finished quilt by looking through pieces of the top cloth that have rotted or torn.

Assembling pieced blocks by seaming them together with a running stitch is called the American method. Today quiltmakers add a 1/4-inch seam allowance to their pieces, but there is some evidence that past quiltmakers used only a 3/16-inch seam. Starting at the beginning of the twentieth century, Log Cabin quilts were assembled using the American method. Crazy quilts and string quilts still use foundation squares.

Trapunto, or stuffing quilts, is a very old style, popular before the Civil War.

Finishing edgings had fashions and fads as well. A quilt with cut-out corners indicates it was made before 1860. Scalloped borders were popular after the 1840s, hitting a peak in the period from 1925 to 1950 and used with the Double Wedding Ring pattern. Fancy borders with cords, braids, tassels, and lace were used on show quilts in the last half of the nineteenth century. Fringed quilts are generally dated before the Civil War. Folded triangles called Prairie Points were used starting in the mid-1800s but were most common after 1925.

Finishing strips made of bias binding point to the twentieth century. Twill tape was used before the Civil War.

You have to be careful dating a quilt by its border or finishing. So many quilt tops were completed years after they were made that the border might be made from a much newer fabric or with a newer technique or style. If you find a quilt with a new border or edging it's customary to date the top and the border separately and document when each was made.

There were other special techniques of quilt construction popular for brief periods. Victorian puff quilts were made from satins and velvets at the end of the nineteenth century. Squares were cut and the corners folded to achieve a cup shape. These were stuffed and then whipstitched together.

The yo-yo quilt was popular from 1925 to 1950. This was not a three-layered quilt. Circles of scrap bag fabrics were cut. The outside edge of the circle was gathered together and the result pressed flat. The circles were sewed together with the small gathered opening to the back. These were novelty quilts and used primarily for decoration. The many spaces between the yo-yos wouldn't keep anyone warm. Some of these quilts were backed with a plain colored cotton.

The Cathedral Window quilt is another nonquilted decorative top. Squares of cloth are folded and refolded with other cloth stitched in the middle. Usually muslin, or a plain-colored fabric, was used for the window part and scrap bag fabrics were used for the centers. Although the pattern dates to 1910, it was most popular in the 1960s and 1970s.

This close-up of one yo-yo shows how fabric circles are gathered and fastened, then stitched together to form this nonutilitarian but whimsical quilt top.
Quilt courtesy of Joan Halla

Quilting

Quilts that are tied aren't technically quilts. They should be called comforters. Tying was a shortcut—it took much less time to tie a top than to quilt it. Comforters were made for utility. Another reason a top was tied rather than quilted was because of the weight of the fabrics used. Heavy velvets and wools were difficult to quilt through, so they were tied instead.

Earlier quilts had more stitching than those made after the introduction of polyester batting. Wool and cotton batts tended to shift in washing and lump in unquilted areas. Quilt designs were stitched no farther apart than half an inch to prevent the batting from shifting.

Quiltmakers were, and still are, very picky about the designs for stitching their quilt tops. There was plain quilting using diamonds; single, double, or triple rows of diagonal lines referred to as crossbars; and clamshell shapes. Fancy designs included floral bouquets, pineapples, spiderwebs, oak leaves, cornucopias, princess feathers, wreaths, and stars. There were quilting sampler quilts created before the Civil War that, like appliqué samplers, used a variety of quilting patterns.

Stipple quilting dates to the first half of the nineteenth century. Hundreds of stitches and stitching lines were used to accent plain areas, unquilted in the overall design. Fan quilting, with its groups of concentric half circles, is a clue to the latter part of the nineteenth century and the early years of the twentieth. Self-quilting, the method of quilting 1/4 inch away from the seam line around each patch in a pattern, is a twentieth-century technique, as is machine quilting.

Thread colored to match the color of the fabric has always been used for quilting. White is a favorite color, while the Amish use black thread. Patterns were often penciled on the quilt top, but quiltmakers also used stencils or paper patterns they traced with a wheel. Two of our sources mentioned the use of a chalk-covered string that was snapped down on the quilt top once it was in the frame to mark the straight diagonal lines of crossbar quilting. But it does seem, to us, that this is a highly inaccurate method of marking quilting lines, not to mention messy.

The way some quiltmakers signed their quilts gives us some idea of its age. Fast inks that didn't corrode fabric were available in the late 1830s. The advent of these new inks might have contributed to the craze for autograph quilts in the 1840s and 1850s. Signatures during this later period were elaborate and included verses and small drawings. Cross-stitch was used up until the 1850s. Embroidered signatures are more commonly found on quilts after 1875.

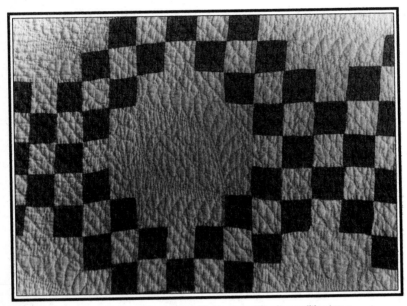

This close-up shows the detail and beautiful leaf and feather quilting on a rose-on-white Double Irish Chain. Look carefully and you can pick out the appliquéd corners on this 1840s quilt.

Appliquéd signatures were used in all quilting periods but were most common from 1840 through 1900. There was a short period, from 1840 through 1850, in which stamped and stenciled initials and dates were used. Signatures were also worked into quilting patterns. These are difficult to find and require close inspection of the quilt top and borders. Quilted signatures and dates are uncommon in twentieth-century quilts.

Thread

There is some discrepancy in the earliest date that cotton thread was manufactured. One source said it was first produced in a factory in Paisley, Scotland, in 1812. Another source noted a story about Hannah Wilkinson Slater, wife of Samuel Slater, the man who memorized the equipment blueprints for cotton-producing machines and then opened the first mill in the United States in Rhode Island. The story goes that Mrs. Slater recognized that the cotton yarn spun for the cloth in her husband's factory was also suitable for sewing. Her husband started marketing his thread near the end of the eighteenth century.

For most of the 1700s thread was made from silk, wool, or linen rather than cotton.

A better way to pin down a quilt's age by the thread used in it is to count the ply. Inspect the quilt for a loose piece of stitching thread. Note the twist to the thread and twist the end in the opposite direction. Count the number of individual strands that unwind and you have the ply count. The invention of the sewing machine created problems with thread then available. Three-ply cotton thread was available after 1800 but it wasn't strong enough to withstand the rigors of use in a sewing machine. A simple six-ply thread was produced after 1840 that was stronger and solved the problem. Around 1860, a complex six-ply thread was introduced. Instead of just twisting six strands of yarn together as in the simple six-ply, the complex took three strands of two-ply thread and twisted them together. When you unravel the thread end you find in your quilt note if it's simple or complex six-ply.

There's a fairly simple way of finding out if repairs have been made to an antique quilt, or if new borders or bindings have been added. Thread made after 1963, because of the synthetic dyes and methods, will glow when put under a black light.

Batting

Cotton and wool battings were used in quilts from their very beginnings up to the 1950s. Whether a cotton or wool batt was used is not a date identifier because both were used equally as often. Some wool batts inside cotton quilts shrank so badly that they actually pulled the quilt in and made it smaller. Puckers cover the top and back. These quilts are sometimes described as gathered. But you can't assume that a quilt you find in this condition has a wool batting. The gathered effect is also possible to reproduce by improper washing in hot water.

There is a raging controversy, however, over whether or not cotton batting can be used as a dating tool. Adelaide Hechtinger, in her book *American Quilts, Quilting, and Patchwork*, published in 1974, states that if there are cotton seeds in a quilt batting it could be dated as early as 1793. Hechtinger's rule of thumb is that if there are seeds every few inches this dates the batt to around 1850. A batting with two or three seeds to the square inch is probably from before 1830. She also advises knowing where the quilt was made. A quilt made in the North would have more seeds left in than one made in the South because Southern quilters had access to the cotton gin more than did Northerners. Hechtinger also notes that it's not easy to date cotton batting after the 1830s because all cotton was ginned and therefore free of seeds. You can test to see if your quilt has cotton seeds in it by squeezing it between your fingers or by holding it up to the light.

Well, in our opinion, the seeds-left-in-the-batting theory just doesn't make sense. Early quilts were closely quilted. The stitches were small and even and the patterns close—not more than half an inch apart—to prevent the batting from shifting and lumping in the wash. Cotton seeds, at least the ones we saw and felt, are about the size of orange seeds. They're big, thick, and round and would be impossible to quilt around in those close patterns. Quilts were too important to the maker's sense of artistry and creativity to allow even one cotton seed to remain and foul up her quilting!

We don't agree that there were so many seeds left in cotton batting that you can safely use them to date a quilt. But there was plant debris. These were seed husks, small pieces of stems and leaves—all the pieces too difficult to remove by hand or by ginning. Cotton cleaned by machine was not refuse-free. At times it wasn't even seed-free! In 1897 there were various qualities of cotton batting ranging in cleanliness and whiteness available to the quiltmaker. A cheap batt, presumably the least free of debris and not a pure white, sold for eight cents a roll. The best batting sold for a quarter a roll. When you hold a quilt up to the light and see small dark spots in the batting they are probably a clue to a cheap batting rather than to a date.

The first commercial cotton batting, produced by Stearns & Foster, was on the market in 1846. This company is still in business today producing both cotton and polyester battings under the name of Mountain Mist. Polyester batting was first introduced in the 1950s but didn't gain popularity until the quilting revival of the late 1960s. Quilts filled with polyester batting have a different look to them. They're puffier, with more loft in the unquilted areas than cotton batting gives. Polyester batting will spring back after compression, and the whole quilt feels smoother and slippery when rubbed. Polyester batting doesn't shrink, shred, or shift in washings, so it doesn't require the amount of close quilting that cotton and wool demand. The presence of polyester batting means that your antique quilt was very recently an unfinished top.

It was also mentioned that some earlier, cheap quilts were filled with newspaper. We agree with Brackman that the paper felt and heard inside an antique quilt is probably there because it wasn't removed from a foundation-style assembly before it was quilted. Both conclusions go counter to the care and attention an expert quiltmaker gives her art, but paper inside quilts does exist. We just prefer the second explanation to the first.

Borders

Borders are the picture frames of quilts. Not all quilts have borders, but those that do are more valuable to a collector. Generally, borders were only applied to best quilts, which is why so many of the quilts that survived to today have them. It's probably also why we prefer our quilts with borders.

A border of chintz was typical on early quilts. An unpieced border of chintz is a good indication that the quilt was made before the Civil War.

Conventional appliqué on borders became popular after the 1840s. Appliquéd borders of chintz using the Broderie-Perse method were common

This scrap bag Shoo Fly quilt houses some feed bag fabrics and zigzag sashing between the blocks. Done in the 1930s, this graphic look has outline quilting on the blocks and fan quilting in the sashing.

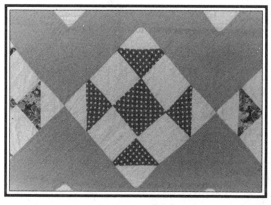

In close-up, the assembly can be seen: mostly good with only a few spots like this one with the junctions not matching. The sashing is very well done.

before 1860. The chintz bouquets, baskets, and bows used were sometimes connected with swags of matching fabric. The swag-style border was also popular in the 1930s.

Zigzag borders framed quilts in the 1880s but were also used before 1850 and after 1930.

Pieced borders in the Sawtooth and Flying Geese patterns were used in all periods of quiltmaking. Sawtooth borders in the quilt top, usually forming the Feathered Star patterns, began being used in the Victorian period. Triangle and cone borders were popular pieced patterns in the second quarter of the twentieth century. Strip borders were comprised of two or more long pieces of different fabrics, which were then quilted in a cable or feather design. Their use is connected to the invention of the sewing machine. They were always popular in Amish designs.

In twentieth-century quilts you'll often find a pieced border framing an appliqué top, or an appliqué border around a pieced top.

Backing

The preferred backing fabric for a quilt has always been white cotton or muslin. Dating a quilt from the backing isn't accurate because many tops were finished long before they were assembled into the fabric-and-batting sandwich and quilted. A clue to an early nineteenth-century date is the presence of two lengths of a loose-weave cotton sewed down the middle to make one large piece.

When feed, flour, and sugar sacks came printed with designs and labels, they were saved and stitched together for the backing fabric. A quilt with many squares of fabric stitched together to form the back might be made of feed sack bags. If you look at them closely, you might even be able to see the brand names that were originally printed on them, although when a quiltmaker saved these bags, she generally bleached them to remove the brand name labels. Another way to tell if your quilt has feed sack fabric is to look for the line of holes that marks the original stitching that formed the bag. Feed sack fabric was available from the latter part of the nineteenth century well into the twentieth. Cotton feed sacks with prints on them, or with quilt patterns, date from the 1930s and 1940s.

Overall Design

One design trait of the late 1700s was the use of the medallion style, a central motif cut from chintz, appliquéd, and surrounded by strip borders. There was also simple patchwork using mixed fabrics with different weights and textures together. Four-block quilts were made from four pieces of cloth, each block one yard square. To these were stitched large appliqué designs. One source stated that this design was a regional variation exclusive to Pennsylvania quilters, but another noted that it was the precursor to block-style quilts.

The set of a quilt is the way block-style quilt tops are put together to form an overall design. We've already noted that the framed medallion set was popular before the 1840s, but it's still used today by contemporary and Amish quiltmakers. When block-style quilts caught on because of their ease of assembly, they were first placed, or set, right next to each other. This style is still used in geometric and puzzle patterns where the blocks must be adjacent to get the full effect of the optical illusion. When appliquéers turned to block-style quilting, they added inner frames, called sashings, to their blocks. These strips of

Made by a boy who was recovering from a long illness, this blue and rust Stripes Bar quilt is from the 1930s. A simple-looking One-patch pattern, it nonetheless has many block junctions to be matched.
He did a pretty good job.
Quilt courtesy of Pam Sperry

fabric were generally narrower than the outside border strips. Blocks could be set straight, which resulted in horizontal and vertical sashings, or on point, which created diagonal sashing lines. "Strip sets" refers to Wild Geese, Roman Coins, or bar patterns where scrap bag pieces are joined together in long strips and then sashing strips of contrasting colors are added between. The whole is then framed with a border. Strip sets are a clue to early nineteenth-century quilts up to the Civil War, but they were also used by the Amish through the middle of the twentieth century.

We covered what must appear to be a lot of material in this chapter to help you date the quilts you see and want to buy. We left as much, probably more, out! The study of quilts might seem daunting at this point but it really isn't. After a while, you'll be dating with the best of them, arguing with collectors and dealers over the fine points. It becomes instinctive after a while, and we were proud when we noticed that we were capable of doing it ourselves. Developing instincts for recognizing and dating a valuable quilt takes time, but it's well worth it.

CHAPTER FOUR

CONDITION

Finding quilts in pristine condition is difficult now and it's going to get harder. As the supply of antique quilts diminishes, more and more quilts that have seen moderate to heavy wear will show up on the market. As we'll see, these quilts, because of special qualities, may be more valuable than an ordinary quilt that's never been used or washed.

All things being equal, a beautiful, well-executed quilt that has never been washed is of greater value than one that has. Unlike the judging rules of contemporary quilts, a quilt that still shows the marks the maker made to guide her quilting stitch is more valuable than one that doesn't because it proves the quilt was never washed. Marked, unwashed quilts are extremely rare, which explains their increased value.

The condition of fabrics in the quilt gives clues to the amount, if any, of use and washing. Unwashed fabrics appear crisper, stiffer, than washed ones. Their colors look truer, fresher, and brighter. Some color fading occurs every time a quilt is cleaned, and fabrics that look softer, feel smoother, and have slightly duller colors than new fabrics are the result of washing. When all the colors in a quilt look faded, it is probably due to many washes.

The look of a washed quilt is different from that of a new one. First, look at the seams and unquilted sections of the quilt. If these appear slightly puckery, or more puffy, this is a clue that the quilt has been washed. Unwashed quilts, if assembled correctly, should be fairly flat and smooth overall; seams should be straight and not have a gathered look. The batting should be evenly spread with no bunches or lumps. In a never-washed or hardly-ever-washed quilt, you can feel compressed batting under the quilt stitches. In one that has been washed many times, the quilting thread may have shrunk slightly, pushing the batting to either side of the stitching line and forcing more batting into the unquilted areas. The thread in seams can also shrink, giving the unquilted area of the quilt more loft, or height. The whole effect of washing a quilt makes it appear and feel softer, and look as though it needs a pressing. These small wrinkles, crinkles, and puckers are the best indication that the quilt has been washed many times.

Washing can, conversely, add to the appeal of a quilt. Those very same wrinkles, crinkles, and puckers add more texture to the quilt top and may actually increase its visual impact. Certainly the fact that this was a much-beloved quilt to someone adds to its nostalgia appeal. In some cases, particularly with the bold colors of the Amish quilts, washing may soften colors rather than fade them, and this can also increase the visual appeal of the quilt.

Another clue to washing is to check the batting. Before the arrival of today's polyester battings, quilts were filled with cotton or wool. As we saw in chapter 3, cotton and wool batts required substantial quilting to prevent finding all the batting in a lump in one corner after the first wash. Polyester batting stays in place, even after washing, and this is one reason newer quilts generally have fewer quilting stitches across the top.

Make a sandwich of your hands on the top and bottom of a quilt. With fingers and palms facing each other, move your hands along the quilt and feel for batting lumps. Some will be obvious, others less so, feeling more like an extra thickness was included rather than an obvious lump. Sometimes the bunched batting is visible to the eye. Check the bottoms and edges of any large unquilted areas of the quilt and you may find lumps of batting resting there comfortably after giving up the battle with the wash. You can even spot batting lumps by holding the quilt up to the light and noting the dark spots in the quilt. Shifted batting decreases the value of a quilt simply because the collected lumps may be so noticeable that the quilt won't hang well on a wall. It's evenness of warmth on a bed is also diminished. A quilt with lumps of loose batting means there are spots with no batting at all. Some of the quilt will keep you warmer than other parts. Don't despair if you fall in love with a quilt with bunched batting. These quilts should also be preserved, but their prices should reflect their fair condition. And the quilt can be repaired. How to fix it, and whether you should, is the subject of chapter 6.

Another clue to an unwashed quilt is the presence of sizing or glazing on the fabric. Fabrics were sized and glazed to add stiffness. Chintzes were usually glazed but held their sheen longer than other glazeds. After repeated washings, the glaze wears off, leaving the fabric softer and more pliable than when it was new. Look for the surface sheen that indicates that a fabric was glazed or sized. If it's still there, then the quilt has not been washed, or at least has not been washed too often.

Don't reject a quilt simply because it has stains. Many stains can be removed by washing with little or no damage to the quilt. If a quilt has been washed before, and you have that confirmed by the dealer you bought it from or determine it yourself from the above indications, then you can follow the directions in chapter 7 to wash out the stains and surface dirt. If you've purchased a never-washed quilt with stains, ask your dealer to recommend an expert quilt cleaner. There's no greater disaster than to wash a quilt for the first time only to find that the colors ran and ruined it. Not all quiltmakers, either antique or contemporary, washed their fabrics before making their quilts. Don't take the chance of washing an unwashed quilt yourself. There are cleaners who specialize in quilts and who can safely clean the quilt for you. Your dealer should be able to make a recommendation. If not, check with your local historical society or a museum for a recommendation.

Often, the dealer has already cleaned a quilt before it's offered for sale simply because it'll sell better with the stains and dirt removed. It's fine to say that stains should not sway your decision to buy an otherwise exceptional quilt, but many people, especially first-time buyers, are turned off by a stained quilt. Make sure you ask the dealer if a quilt with stains has already been cleaned. It might be that the stains are permanent, in which case the price should be lower than the same quality quilt without stains. A reputable dealer should tell you up front if a cleaning has been attempted and failed. Mildew, for instance, is one stain that is almost impossible to remove. If you can live with the stains, consider yourself lucky for getting a great quilt at a wonderful price.

Fabric deterioration is another factor to carefully consider in the quilt you select. Tears, rips, and puncture holes are obvious indications of heavy use. As we'll see in chapter 6, these can be repaired, but they really should decrease the

The size of the blocks in relationship to the overall size indicates that this piece was not made as a crib or small quilt. With a new border, this Ohio Star quilt with lattice sashing now makes a nice wall hanging.

value of a quilt. Here again, many times a dealer will go ahead and repair a quilt before it's offered for sale. If this was done, the dealer should point it out to you.

"You can do anything you want to a quilt," said Connie Sprong of the Quilt Loft, "as long as you tell the customer you did it." Repairs already made to a quilt should be noted before the sale and the price should reflect them. A repaired quilt is not as valuable as one in original condition no matter how well the repairs were done. Badly damaged quilts offered for sale as is, with their rips, tears, and wear left alone, are best known as cutters. Most dealers will go ahead and repair a quilt that shows promise. The less unique quilt that needs work will be offered at a reduced price as a cutter. Or the dealer will go ahead and cut the quilt, using the good sections to make smaller wall hangings, crib quilts, or other items. There are quilt sellers who repair quilts and pass them off as original work and fabric. This is frowned upon in the industry and these dealers are few and far between, but they do exist. All the more reason to buy only from a dealer you trust who was highly recommended to you.

Worn spots on the top of a quilt can also be repaired or left as is. After all, one of the reasons we buy quilts is for their nostalgia and sentimental value. The fact that a quilt is worn thin proves it was well loved by its previous owners. Worn fabric pieces within the quilt top should be carefully inspected. If the worn spots affect all the different fabrics within the quilt top, the wear is probably from use. Some frayed, thin, and weakened fabrics are the result of inferior dyeing. This shows up particularly with the acid reds of the late 1800s. If the worn spots on your quilt top show up in only one of the fabrics and all the pieces of this same fabric show wear, it is probably the result of these acid dyes. This fabric deterioration marks a specific time period so well that the wear has little effect on the price.

Silk crazy quilts, even when the fabric starts turning brittle and the pieces are frayed, may be of greater value than another quilt in perfect condition. The silks and satins used in these quilts during the Victorian period just haven't held up as well as other fabrics. But, once again, they are such excellent examples of a specific period of quilt history that they retain their value even in fair to poor condition where a cotton quilt would not. Because the silk crazies will continue to deteriorate to the point where they can't be used at all, even to hang, wool crazy quilts will supplant them and continue to increase in value because the wool crazies can be hung and used to illustrate the same period of quiltmaking.

Bindings are generally the first part of a quilt to show the effects of wear, washing, and use. As the outside edge of the quilt, the binding is the part that rubs along the floor most often. It is also the part most often grabbed when we

This Strip or Ribbon quilt was made in the 1860s and shows much fabric deterioration, splitting, and loss. Silks, satins, and velvets of that era did not stand up well to the passage of time.
Quilt courtesy of Florence Atwater

snuggle into a quilt, pulling it up around our neck and shoulders. The binding is the most frequently repaired and replaced part of a quilt.

The Dresden Plate quilt pictured on page 77 was made by Liz Greenbacker's great-grandmother in the early 1900s. It has mildew stains, some of the plate sections are rotted away so that only the seams are left, the sashings have worn through on the outside blocks, and the binding has already been repaired once.

Originally this quilt was self-bound. That means that the backing fabric was turned over to the front and stitched down as the binding. When this frayed and wore out, a less expert seamstress repaired it by simply folding an inch or two of the quilt to the back and stitching it down. The uneven, highly visible stitches in blue thread show that this repair was done by an inexpert seamstress. Whoever repaired it wanted simply to keep using the quilt, because she ignored the design elements of the quilt by folding over parts of the Dresden Plate patterns of the blocks and the chain quilting in the borders to make her new binding. Because of the way she fixed it, when viewed whole, this quilt looks as if it never had left or right borders, and the top and bottom plate

This little appliquéd red flower has a yellow center, green leaves, and is a perfect example of fabric deterioration in certain colors. The red fabric has literally split along its woven threads, exposing the white ground fabric.

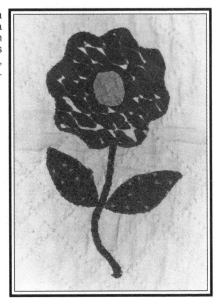

blocks look like parts were lopped off. Inspecting the back shows the extra fold in the edges of the quilt and reveals the original self-binding.

Unfortunately, Great-Grandmother's beautiful Dresden Plate quilt, so indicative of the pastel period, wouldn't be regarded as worth much more than a cutter to a dealer. It looks suspiciously like one of the quilt kits of the period; it has large patches of mildew stains that won't come out: it's been much used and shows it; the fabric deterioration in the plate patches is extensive and the result of wear, not inferior dyeing; and the repairs did little more than accelerate the wear along the edges of the quilt so that now the sashings as well as the bindings and borders need extensive repair. But it will never become a cutter because of its sentimental value. This quilt still has many possibilities and we'll refer to it extensively in chapter 6, on repair and finishing.

As with other repairs, a dealer should tell you if the binding has been replaced or if it is original. A quilt with its original binding in good condition should be valued higher than a quilt with a poor binding or no binding at all. A quilt with an original, but poor, binding should be valued higher than a quilt with a replaced binding even if period fabrics were used for the repair. The rule of thumb is that if it's not original, it's worth comparatively less than a quilt that has all its original parts. Some dealers don't point out a replaced binding. Customers really want quilts in excellent condition, and the tempta-

Showing much use and wear, this predominantly blue Dresden Plate has a torn binding, tears on the back, many tears and splits on the front. The inset shows one of the plates with an uneven center, but some nice cable and outline quilting. This quilt presents a serious problem for the quilt repairer; stabilization is probably the best that can be hoped for.

tion to replace a binding and pass it off as original is a great one. The dealers we talked with and visited all noted on their price tags any repairs or replacements they had made to a quilt and their prices always reflected those changes. Remember to ask questions. If repairs aren't noted but you're pretty sure they've been made, you'll want to question that dealer thoroughly on all aspects of the quilts for sale.

Color loss, or fading, can be caused by washing or overexposure to bright lights or direct sunlight. If the fading shows all over the different fabrics in the quilt, in other words evenly over the top, the fading is probably from use and cleaning. If there are streaks of fading over the quilt top they are probably the result of exposure to strong light. Remember this when you display, hang, or drape the quilts you've bought. Any bright light, and certainly direct sunlight, will fade the parts of the quilt it plays on the most. Color loss devalues a quilt. A faded, streaked quilt is less valuable than one that has faded evenly overall, and the unfaded quilt is more valuable than the one that has faded from use and washing.

There are exceptions. As already mentioned, Amish quilts, with their bold colors and combinations, tend to soften and mellow with use and washing. Streaks of fading caused by sunlight or bright display lights will devalue these quilts, too, but washing sometimes adds to their visual effect rather than detracting from it. An unwashed Amish quilt has its own appeal of sharp, crisp color, while the washed quilt may make the colors glow in a way the unwashed ones cannot.

There is also a green, used in the late 1800s, that has had a tendency to fade to a mustardy-tan color that is so indicative of the period that the design has to be pretty awful to devalue the quilt that incorporates it. It's seen mostly in appliqué and can be readily recognized as the stems and leaves of the flower designs. It sometimes shows up in pieced geometric quilts, too. The color faded so uniformly that it was once thought that it was the color of choice. But so many Rose of Sharon and Whig Rose quilts showed up with the same tan fabric, and it seemed illogical that so many quiltmakers would choose tan for stems and leaves, that investigations revealed that it had been green and then faded to the tan color. In some cases, you can see the original green by slightly lifting the piece to see the seam allowance underneath. This may be a shade of the original green that hasn't faded to the tan because of less exposure to light and washing solutions. This faded-to-tan green is another exception that proves the rule. Although color loss normally devalues a quilt, this faded green is so indicative of a quiltmaking period and style that it shouldn't devalue the quilt. Sometimes the faded pieces enhance the design, and these quilts become more valuable. When these formerly green pieces detract from the design, the quilt might be less valuable—even though they strongly indicate a particular period of quiltmaking history. Your emotional reaction to the quilt will tell you which is which. If you still like the impact of the quilt even with the odd-colored

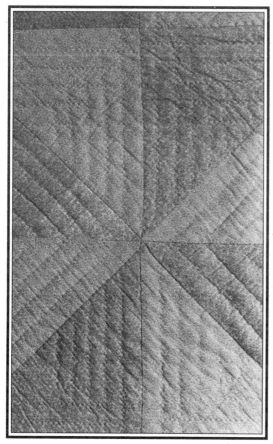

Some color loss has occurred in the point of one triangle and overall on this pink-and-green Diamonds quilt, made in the early 1800s. Note the excellent straight-line echo quilting and the perfectly matching points of the pieces.
Quilt courtesy of Betty Wilson

stems and leaves, then the faded color works for you. If it doesn't hit you, then the fading detracts from the quilt's appeal.

A quilt with permanent crease lines was improperly stored. As we'll see in chapter 7, quilts should be stored in cloth and refolded at least twice a year to avoid making permanent creases in the fabric. These creases devalue a quilt. Again, it isn't reason enough not to buy and preserve a good quilt, but all things being equal, creases should mean a lower price for the quilt than it would fetch without them.

Remember that condition counts less than you think. The truly unique quilt will overcome stains, rips, frays, poor repair, and fades. But as you become more and more knowledgeable about quilts and quilt collecting, you'll be able to judge the condition of a quilt, know when one has been repaired, and therefore, know how it affects the price. If nothing else, it helps you find a reputable dealer. The dealer who notes repairs and replacements, cleanings, and permanency of stains on the quilts for sale is dealing honestly and is one you can trust.

CHAPTER FIVE

WORKMANSHIP

Workmanship means the quality of work within a quilt—including stitching, assembly, quilting, fabric choice, color balance, and design—and how these factors affect the value of a quilt.

The most easily recognized and evaluated aspect of workmanship in a quilt is the quality of the quilting stitch. A quilt is three layers: top, batting, and backing. It is the thickness of the batting and the weight of the fabrics used for the top and backing that determine the degree of difficulty in sewing the quilting stitch. Obviously a heavy wool quilt with a thick batt is extremely difficult to stitch through and can result in relatively large stitches. This is the reason why wool and velvet crazy quilts and Log Cabins are tied rather than quilted. Their thickness prohibits the fineness of stitching that the expert quilter demanded of herself. In fact, most of the crazy quilts and Log Cabins are not quilted because they have no batting.

In cotton quilts, with medium to light batting, quilt stitches should be small and even. Except for the miniaturization period, when for a short time, the number of tiny pieces in a quilt rather than expert stitching determined a quilt's worth, quiltmakers have always competed to make their quilting stitch the smallest of their peers. One of our sources stated seeing a quilt with twenty stitches to the inch! We saw several quilts with ten stitches to the inch, fewer with twelve, and most were in the six-to-eight-stitches-per-inch range. A quilt with ten or more quilt stitches to the inch should be a little higher priced.

As important as the number of quilt stitches per inch is the uniform length of each stitch. All else being equal, a quilt with stitches of varying lengths throughout should be valued less than one where the stitches are all approximately the same length. These are the hallmark of the expert quilter.

Even if the stitches are relatively large or uneven, sometimes the amount of quilting can compensate for the lack of expert stitching. A Lone Star with its plain set squares covered with princess feather stitching, wreaths, cornucopias, or floral quilting designs is of greater value than one with mere outline stitching. An overall quilt pattern such as the single, double, or triple parallel rows of stitches that run diagonally across the top makes a quilt more valuable than if the quiltmaker merely stitched quarter-inch outlines around the block patterns. A whitework quilt (also called whole-cloth and sometimes miscalled trapunto) is one of the most valuable because its pattern is derived from the quilting and not from any pieced or appliqué pattern sewed on the top. *Whitework* is a term held over from the past, when these quilts were done only with white thread on white cloth. There is a trend in recent years, and always among Amish quiltmakers, to use a ground fabric and thread of a color instead of white.

A good quilting design should add to the surface texture of the quilt, either highlighting or contrasting the patchwork pattern chosen for the top. While, technically, quilting is only to hold the three layers of the quilt sandwich together and keep the batting from shifting and lumping, this is another area where quiltmakers rapidly added beauty and expertise. Hundreds, perhaps thousands, of hours went into exceptionally worked quilts, and it's likely that at least half of that time was spent solely on the quilting. Expert quilting adds greatly to the value of a quilt even if other elements are not exceptional.

Appliqué stitches should be virtually invisible. Again, these stitches should be small and even. To check appliqué stitches, pull (lightly, please!) on the appliquéd patch to lift it slightly from the ground fabric. Note the placement of the stitches. Tight, small stitches that can be seen only while lifting the appliquéd patch are the most desirable. Curves and corners on appliqué should be smooth and unfrayed. Fraying on the inside curve of an appliqué patch indicates an inexpert maker who left too little seam allowance or didn't correctly slit the seam to make an even, flat curve.

There is one exception to the invisible appliqué stitch. In the approximately twenty-year period after the Civil War when the sewing machine was invented and became popular, some quiltmakers showed off their fascinating new technology by appliquéing with a topstitch done by machine. If you can accurately date a quilt with machine appliqué to this time period, the topstitching should add to the value instead of detract from it. However, this is a matter of opinion and some quilt dealers and collectors may think differently. Although machine assembly does not detract from the value of a quilt, some collectors still devalue a quilt with machine appliqué. We choose to honor history and the advent of the new technology by according these quilts a higher value. Quilts with machine quilting, no matter when they were made, are less valuable than those with hand quilting because the machine stitch simply isn't as well done, or as time-consuming, as hand stitching.

The next most obvious example of good workmanship is the alignment of the sashing strips. These strips of cloth used to separate individual quilt blocks from each other should match perfectly on the horizontal and the vertical.

This beautiful example of a Trip Around the World shows great use of the lights and darks, and has a print border that pulls it all together. Made in the 1940s, the quilt is machine-quilted in straight lines.
Quilt courtesy of Brian Comstock

Sashings strips that are offset from each other represent poor piecing of the block.

Inaccurate cutting or piecing of the patches in a design might make each block a different size than the others and force the sashing out of line. Puckers in the corners of individual blocks or along the outer seam line can be the result of forcing a too-big block to fit the sashing. Conversely, puckers or gathers in the sashing might have been necessary to fit a too-small block into the quilt top. Generally, sashings are the same color throughout the quilt, and a piece of a different fabric within a sash might mean the maker ran out of the right fabric.

Unaligned sashings usually indicate poor workmanship and would make a quilt less valuable than one with perfectly aligned, uniform sashing strips. The Basket quilt pictured on pages 85 and 86 illustrates poor sashing. There are two

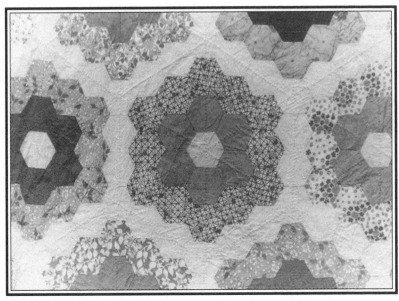

A close look at this quilt reveals minimal but precise straight-line machine quilting. The wide variety of wonderful 1930s prints can also be seen.
Quilt courtesy of Helen Warner

bulges in the two left basket strips that are the result of poor sashing assembly. When quilt blocks are forced to fit a sashing, or vice versa, these bulges appear in the quilt. Unless tucks and gathers are used, even quilting won't flatten the quilt and quilts should be flat. Also note that the sashings throughout the quilt are slightly wavy and even some of the baskets are distorted because of the quiltmaker's attempt to force them to fit the sashings. Several vertical sashes are also out of line. Can you find them?

There is an exception, however, to the rule of perfectly aligned sashings. African-American–style quilts, discussed in chapter 15, often use unaligned sashings as incorporated design elements. Using different fabrics within the sashings, instead of the coordinated fabric in traditional quilts, is also a design selection in the African-American–style quilt. Quilts that show these design elements should not be devalued because of them. We must, instead, be aware, as is made clear in chapter 15, that they are part and parcel of the maker's art and not a reflection on the workmanship. Even in these quilts, however, puckers and gathers should not exist. Seams should be flat and even.

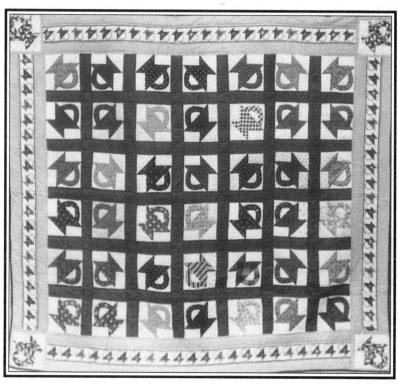

It's hard to believe that this Basket quilt, which looks so good in this picture, has so many problems. It actually looks much better from a distance than close up, a thought you should keep in mind when looking at quilts.

Quilt courtesy of Betsey Comstock

For your next clue to good or excellent workmanship, inspect the individual blocks in a pieced top. The points of each pattern piece that makes up the square should match with the others. Probably the most notable example of poor workmanship can be seen in a Lone Star, either bed-size or block-size, where the diamonds' points don't match. If the middle diamonds of a Lone Star (or Star of Bethlehem, as it's called in the Northeast), don't match, each succeeding strip of diamonds will be successively off point. The quiltmaker who didn't rip out those patches and start over is guilty of inferior workmanship and that quilt is not as valuable as one where all the points match and align perfectly.

A closer look reveals some of the problems with this Basket quilt. The sashing is a major one: not only doesn't it match anything on the quilt, but it is poorly applied with puckers and uneven junctions. When buying a quilt, one must look beyond what first meets the eye.
Quilt courtesy of Betsey Comstock

The more complex the pieced block, and the better the workmanship, the greater the value of the quilt. This is particularly true in Compass Rose quilts or Dahlia quilts, which are difficult to piece and keep points matched. Many pieced blocks use curved pattern pieces, and these are even more difficult to match perfectly because some of the edges are cut on the bias. As a rule of thumb, if the points match the quilt is more valuable, and the more pattern pieces there are in a pieced block, the more valuable the quilt.

The choice of fabrics is the next item to inspect while you're deciding to buy a quilt. Quilts of cheap cottons or the chintz of the late 1800s that was so bad it gave rise to the term *chintzy* applied to anything, or anybody, cheap, will be of less value than quilts made with quality cloth. The Basket quilt we've already mentioned is a multigenerational quilt assembled with sashing strips made of truly inferior cloth. Already wearing thin, the sashings preclude use of the quilt and even make it foolhardy to hang it for any length of time. We're assuming the woman who added the strips was not an expert quiltmaker or seamstress, for if she was, she would have picked better fabric for this important

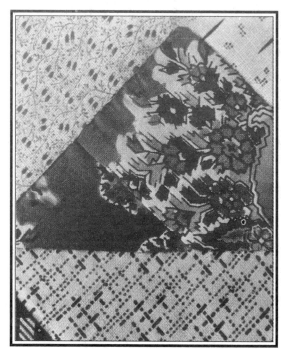

This close-up of an 1880s Ocean Waves patch shows the lengths to which an expert quiltmaker will go in order to have a polished look. One tiny corner was pieced together, not only to get a whole triangle, but a whole triangle with the printed pattern of the fabric matched.
Block courtesy of Miriam Zimmer

part of the quilt. The blocks are made of strong, high-quality shirting fabrics assembled with small, expert hand stitching, leading us to conclude they were made by another woman who knew the feel and desirability of good, strong cloth and who was much more experienced.

Cloth that is rotted or fraying may or may not be the result of poor fabric selection. Rot and deterioration overall are probably strong indications that the quilt was not properly stored, washed, or cared for. But, as we saw in the section on dyes and dyeing in chapter 3, some fabric deterioration can be the result of the old acid dyes used to print the fabric. For some periods of history quiltmakers used the best fabric available but because of inferior technology it just didn't last. Quilts with overall fabric deterioration, or poor fabric selection, are less valuable and should be priced accordingly.

Some aspects of design are considered part of workmanship: block arrangement, color balance, and borders.

How a quiltmaker arranged the blocks in a quilt attests to her artistic eye. Most Basket blocks are arranged with the handles or flowers pointing in the same direction, but some quiltmakers place them in sets of four with the

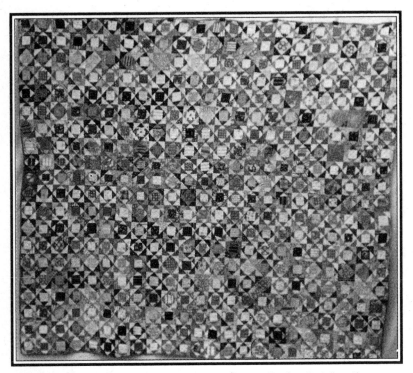

The abundance of different fabrics on this Hourglass quilt takes its toll on the eyes. Created in the early 1900s, it has nearly every color imaginable but strikes one as predominantly brown.
Quilt courtesy of Doris Dean

handles pointing to the inside. If the entire quilt top is assembled in multiples of these groups of four, this is also a pleasing design. The Basket quilt pictured in this chapter is assembled in groups of four. Note that the baskets in the bottom row point down. This is an odd row, no doubt to make the quilt the right length for a bed. The quilt would have been more balanced, more visually pleasing, if that last row had been eliminated. Then, not only would there be even multiples of groups of four, but the top row of baskets, pointed down, would have been balanced by the bottom row of baskets pointing up. This may seem a minor consideration, but it's something to watch for when you see a quilt you like but something in it just nags at you. That odd sensation that there's something not quite right about the quilt may be that the pattern balance is off even in a small way.

A close-up of the Hourglass quilt shows less-than-perfect assembly with many unmatched junctions and wavy seams. With all those small pieces, we can probably forgive the quiltmaker, though. She did keep an interesting scrap bag.
Quilt courtesy of Doris Dean

Many quiltmakers obviously arranged, rearranged, and re-rearranged their finished blocks to find just the right order for piecing them together into a top. Many quilt patterns create totally different visual effects by simply turning them inward or outward in relation to each other. Few quilters assembled the Pine Tree in any way other than upright—looking like a tree. There are a few, however, who assembled the blocks in groups of four, like the Basket quilt, and created a stunning optical illusion. Generally, when a quiltmaker assembled a pattern nontraditionally and the result was a startling re-creation of a traditional pattern, these quilts are more valuable. They are yet another testament to the fact that quilts were created, not just made.

Color balance is another design aspect that greatly affects the visual and emotional impact of a quilt. Working with scraps and leftover fabrics, most quiltmakers didn't have the luxury of large lengths of coordinated fabrics such as we use today or that were available to the wealthy. Scrap bag quilts are by far the biggest percentage of quilts available. Antique quilts of coordinated fabrics are rarer but not impossible to find. Because their color balance was built in right from the beginning of the work, coordinated-fabric quilts may have greater visual impact and therefore more value.

But just as they did with their patterns, quiltmakers worked with their scrap bag blocks, shifting them around the top of the quilt, offsetting a light block with a dark, constantly rearranging them so that the colors blended, contrasted, and moved the eye across the top of the quilt. This is not something they did unconsciously. Blocks were not merely pieced, thrown in a pile, and then picked up in turn and sewed together. The expert quiltmaker would have spent considerable time arranging the blocks to get the best possible, most pleasing, use of color—even if it was done by instinct alone.

Let's return to the Basket quilt as an example of color out of balance. It seems unfortunate to use such a pretty quilt as a bad example. It isn't that this quilt is a poor one. On the contrary, it's quite pleasing. But it isn't exceptional. We can see that all the elements for an exceptional quilt are there, they simply weren't assembled in the best possible way. It could have been so much better.

In the Basket quilt, there are three blocks made with red fabrics. Two are dark red and one is a red-and-white print. If we could change this quilt, we'd start by placing those blocks in different positions. The two dark reds could have been placed opposite each other in the center grouping of four blocks with two of the dark blue blocks. This would have drawn the eye immediately to the center of the quilt. Or the two dark reds could have been in opposite corners of the quilt; say, the top left and the bottom right. This would have drawn the eye diagonally across the quilt. There are also enough light and dark blocks to have arranged them in groups of four with two light and two dark opposite each other. This way, each group of four would have its own color and contrast balance. There are a black-and-white stripe and a black-and-white check we'd love to move opposite each other and contrast with darker blocks. But the quiltmaker, and here we're assuming it's the same woman who picked the sashing fabric and put the blocks together, didn't pay attention to the light and dark options available to her. Some of the groupings have three dark blocks and one light block. Others have two lights on one side and two darks on the other, rather than the more balanced look of placing them opposite their "twins."

Why wasn't this quilt better assembled? The elements are all there to make this a truly stunning, therefore valuable, quilt. But this is a multigenerational quilt, as we noted before. The woman who assembled the quilt top must have found the completed blocks stored away and finished it out of sentiment or because she hated to see the work already done go to waste. Perhaps, after finding the blocks, she decided to make her first attempt at quilting. The fact that her descendants found the completed top unquilted suggests that she fell prey to the same problem her ancestor did, a lack of time, energy, or desire to finish the quilt. Instead of being taken apart, rearranged, and given new sashing, this quilt was left as is to preserve the work of those past generations. And whatever problems it might have in design and color balance, it is still a family quilt. To take it apart and reassemble it would decrease its value to the family because it would eliminate all the work done by the second quiltmaker who worked on it. A large part of the sentimental value of this quilt would be lost. The fact that two ancestors, and now a third, worked on this one quilt, enhances rather than detracts from its value as a family heirloom. (This is further discussed in chapter 6 on repairing an antique quilt.)

Another aspect of color balance is contrast. In a quilt like the Log Cabin, contrast is the strongest design element. Each Log Cabin block is divided in half on the diagonal, with darks on one side and lights on the other. If fabric colors are chosen that are too close in tone and don't offer enough contrast, the prime effect, the interplay of light and dark, of the Log Cabin is lost. Assembly of the Log Cabin blocks in the jagged Streak O' Lightning, the squares of Barn Raising, or the rows of Straight Furrows, should highlight the contrast between light and dark fabrics. If the dark and light rows are not obvious and easily distinguished, then the quiltmaker didn't arrange her colors within the blocks with enough contrast. A Log Cabin with obvious light and dark contrast, pleasing to the eye, is more valuable than one without that contrast.

Other quilt patterns rely on contrast for their optical effect. The Tumbler pattern is one. This is a one-patch design, like the Hexagon. Tumblers look like a profile of a glass, hence their name. It's basically a rectangle that's wider at the top than at the bottom. Half the pieces are cut from light-colored fabrics or prints and the other half from dark. A light piece is sewed to a dark upside down piece, and the alternating pattern is continued until there is a row long enough to fit the dimensions of the quilt. The second row starts so that its pattern of light and dark is the opposite of the first row. Tumblers were often made as charm quilts (with no two fabrics repeating anywhere in the top). If the fabrics contrast well, the effect is a kaleidoscope of light and dark colors and print textures. If they're too close in shade, the effect is lost in the jumble of similar color tones.

The Hexagon is another one-patch design sometimes used for a charm quilt but more often seen in Grandmother's Flower Garden quilts. In these, the hexagons are arranged in circles to form the flower. Each circle is usually the same fabric, or at least the same basic color even if in different tones. In this pattern there are three or four circles of color to make the flower and the circles can be arranged with alternating light and dark rings, can go from light in the center to dark on the outside, or the reverse. The flowers are then set off with another row of white hexagons. Traditionally, small green diamonds joined the flowers together, but more often the white row that sets off the flower is also used to join the blocks together.

We saw one spectacular scrap bag Nine-patch Variation that was so well planned that each block was assembled with a light and dark side, divided on the diagonal like the Log Cabin block. When assembled in the Straight Furrows style, these Nine-patch blocks produced dark and light bands that were highly contrasted and visually pleasing. Yet the entire top was the usual mix of scrap bag solids, prints, dark and light fabrics, and done in the simplest quilt block.

Remember that the use of color is controlled by the quiltmaker. Sometimes what seems to our eye as unbalanced may just be the planned effect of the artist. If a color or piece of fabric leaps out at you, determine why. Perhaps that odd bit of orange or that dark grouping of fabric pieces was intended to draw your eye to that portion of the quilt. Maybe that's the signature or date patch; maybe the pieces are from the clothing of someone special to the quiltmaker and so, to the maker, deserved special placement. Perhaps the artist's eye saw something else in the pattern that she wanted to point out. Sometimes oddly placed color creates a whimsical quality in a quilt that makes it all the more valuable. Of course, sometimes a quilt is just out of color balance, like the Basket quilt we've discussed. That doesn't mean it shouldn't be bought and preserved. It just means it will fetch a lower price.

Borders enhance a quilt's value just as a frame enhances a painting's value. A properly designed border, in the right color scheme, once again draws our eye to the important part of the quilt, its pattern. Prairie Points and Saw Tooth borders are rare because of their degree of difficulty, and they therefore increase the value of the quilt to the collector. A good border, like a good frame, adds to the overall beauty of a quilt. It shouldn't be so noticeable that you see the border and not the quilt, and it shouldn't be so weak that it fails to highlight the design of the quilt top.

These are the basics of workmanship. Look for your own examples of good and bad workmanship, quilting, design, color balance, and borders. Learn to analyze the quilts you see—both the ones you like and the ones you don't like. Instead of trusting only your instinct, judging solely on immediately liking or not liking a quilt, soon you'll be able to distinguish why a quilt appeals to you and why it doesn't. But don't lose track of those instincts! Emotions play a large part in the appeal of a quilt, and we don't want to get so educated that we pay attention only to technique. The overall impact of the quilt on your sensibilities is of far more importance in your decision to buy it than all its technical aspects combined.

CHAPTER SIX

REPAIR AND FINISHING

Repair

There are several levels of controversy over the repair and restoration of quilts. At the first level there is discussion over the terminology. Some quilt historians, such as Stephanie Hatch, a director of the New England Quilt Museum, feel it's impossible to restore a quilt.

"*Restore* means to return a quilt to its original state," said Hatch. "That's impossible. You can't restore a quilt but you can repair it." Despite this fine-tuning of terminology, there are still many people repairing quilts who call themselves quilt restorers. In fact, most professionals who repair quilts still use the term *restoration.* As a technical point, we agree with Hatch that *repair* is the proper term, so this chapter will refer to repairing a quilt, not restoring it. Remember, though, that there are people who still refer to the repair process as restoration. When you're looking for an expert to repair your quilt, look for the title "restorer." After reading and reviewing this chapter, you'll know what questions to ask a professional to make sure the repairs to your quilt are done the way you want them done.

At the next level of controversy some historians, dealers, and collectors are very particular about how repairs are made to a quilt. The preferred method of fixing frayed, rotted, or deteriorated fabrics is to either stabilize them or appliqué appropriate fabrics over them. It is considered tampering with the history of the quilt to remove a damaged piece of fabric and replace it. Quilt purists believe that only fabrics of the same period as the ones in the quilt should be used to repair it and then they should be appliquéd over the original damaged piece. This way, if at some point in the future your quilt needs to be closely examined for its historical or technical significance, the original fabric is there, underneath the new, to be studied. As our knowledge of quiltmaking history grows, these pieces of fabric and the way the quilt was assembled could add a great deal to quiltmaking lore, so many experts believe that as much as possible of the original work should be left in the quilt.

On the other hand, there are those who believe that errors in judgment on the part of the original quiltmaker should be corrected. Lila Lee Jones refers to her collection of twenty-six antique quilts as "rescued" heirlooms. Jones has found quilts at garage sales and auctions. She has no compunction about replacing odd fabrics.

"I attended a garage sale where I purchased a feed sack Snowball quilt top with one ghastly pure-white snowball amid all the creamy muslin snowballs," she wrote in *Quilt Craft* magazine. "I replaced the stark-white block with muslin. . . ."

A quilt historian would argue that a valuable piece of information was lost because of replacing that one white snowball. Why was it there? Did the quiltmaker simply run out of muslin? If she did, why didn't she just get more? Was she too far from town? Was she out of money? Was the one white snowball made from a family fabric that had sentimental meaning? Or was it actually a design element included on purpose? Perhaps this quiltmaker remembered and believed the superstition that a perfect quilt, or a perfect anything, meant attempting to imitate God. Rather than invite His wrath, perhaps she purposely included the one white snowball as an imperfection? Even if the imperfection were left in, we may never know the real answer, but the absence of the single white snowball means no one will ever ask the questions, and it is over this that quilt historians object to the removal of original fabric no matter how damaged its condition or jarring its effect.

Yet we're sure that Jones, and others, would agree that a quilt that smacks the artistic sensibilities so strongly as the one with one white snowball among the muslin would mean that that quilt is headed for the garbage heap and will be lost to history. If a quilt doesn't appeal to us, its chances for preservation are severely limited. It wouldn't be cared for or displayed. It seems far better, in this case, to fix a quilt so that most of it will be used and preserved rather than throw it away. Quilts that are badly worn or have poor design elements, like this Snowball quilt, can be purchased cheaply. They're worth less because of their poor condition. Since they're already devalued, what's the harm in repairing the quilt so that it can be used with pride?

We'd agree with both statements. Certainly a quilt that is damaged but is of great historical, technical, or family significance should be preserved as is. It is a record of its time and maker. If we are to learn anything from these exceptional quilts they should not be tampered with no matter how noble the intention. Only when left alone can these quilts reveal to us the full extent of the maker's intent and art.

Museum-quality quilts, damaged or not, should be left as is. But we also believe that badly damaged but beautiful quilts should not be discarded. If this means a new binding, new borders, new fabric pieces, then so be it. Ultimately it is the decision of the owner, you, that is the final determination on whether or not a quilt should be repaired or left alone. In the next chapter, we'll see how to care for a quilt so that any further damage is avoided.

Some quilt damage is permanent. Discoloration, color loss, color migration, and dye deterioration are permanent—as are mold and mildew stains. These types of damage can only be covered up. Permanent damage should affect your decision to buy a quilt. Think carefully before you buy a damaged quilt about what it will take to repair or stabilize it. Once you've bought it, you can follow the advice in this chapter on how to cover over the damage or learn to live with it as is.

If you decide to repair a quilt, make sure you know how or find a professional that does. Most experts agree that you should use period fabrics to repair a quilt. Once you know the approximate time period your quilt was made, you can begin hunting for replacement fabric from that same era. Most quilt dealers have a selection of period fabrics they use for their own repairs and make available for sale. At the very least, if you've established a relationship with dealers, tell them what you need and they'll keep an eye out for it as they search for more quilts. We'll talk about cutter quilts later, but they are also a source for period fabrics. A cutter with usable fabric from the same time period as your quilt can be taken apart to provide you with period material. While you're looking for period fabrics, keep an eye out for thread, too. To be strictly accurate, you should use 100 percent cotton thread of the same weight and color that was used originally.

The Basket quilt discussed in the last chapter was finished using new material for the borders. Although author Liz Greenbacker didn't change the sashings or the baskets, leaving them as the original work of the previous two quiltmakers, if she were to finish that quilt today, after researching this book, she'd finish it with period fabrics rather than new. The quilt isn't ruined. It's a beautiful example of a multigenerational quilt. It just isn't accurate. If you can be accurate, do so. There are sources for period fabrics and these should be used if possible. There are also sources for new fabrics in period colors and designs. If all else fails, you can use some of these reproduction fabrics. Your common sense should prevail. The important thing is to preserve the quilt as closely as possible to its original design, fabric content, and artistic intent.

Before you begin your repairs, you should document the quilt thoroughly. Make a graph of the quilt, noting the blocks and fabric pieces that need repair. It's also a good idea to photograph the pieces you'll cover with fresh fabric. Get high-speed film for use in low light to take these pictures. A camera flash will contribute to the deterioration of your quilt because it is a high burst of intense light. Also photograph the bindings or borders that need repair. When you finish the repairs, take pictures again of the same spots with the fresh fabric. If you do the work yourself, keep notes on how it was done and any special problems you encountered. Note, also, where you found the replacement fabrics. At the end of your repair project, you'll have detailed records of the process. Keep these together with any documentation you have of the quilt and its maker. This should include any personal stories about the quiltmaker, where and when the quilt was made, where and when you bought it, and how much it cost. You can keep all this documentation in a separate folder or you can stitch a muslin pocket to the back of the quilt and keep it there. With this last method, remember to wrap the documentation in acid-free paper so the oils from the paper and the chemicals from the photographs won't seep through to damage the quilt further.

To begin your repairs, you should never remove the damaged piece of fabric in a quilt top. The Tumbler quilt on the opposite page was repaired using period fabrics, already cut by the original quiltmaker and found with the quilt top. But here again, the repairs are inaccurate. Although period fabric was used for the repair—and finding the pieces pre-cut with the top meant that these were the same pool of fabrics used originally, a rare find—the old frayed and stained pieces were removed. Our determination of this quiltmaker's decisions while making her quilt is diminished because these fabrics were removed. In justice to the quilt, period fabric was used and replacement selections were made based on the other pieces in the quilt.

So don't remove those torn, worn pieces from your newly acquired quilt. Instead, measure carefully and prepare a cutting template for the exact size and shape of the piece that needs replacing. After washing the fresh fabric, cut out a piece using the template and adding a 1/2-inch seam allowance around all sides. Lay the new piece over the old one, turn under the seam allowance, and pin it down. Make sure that all of the damaged piece is covered and that the new piece doesn't overlap any of the adjoining pieces. Leave the replacement piece slightly loose, with a small bubble to it, to accommodate quilting stitches if needed. Blindstitch the new piece down. Continue covering the worn spots on your quilt, exactly matching the pattern pieces of the original, until all the damaged pieces are covered.

We saw two whimsical exceptions to covering damaged pieces exactly as they were originally cut. One was a cotton crazy quilt with the squares separated with solid sashings inexpertly pieced and unaligned. Both the sashings and the appliquéd replacement fabrics used to cover the holes in them actually add to the light and frivolous nature of the quilt. Instead of detracting from

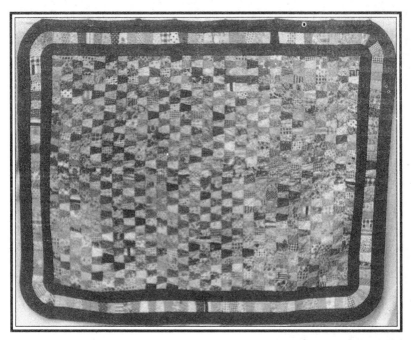

This classic example of a One-patch Tumbler quilt was a top that was found by a family, with enough extra pieces to finish the quilt in 1989. After forty years in storage the quilt began a new life. The dark blue border is new, but the blocks are all 1930s.
Quilt courtesy of Nancy Groves

the beauty of the quilt, the irregular-size squares and rectangles of the unaligned repair pieces add a further touch of humor and movement.

The second nontraditionally repaired quilt is a Double Nine-patch that obviously needed a new binding. Most of the top in the quilt was in good shape but a few blocks needed replacing. On page 100, we can see one of these blocks was repaired the correct way, by appliqué, but the repairer didn't shape the replacement block to the exact size of the original. This occurs in a few places and jars the symmetry of the quilt. But it is the repair of the border that gives this quilt a whimsical look. The owner repaired it following accepted technique. She appliquéd the replacement pieces and even quilted through them after they were applied. But she replaced the binding in small strips rather than by using ones the same length as a side. And she pieced each strip on individually so that, as you can see in the photo, some of the pieces are wider and extend farther over the top of the quilt than others. These repairs give this quilt a

A sister to the previous Tumbler quilt was found at the same time. This close-up shows the variety of printed fabrics used in its creation, and the shape of the Tumbler blocks.
Quilt courtesy of Kathryn Robinson

decidedly African-American style (see chapter 15) that should make any viewer smile. The workmanship on the repairs is good. The replacement fabric is not from the same period, but the repairer did select new fabrics that matched the intensity and tone of the original scrap bag fabrics. Neither of these quilts is repaired according to the "rules," but in these two examples the results make us happy they weren't. They're offbeat and irregular but the workmanship is good and the end results are pleasing to the eye.

Bindings are usually the first spot on a quilt to wear. The Dresden Plate quilt discussed in chapter 4 needs to have its binding replaced. One attempt at repairing the binding has already been made by simply folding the quilt around on all four sides and slipstitching the edge down. This repair will be removed. Since the border is also badly worn in spots, and is the same fabric as the binding, repairs will have to wait until suitable replacement fabric is found. Ideally, the owner should wait until she finds the exact fabric to match the original. This is probably impossible. A decision will have to be made to replace both the borders and the bindings with similar period fabric, or to just replace the binding with a coordinating piece.

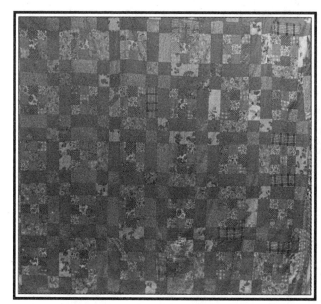

This tied comforter has a heavy blanket inside and shows signs of heavy use. Probably made in the 1920s, this piece holds some very interesting nonprofessional repairs.
Quilt courtesy of Laura Caro

Dealers regularly replace worn bindings on quilts. It improves their salability, if not their accuracy or originality. Replacing a binding is not as serious, except to purists, as replacing other parts of a quilt. As with all repairs made to a quilt before it's sold, the dealer should note it in the documentation of the quilt so you know when you buy it that repairs have been made, what fabrics were used, and if the repairs were made by hand or machine. The price should reflect the repairs because the quilt is no longer completely original. But, as we've discussed before, a repaired quilt is far preferred to throwing one away, and as long as the dealer notes the repairs, you can feel confident purchasing it.

As you make the initial inspection of your quilt, documenting the damaged parts that need to be covered or replaced, you should also note the way it was made. Check the length of the assembly, appliqué, and quilting stitches. When you make your repairs and when you re-quilt it, your stitches and workmanship should match those of the original maker. "Study the back for the stitching," advised Hatch. "How often did she backstitch? How did she do the corners? There's an idiosyncrasy with every quilt that should be recognized."

Once you've documented the workmanship of the original quiltmaker, your repairs should reflect that same level. You'll destroy the integrity of the quilt if you replace long, uneven quilt stitches with your usual tiny, even ones. Hatch, and other quilt experts, agree that repairs should be made duplicating

A closer look at the same quilt reveals some unusual repairs that contribute
to an interesting look. While not quite in keeping with purist repair standards,
the calico patch on the square and the floral fabric appliquéd over the edge
do serve the purpose of repairing this quilt.
Quilt courtesy of Laura Caro

the stitch length, quilting pattern, and workmanship of the original maker. If
not, the repairs will stand out, jarring the overall unity of the quilt.

"I'm more concerned about restoring and preserving these quilts made
with both dedication and an obvious love of design," said Dixie McBride in a
recent issue of *Traditional Quiltworks* magazine. McBride's antique quilt collection now numbers over a hundred and she repaired most of them herself.
"Although all textiles eventually deteriorate, these quilts should be cared for and
preserved as whole quilts as long as possible."

Which brings us neatly to the discussion of cutter quilts. While we agree
that every attempt possible should be made to preserve a quilt as is, it's not
always feasible. Some quilts are just too badly worn, overused, and uncared for
to save whole. These are called cutter quilts. It's an apt title, for a cutter quilt
is taken apart and its good pieces used elsewhere. These salvaged pieces can be
used as period replacement fabrics for less-worn quilts. Or, if they're large
enough, they can be cut down to crib or wall hanging size, rebound, and sold

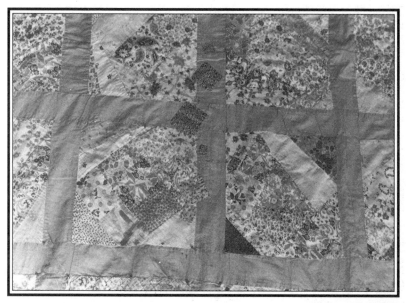

This close-up of a cotton crazy quilt shows some unusual repairs. Patches appliquéd over tears in both the squares and the sashing almost seem to add to the abstract look of this quilt. Self-fixes for a home problem, this is probably not something you'd want to do to, say, an 1850s Turkey Tracks.
Quilt courtesy of Laura Caro

in their new form. There's no doubt that the Basket quilt discussed in chapter 5 would have had its inferior sashings removed by a dealer. The Basket blocks themselves, with good workmanship and in excellent condition, could then be sewed into a new quilt or sold as a set. Because this quilt remained in the same family, and the sashings represent the work of the second generation that worked on the quilt, they were preserved as is. A dealer, sentiment aside, would not have left those inferior fabric sashings in.

Cutter quilts have been taken apart to make pillows, pocketbooks, totebags, and stuffed animals. Salvaged sections of worn quilts have been incorporated into clothing. Even designers, such as Ralph Lauren, have bought quilts to cut down for their clothing lines. The problem is that many people cut down quilts that should not be considered cutter quilts. Many quilts that should have been preserved whole are now gone forever. There is strong feeling among quilt historians, such as Stephanie Hatch, that there is no such thing as a cutter quilt.

"If it's that far gone, I'll buy it for study purposes," said Hatch about damaged quilts. "But it has to be very far gone. I will buy a quilt to find out

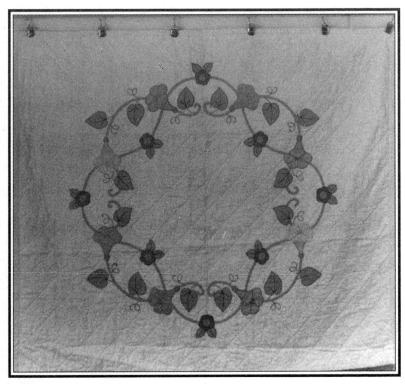

It would have been a shame to let these appliquéd Morning Glories from the 1930s go, so this quilt was salvaged from a larger quilt with badly damaged edges.

how it's constructed. Just as a painter takes anatomy, a quilter must understand what's inside a quilt. But you shouldn't make teddy bears out of any quilt!"

"That's definitely a purist attitude," said Diane Reese of the Quilt Loft when we discussed the theory that no quilt should be classified as a cutter. Reese has been repairing quilts for over five years. "We tried the historian route and it didn't work. You do have to be a little practical in this business." Reese explained that some customers, particularly first-time buyers, simply won't buy a quilt with damage. To recoup their investments, quilt dealers must sometimes repair a quilt or cut it up to salvage usable pieces. She's very careful, however, to cut only those quilts that are classified as cutters.

A quilt placed in the cutter category should have a lower price than even most unquilted tops. Because they're so cheap, they're the perfect investments

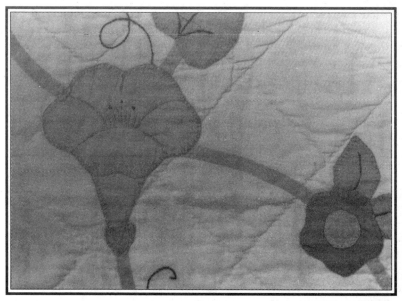

A closer look shows the appliquéd stems and overcast stitching carefully done on the gold-and-green flowers. Even with little quilting and a good amount of fade overall, this quilt is a gem.

for study, salvage, or repair. Don't overlook the cutter quilt while you're searching for additions to your antique collection. If you have any knowledge of quilting, or some sewing background, a cutter can be the perfect place to learn about quilts and teach yourself accurate repair techniques. And you'll be preserving a quilt, even if only in parts, that otherwise would be discarded.

What do you do with an antique quilt you don't want to repair or one for which repairs would destroy the historical significance or design elements? For instance, a silk crazy quilt, considered the primary representative sample of quilting from the Victorian era, with frayed, cracking, or shredded fabric, shouldn't be repaired. Because the silks in these quilts deteriorated so badly, period fabric in good condition is extremely difficult to find. Crazies are also particularly design-sensitive. Only the original quiltmaker would be able to explain her choices of shapes, colors, and textures. And the very nature of the fabric deterioration makes these quilts almost impossible to preserve by any of the methods we've discussed. You can't vacuum them. The shredded fabric would be sucked into the cleaner, and surrounding fabrics, which appear undamaged, could ravel and shred under the stress of vacuuming, thus furthering the deterioration of the quilt top. Silks, velvets, and wools from this period—or any period, for that matter—should never be washed. It's doubtful that you'll find a professional cleaner, even one with experience in chemically cleaning quilts, who will agree to clean one. The unique design elements of these quilts shouldn't be covered up with replacement cloth, period or not. But something must be done.

It's called stabilizing. There's an excellent discussion of how to stabilize a quilt in Nancy O'Bryant Puentes's booklet *First Aid for Family Quilts*. Puentes advises using either Crepeline, a special single-filament silk fabric, or nylon tulle, also known as bridal illusion. You might have to dye these fabrics to match the colors you need to cover. The process is much the same as covering a damaged piece with a replacement piece. A piece of tulle or Crepeline is cut to the size of the damaged piece and sewed, through the seam line, over the top of it. Unlike covering with fresh fabric, no seam allowance is added. The effect of this method is to hold the damaged piece in place. This thin layer will protect it from further shredding from handling and keep the shredded pieces in place. It won't stop the deterioration process, but it will slow it down because the original fabric will have a protective layer, a buffer, over it. Using tulle or Crepeline over damaged pieces gives them a slightly frosted look but the addition should be almost invisible until the quilt is inspected closely.

Stabilizing is one instance where tiny stitches shouldn't be made. As Puentes points out, the smaller the stitch, the more tiny holes are made in the fragile fabric. These holes will eventually accelerate the deterioration. Use larger stitches to prevent adding to the damage. We strongly recommend Puentes's booklet for anyone contemplating stabilizing, repair, or cleaning of a quilt.

Don't assume that an expert quiltmaker is also an expert quilt repairer or restorer. Although the same basic techniques are used when making a quilt, repairing one takes different expertise and knowledge than making one from scratch. There are questions you should ask anyone you hire to repair your quilt. Will period fabrics be used? Who determines what will be repaired and what will be replaced? Insist that original fabrics remain and that pieces are covered, not replaced. Ask that the original workmanship be duplicated, even if it isn't up to perfect quiltmaking standards. If you just want your quilt stabilized, make sure the repairer knows what that means and has the right materials for the job.

If you're having your quilt professionally cleaned, make sure the cleaner has experience with your type of antique quilt. Establish who does the stabilizing before your quilt is cleaned, you or the cleaner. Most often, you'll be responsible for stabilizing a quilt before cleaning. A cleaner with experience should be able to tell you what parts need stabilizing before cleaning to prevent damage. Any fabric that is stiff and dried with age should be softened, stabilized, or left completely alone. These fabrics are prime targets for rips and frays when cleaned.

Repairing your quilt can be expensive when you hire the work out. Learning how to do it yourself, starting with new sample fabrics to practice the techniques, isn't difficult and just may spur you on to a new hobby or business.

Finishing

There are many excellent quilt tops available for sale. The same rules of workmanship apply to a top as they do to a finished quilt. Appliqué stitches should be small, even, and invisible. The design should be pleasing and color balanced, or so unique that its whimsical quality compensates for any other flaws in design. The fact that a top is machine pieced should not detract from its appeal or value. Sewing machines have been popular for over a hundred years. Many quiltmakers today machine assemble tops because it saves a great deal of time compared to hand assembly. Quiltmakers of the past knew this too. As long as the seams are flat and even and the points match, a machine-assembled top is valuable, too. Not only are you preserving a quilt, you're contributing to its historical value by finishing it and adding a new multigenerational quilt to the current stock of antique quilts.

Check fabrics for colorfastness in your quilt top. (Chapter 7 tells you how.) A top that is stiff or dried with age may be saved by soaking in a mild fabric softener and warm water several times. Be sure to rinse the top completely of the fabric softener before you dry it. Dry a top the same way you dry a quilt. Spread it on a sheet outside on the ground in the shade. Place another sheet over the top. (See chapter 7 for discussions about care, cleaning, storage and display.)

Inspect your quilt top closely. Check for any damaged pieces of cloth and repair them first, following the methods discussed earlier. Then note the design, colors, and prints in the top. You'll be hunting for period fabrics in like colors and prints to add a border and bind the completed top. You'll also want to research the pattern. By studying other quilts made from the same pattern, you can decide on an appropriate quilting design. Perhaps you can find a top with the quilting lines already marked on it. If you do, you've got a real treasure. Not only do you have the original piecing but also how the quiltmaker intended to quilt it, too! Marked tops are rare. To be historically accurate, your research should reveal a quilting pattern appropriate to the period of the quilt. Since you're actually finishing a multigenerational quilt, you might want to exercise your own artistic sense by designing the quilting pattern yourself. There are many good books on quilting techniques. We'd recommend any by Jinny Beyer or Michael James for teaching yourself quilting skills.

Completed squares are also available for sale. These may be the salvaged remnants of a cutter quilt or may have been found intact. Apparently many quiltmakers of the past started projects they couldn't, or wouldn't, finish. It's interesting to contemplate why these unset squares were left forgotten just as it's interesting to speculate on why a woman would complete a top and not quilt it. Did she not like the squares once they were done? Did she run out of fabric to finish it? Maybe she couldn't find the right color or print fabric for the sashings, border, or binding and placed the squares aside until she did. It is just this speculation that makes the search for quilts and their repair and finishing so intriguing.

Squares are probably the cheapest way you'll find to own an antique quilt. As the most basic part of the quilt, they're certainly the best way to learn how to quilt and still retain a piece of history. There's something very appealing to adding your own work and artistic sense to a quilt started decades earlier. If quilts have their maker's soul sewed into them, then by acquiring completed squares and finishing them into a whole quilt, we can add our own piece of ourselves to the original work. We think a greater joy is rarely found.

One note about adding fabrics to tops and squares. You'll inevitably have to add fresh fabric for borders, bindings, and in the case of squares, for sashings. Fresh fabrics will look, well, fresh. They may be brighter, cleaner, stiffer than the original fabrics even if from the same period. After all, they haven't been washed, used, caressed, or folded as much as the fabrics in the top or squares. They'll look newer. Resist aging the fabrics with tea-dyeing, café au lait, or microwaving. These are methods used to make new fabrics look old. Tea-dyeing was used frequently around the Bicentennial to give new fabrics an old look, but the tannic acid in tea causes the very deterioration of fabrics that we want to arrest in antique quilts. By tea-dyeing, your brand-new fabrics will look as old as the original quilt fabrics but will also probably deteriorate faster. Be careful in your selection of colors for replacement fabric so that they more closely match the original and stay away from tea-dyeing or other artificial means of aging fabrics.

Whether you're preserving, stabilizing, repairing, or finishing your antique or family heirloom quilt, remember that there are professionals willing to help.

When assembled in a diamond shape, the traditional Grandmother's Flower Garden hexagons become a Diamond Field patch. These blocks would make a nice crib quilt or lap quilt when assembled and quilted.

Of course they charge a fee, but at least you'll know you're not alone as you do your part to preserve a piece of your past. Quilt repairers and restorers have the same love of quilts as you do and they treat every quilt they meet with the respect it's due. As with all other aspects of quilt collecting, get credentials and recommendations for the professionals you choose to work with.

And don't be afraid to study, research, and practice quilt repair so that you can preserve your prized quilts yourself!

CHAPTER SEVEN

CARE, CLEANING, STORAGE, AND DISPLAY

❖

Cleaning an antique quilt is so hazardous to its health that it should be attempted only when absolutely necessary—and even then only after you've investigated all the methods available to you. Keeping any quilt clean, antique or new, actually starts much earlier than the first wet or dry wash. Much of the advice in this chapter is geared to preserving quilts and reflects a purist attitude toward that end. Caring for any quilt is not easy. What follows is the ideal, and if it seems like hard work, it is. How much of this advice you follow depends on your resources, common sense, and emotional attachment to your quilts. You can cut corners if you like, but you must realize that in doing so you may also cut short the life of your quilt by taking a shortcut in its care, cleaning, storage, or display.

Determine, first, how and where you're going to use your newly acquired piece of American history. Quilts are much more fragile than most other antiques, and use wears them out quicker than it will a Hitchcock chair, a Revere tankard, or Depression glass. Textiles wear, deteriorate, and rot much faster than their antique counterparts, so give careful thought to their use.

If you're going to use an antique quilt on your bed, never sleep under it. That's the advice of Larry Zingale in the video *How to Buy Antique Quilts* (Warwick, N.Y.: Hilltop Productions, Inc., 1988). At night, take the quilt off the bed, fold it, and place it on the foot of the bed or drape it on a quilt rack, but don't actually spend the night tossing and turning under it. If it's nighttime warmth you're after, buy a new quilt and use it—understanding that you'll wear it out sooner than you would if you took it off the bed at night.

To enhance the life of a quilt you do sleep under, Laura Fisher advises turning the quilt frequently so that a different edge is at the top of the bed. As you sleep with a quilt, your body oils rub into the fabric along the top edge. By changing the direction of the quilt frequently, this wear will take place evenly on all edges of the quilt, thereby prolonging its looks and life.

Whether you display your quilt on a bed or a wall, check the light in the room. Ultraviolet light is the most damaging element of your home environment on a quilt. Keep your quilts away from fluorescent lights or invest in filtering sleeves or shields for these lights. If you want to be absolutely sure your quilt won't be damaged by the sun's ultraviolet rays, you can replace window glass with UV-filtering glass or Plexiglas. If the cost of that seems prohibitive, you can cover the windows and doors with a Mylar polyester film or treat the glass with a polyester film or a liquid metallized coating. If you're contemplating adding storm doors and windows, install those with rigid acrylic made for filtering ultraviolet rays.

Never display or hang a quilt on a bed or wall that gets direct sunlight or is near hot, bright lights. The visual effect of a skylight on a quilt beneath it may be stunning but it can cause overall fading—or worse, patches of fading that will leave the quilt looking streaked and blotchy. It doesn't take long for fading to occur.

As for the temperature and humidity in your house, if you're comfortable, your quilt is too. Maintain a temperature that's comfortable for you. If you're sweating from an increase in humidity, your quilt is also at risk. Place a fan in the room with the quilt to increase air circulation and to help avoid the formation of mold or mildew on the fabrics.

A quilt that's hung, or displayed on a bed but not slept under, will benefit from the regular vacuuming and dusting you do normally in the house. If dust and dirt don't accumulate anywhere else in your home, they won't collect on your quilt to damage it either.

How much use your quilt gets determines how long it will last, and only you can make that decision. Nancy O'Bryant Puentes writes that you should decide which of your quilts will get heavy use and which will get light use. The decision is yours, based on the knowledge that those quilts that are used heavily will wear out quicker than those you use only for display. Sleeping with a quilt, using one as a rug on the floor for a toddler, letting pets sleep on them, will mean a much shorter life for any quilt, antique or new. Make the decision early, for much of the responsibility of preserving a quilt lies in how you use it.

Expect to clean a display quilt only once about every five years. If you've cared for it, and stored it, properly during that time, you shouldn't have to clean it more often than that. Even a stored quilt with a musty smell can be improved simply by an airing rather than a wet wash. Place the quilt on a sheet outside, on the ground, in the shade. Place another sheet on top of the quilt. Leave it out for several hours. If you can't air the quilt outside, spread it on a bed and place several fans in the room to provide good air circulation. Leave it until the smell goes away or you determine it really needs a washing. If you rotate your display quilts, they'll get the airing they need while they're on display.

If a quilt does need to be cleaned, there are several steps to take. First, try vacuuming the quilt rather than going directly to a wet wash. A good vacuuming may remove most or all of the surface dust and dirt apparent on the quilt and some that isn't apparent but that can still damage the quilt. Never vacuum directly on the quilt, and never vacuum, or wash, a quilt that hasn't been stabilized (refer to chapter 6 to review the stabilizing process): the suction from the vacuum will pull and damage the fragile fabrics. Instead, cover the rough edges of a square of fiberglass screening with twill tape. Place this over a section of the quilt and vacuum through the screening, using your upholstery attachment on the vacuum cleaner. Dirt and dust will be lifted off the quilt but the fabrics won't be damaged from the suction. Proceed, vacuuming all sections of the top and back of the quilt. Inspect the quilt again. In most cases, vacuuming a well-cared-for quilt is sufficient to clean it.

If vacuuming didn't do the trick and the quilt still needs cleaning, you must first consider the content of the fabric, the condition of the quilt, and whether the colors might run. Never wash a silk, wool, or velvet quilt or a quilt with a wool batting. These quilts need to be professionally cleaned by an expert. Check with your quilt dealer, a professional trade organization such as the National Dry Cleaners Association, a museum, or other quilt collectors for a list of names of professional cleaners with experience cleaning these quilts.

It's a good idea to check for colorfastness even in a cotton quilt that's obviously been washed before. And don't check just one corner of a quilt. You must check all the different fabrics in a quilt to make sure none of them will run. Puentes advises placing a drop of tepid water on a piece of the fabric and blotting with a white paper towel. If there's color on the towel, the quilt shouldn't be washed unless you're ready to accept the consequences of color bleeding to other fabrics and ruining the quilt. If there's no color on the towel, then the quilt is probably colorfast, but Puentes points out that this does not guarantee that the colors won't run.

Harriet Hargrave writes a column called Quiltsense for *Traditional Quiltworks* magazine. In a recent issue, she proposed a four-step method of testing for colorfastness. First rub a dry white cloth over the fabric to be tested. If no color appears on the cloth, moisten the white cloth with cool tap water and rub the fabric again. If there's no color on the white cloth, dampen it with warm water and gently rub again. If there's still no color, mix your washing agent (to be discussed soon!) according to package directions and moisten the white cloth with that. Gently rub the fabric again. If the white cloth is still white, the quilt is probably safe to wash. Even with this method, there are no absolute guarantees that color won't run.

We'll discuss washing a quilt soon, but this is a good time to discuss what to do if you tested for colorfastness and the fabrics in your quilt still ran together in a wet wash. You must, according to Hargrave, not let the quilt dry. Once dry, the bleeding can be permanent. Instead, Hargrave recommends a product called Easy Wash, soaking the quilt for fifteen minutes. If this doesn't work, she recommends Snowy Bleach. Neither is guaranteed to remove the bleeded color, but she's had good results with both products. The important thing to remember when fabric colors bleed is to do something immediately, before the fabric dries and the color damage becomes permanent.

So far you've vacuumed the quilt and decided it still needs washing. You've tested the colors and it looks like they won't bleed. You're ready to wash. Both Hargrave and Puentes recommend using Orvus Paste, which is a natural product and rinses out thoroughly. Whatever you use, make sure it's a nondetergent, mild washing solution. Hargrave cleans her quilts using the washing machine because it's already designed to hold a lot of water. Never use the agitation cycle, but gently move the quilt in the water after it's soaked for about ten minutes. If the water seems particularly dirty, you may have to repeat the wash process. Hargrave advised using the gentle spin cycle to force excess water out of the quilt.

"Spinning will not harm the quilt—it is only centrifugal force, which is not agitating—and it is much easier on the fibers than handling a heavy, dripping-wet quilt." She does not advise using the gentle spin cycle on king-size quilts, but suggests using a front-load washer for anything bigger than queen size. Although we trusted her judgment on everything else, Hargrave was the only expert who did recommend using the gentle spin cycle. Puentes's bathtub method, which we'll discuss soon, seems less stressful on the quilt even though it takes hours longer.

Laura Fisher recommended hand-washing in a tub big enough to lay the quilt out flat. Since that's virtually impossible for anything larger than a small wall hanging, Puentes's method seems preferable. Puentes advised lining a filled bathtub with a clean, light-colored sheet so that the edges hang to the outside of the tub. The water should be warm, not hot. Then add the quilt, placing it in the tub by fan-folding it so that it's flat, not bunched up. Puentes advised soaking the quilt for up to twelve hours, changing the water several times. If the quilt still isn't clean, then she advised washing, using Orvus and following the directions on the package. Use the washing agent sparingly. It's better to wash the quilt a couple of times than to use too much of the cleaning agent. Never rub or wring the quilt, but agitate the water and gently move the quilt to wash it.

You may have to rinse the quilt up to ten times to get all the cleaning agent out of it. An improperly rinsed quilt will attract dirt and you'll be doing this difficult and arduous job again much sooner than is good for you or your quilt. Even if no suds appear after several rinsings, a few more won't hurt as long as you're gentle with the quilt.

Puentes advised leaving the quilt in the tub to drain out excess water. Its own weight will force a lot of the final rinse water out of the quilt. Only after it's drained this way for several hours should you lift the quilt out of the tub, using the sheet to carry it rather than handling the wet quilt itself. Never hang a wet quilt on a clothesline! Its own weight can rip and tear the fabric even in a new quilt. And never dry a wet quilt in the automatic dryer—that's too much stress to place on wet fabrics. Instead, place the quilt on a sheet, or several sheets, spread on the ground in the shade. Puentes "blots" the quilt with heavy towels once it's down on the ground to remove more of the excess rinse water. Then cover the quilt with another sheet, or several more, to protect it from debris, and leave it to dry, making sure you check that it is never in direct sun. Drying a large, heavy quilt can take an entire day. In fact, Puentes states that washing a quilt takes an entire weekend.

Make sure the quilt is completely dry. If the top side feels dry to your touch, Hargrave advises carefully turning it over. Replace the top sheet and leave it to finish drying. Hargrave has dried quilts over bushes. With a sheet already draped over the bush, she placed the quilt on top of the sheet and covered it with another sheet. The quilt dried faster because of the increased air circulation provided by keeping the quilt off the ground. Although this certainly saves time, we'd be a little concerned that the weight of the quilt might push branches through the fabric.

Drying outdoors may add brightness to your quilt. In *Collecting Quilts* (Paducah, Ky.: American Quilter's Society, 1985) author Cathy Gaines Florence advised laying even a dry quilt that appears dull outside on tall grass out of the sun.

"The combination of ozone rays and chlorophyll-laden grass is a natural bleaching process that will further brighten the colors," she wrote.

All of our experts noted that antique quilts deserve extra special attention. Before you attempt a cleaning, if you didn't do it when you bought the quilt, check with the dealer to document the fabric content, what kind of batting was used in the quilt, and to consult on a cleaning method. As we've noted before, sometimes cleaning shouldn't be attempted even if the quilt is stained. But to attempt a cleaning without knowing what's in your quilt or checking for colorfastness is surely courting disaster. Ideally, you should have asked the dealer about cleaning methods and fabric content when you purchased the quilt, but if you didn't, call back and discuss it or hire another expert to evaluate the quilt for you. Quilt dealers and collectors we contacted also agreed that a museum-quality quilt should never be cleaned by anyone other than an expert.

Before we discuss how to hang a quilt, you should know how to store them. Quilts should never hang for more than six months, and some experts recommend taking them down and letting them rest after three months. The rule of thumb is to let a wall quilt rest for as long as it was hung. Storage creates other problems that affect the life of a quilt. If it is improperly stored, a quilt can suffer from rot, mildew, mold, rodents, and insects.

Never store a quilt in plastic, either tightly closed or loosely wrapped. There is always moisture in fabrics from the air and even the most completely dried quilt will have moisture content. Storing a quilt in plastic traps that moisture inside and can lead to mildew and, eventually, rot. Quilts should be stored wrapped in cotton cloth, muslin, or cotton pillowcases. Storing them in cloth allows the wrapping and the quilt to breathe and avoids mildew from trapped moisture.

There is plenty of debate on how quilts should be stored. Some experts feel quilts should be stored rolled, not folded, while others feel folding is less stressful in the long run than rolling. To store a quilt rolled, you'll need an acid-free tube or a cardboard tube wrapped with acid-free tissue paper. Any good quilt shop should know a supplier of acid-free paper products. Roll the quilt with the top out. If any wrinkles or creases result from the rolling, they'll be on the backing and not on the top of the quilt. Roll loosely after placing a layer of acid-free tissue on the quilt so that it separates the rolls of fabric from each other. Then wrap the outside of the roll with cotton cloth.

The problem with rolling a quilt to store it is that there's usually little room in a house to put it after it's rolled. Puentes advises placing the roll diagonally under the bed by supporting the ends of the cardboard roll with blocks so the quilt isn't sitting on the floor. She points out that this area must be carefully cleaned to remove dust, insects, and insect larvae from damaging the rolled quilt.

In most homes, folding a quilt is the only realistic way to assure a place to conveniently store it. When you store a quilt folded, you should take it out of its wrappings and refold it along different lines several times a year. A quilt stored for a long time in the same fold pattern will develop permanent creases along the fold lines and ruin the quilt.

Always store any quilt with acid-free tissue folded inside. Some of the dyes in antique quilts will migrate if they lie on top of other parts of the quilt. The tissue separating the fabric folds will stop this migration. Puentes also advises placing wadded rolls of acid-free tissue along the inside of folds to prevent a sharp crease from forming. Once folded, the quilt can be wrapped in cotton or placed in a pillowcase and then stored in a box. The multiple layers of box, cotton, and tissue paper will discourage rodent attacks as these critters forage for nesting material. Frequent checking and refolding of the stored quilt will discourage insect infestation and damage from their protein-eating habits.

Frequent changes in your display quilts will almost guarantee that they remain in good condition for many, many years. A quilt forgotten, even if carefully stored, is a target for damage. Use your quilts by rotating their display, giving them time to rest, naturally airing them, and keeping them clean.

How you display a quilt also affects its life span. A quilt left hanging for years, even when properly hung, will stretch, distort, even wear and rip along the stress lines. A quilt that's hung should be properly supported at least along the top. With larger, heavier quilts, a support along the bottom is also advised. Never hang a quilt by pushing pins through its top or by using clips. The quilt will sag and stretch in the spaces between the pins and clips and will be distorted. These stress points are the first to wear and tear.

Instead, follow the methods in any good quilt book for sewing a casing or sleeve that is the same width as the quilt along the top, and sometimes also the bottom, edge. Slip a dowel or a curtain rod through the sleeve and then hang it on the wall. Another interesting method is to sew Velcro strips to a wider strip of cotton twill tape. Then sew the tape to the quilt. (With both the casing and Velcro methods, Puentes advises that every third or fourth stitch go through all the layers of the quilt. This means there will be stitches showing on the front of the display quilt, but they will better distribute the hanging weight of the quilt. When casings or strips are stitched only to the backing fabric, the weight of the quilt will wear the backing away and eventually it will rip.) Another batch of Velcro strips are attached to lathing strips, which have been sanded and finished to smooth them. Then the strips are nailed to the wall and the quilt is hung by pressing the Velcro strips on the back of the quilt to the strips on the wall. The advantage to this method is that all four edges of the quilt can have Velcro strips so that the weight of the quilt will be equally distributed on all four sides. Even then, Fisher suggests turning the quilt, if the design allows that, frequently so that a different edge is at the top. This will prevent sagging and distortion of the quilt as it hangs.

In "Hanging Quilts" (*Traditional Quiltworks*, No. 13), Linda Halpin advises placing a sleeve and dowel across the center back of a quilt that hangs on point. The top point of the quilt is hung on a nail in the wall with a loop sewed to the back. The center dowel is hung with nails or the curtain rod attachments that came with the rod.

One expert even advised attaching the quilt to a backing canvas and stretching that over a wooden frame much like an oil painting. For smaller pieces, say a single block or a small set of four blocks, framing is also an option. If the piece is framed under glass, however, make sure that either the glass is not set tight to the piece or the cardboard backing to the frame has small holes punched in it to allow for air circulation. An airtight frame will trap the natural moisture in the textiles and start mildew and mold.

We discussed in the last chapter why some experts think a quilt should never be considered a cutter. If you have a badly worn quilt and don't want to cut it down to just the good parts or to make something else out of it, then be creative in how you display it. A nice quilt rack and some careful folding will display the good parts of a worn quilt quite effectively and you won't have to feel you've destroyed a piece of history. Loft railings and banisters are also effective display areas as long as you remember to check for dust and debris and you rotate the quilts as you would the ones hung on your walls or displayed on your beds.

Just because they're valuable and you now know how to store your quilts, don't keep them in storage. Quilts were made to be used and you should feel comfortable using yours in some way. Like everything else of beauty, quilts take some work to maintain in our lives, but they're well worth the effort.

CHAPTER EIGHT

TRENDS IN THE MARKETPLACE

Quilt collecting has its own history, starting in the early 1900s when quilts made in the previous century suddenly became desirable for hanging on walls. The first quilt collections were, as is stated by Penny McMorris and Michael Kile in their book, *The Art Quilt,* "an important change in status for quilts, which had, until now, been looked upon by art and antique collectors as objects unworthy of display and safekeeping." In fact, quilts were deemed so unimportant by collectors that even in the late 1960s you could pick up a pair of quilts for only $15. Antiques dealers scoffed up quilts, not for their own value but to wrap their antique furniture in to avoid scratches, nicks, and gouges while in transit. Even in the early 1970s, at the very beginning of the nostalgia craze connected with the approaching national Bicentennial, quilts were commonly sold for as little as $25.

All that changed very soon. By the mid-1970s, quilt prices had mushroomed and the nostalgia craze, in full swing during the actual years of the Bicentennial celebrations, had greatly increased demand for quilts. Magazines touted quilts for decorating appeal, particularly with the country or Colonial looks in interior decorating also fostered by a desire to return to simpler looks and lifestyle. After the Whitney Museum exhibit of antique quilts, an important step in classifying quilts as art (see chapter 14), galleries began hanging and selling antique quilts with other art.

By the late 1970s and early 1980s, prices had skyrocketed and supply was dwindling. Quilt owners, who had previously been quite willing to part with Grandmother's quilt, were now reluctant to sell. Finding quilts available for sale became more and more difficult as people realized the value and importance of their family quilts and as more people entered the market looking for quilts to resell. In a quilt-buying frenzy, pickers knocked on doors and begged people to sell what they had. Quilts became regular features in American auctions. This increased demand resulted in astronomical prices. At a January 1988 Sotheby's auction one quilt with an estimated value of $6,000 to $8,000 sold for $13,200. Another quilt, estimated at between $8,000 and $12,000, actually sold for $26,400. The record price paid for any quilt was $176,000 for an 1840 Baltimore Album quilt at a Sotheby's auction in 1987. One year later another Baltimore Album quilt dated 1848 sold for $110,000.

But the late 1980s reflected the downswing in the economy and the higher level of sophistication of quilt buyers. Some exceptional quilts, with high estimated values, didn't sell. More and more quilt collectors were specializing and therefore willing to wait for the exact type and style of quilt they wanted. The days when any quilt would sell at an exceptional price were gone. Buyers became more choosy at each level of quilt collecting.

Still, quilts are affordable. There are many fine examples of antique quilts in the $300-to-$500 range.

"A few hundred dollars buys a good quilt," said an *Antique Trader Weekly* magazine editor. "It all depends on what you're looking for. It's a very hot hobby, rapidly growing, and there's much more interest than before." Subscription numbers for quilt magazines attest that interest in quilts is still growing. *Quilt World* magazine has over 130,000 subscribers; *Quilt Today* and *Traditional Quiltworks* have over 90,000. Contemporary quiltmakers, many times also antique quilt collectors, number in the hundred thousands. *Quilter's Newsletter Magazine* notes 736 quilt guilds in the United States, Canada, Europe, Australia, and the Orient, with almost 70,000 members. The National Quilting Association, Inc. is the oldest such group in the country, and the Studio Art Quilts Association is very probably the newest. Bill and Meredith Schroeder, quilt collectors, founded the American Quilter's Society and in six years had a membership of 75,000. In 1991, they opened the Museum of the American Quilter's Society, featuring the society's annual show, and drew over 11,000 quilt enthusiasts to Paducah, Kentucky, to view, take workshops, and learn about quilts.

Interest in antique quilts isn't confined to the United States. American quilts are sought by dealers in Paris, Switzerland, Japan, and Australia. The quilt-collecting boom hasn't peaked yet in Japan and is only just beginning in Australia. When we spoke with him, James Carroll had just returned from a show in Japan.

"Ninety percent of the Japanese never saw a quilt before, so we were also educating them," Carroll said. "They were cool about the twentieth-century quilts. If you could convince them they were a hundred years old then they got excited. The Japanese want their quilts perfect. They don't want to bring shame on themselves or the recipient so they don't want any imperfections." Carroll also noted different buying habits among the Japanese.

"We sold one crib quilt the first night and then nothing until the last day of the show," said Carroll. "Each day customers came, some right after their tea ceremonies, all dressed in kimonos, and they'd look. Their culture teaches them to be part of a group so they always came in a cluster.

"But the last day we sold a lot of quilts," said Carroll. "They just wanted to think over their purchase, consult each other about it. The wealthy Japanese buyer knows about quilts but the man on the street doesn't." Carroll is a partner in the Quilt Loft in Groton, Massachusetts, but also operates out of his home in New Hampshire. He had the best selection of squares and antique fabric that we saw during our research. He agrees that New England is somewhat picked over for quilts, but thorough searching still uncovers good ones. The day we spoke with him he had just bought two quilts found in a trunk upstairs in a barn. One was from the 1830s and the other was from approximately 1910.

"That's an eighty-year difference," he said. "How did they get there?" Carroll pointed out that those two quilts were indicative of a current trend. Quilts purchased in the 1950s and 1960s are now being released by their owners for resale or passed on to heirs who don't really want them and sell them off. "You have to keep your eyes open."

Current market trends show a move toward collecting more sophisticated quilts by a more knowledgeable buyer. But as we wrote this in early 1992, the general economy had affected the sales of quilts as it had the sales of most everything. The antique quilt market was flat.

"Sales have slowed down over the past year," said Ginnie Christie, a quilt collector and dealer in Albany, Oregon. "The whole antiques market has dropped off, but quilts are slowly, slowly picking up." Christie is also a dealer in antique furniture and she's noted sales are better there. "Instead of quilts, people are buying furniture they can use."

"People still want the $500 quilt for only $150 to $200," Christie said. "They don't appreciate quilts here like they do back east. I have a few customers willing to pay what a quilt is worth but many look at the price and say: 'Oh lord, Marj, I've got one like that at home in a trunk!'" Quilts have appreciated in value about 10 percent yearly for nearly a decade, making them a decent investment, and as far as affordability goes, quilts are still among the most affordable of collectibles.

Laura Fisher, of Laura Fisher/Antique Quilts and Americana in New York City, had a different view of the market.

"The trend is that interest in quilts continues to grow unabated," Fisher said. "The market is healthily and heartily growing. Of course, people want the scarcest and the rarest, but those are the serious collectors. For the general public, I sell everything and don't see any trends. On the same day I'll have someone in the shop looking for an appliqué and someone looking for a nineteenth-century geometric.

"Prices are up for the best, for the unusual, for the truly unique," said Fisher. "But they're not up exorbitantly for the general body of quilts." However, Fisher didn't want to discourage anyone from buying an antique quilt because of the prices. "Prices are going up in a reasonable and anticipated way given that there's less material available. The rise in quilt prices is no more unrealistic than the rise anywhere else, even in manufactured goods. It's exciting to see the rare and unique move up into the realm of art and affording the quilt its due, but there's still plenty out there that is affordable. The prices of new things are right up there too, and people are finding that they might as well get a quilt for the same price, have something they can use, and have it increase in value, too. People are still buying quilts and they're buying them all over the world."

"People do go for the best," said Margaret Cavigga of Northridge, California. Cavigga specializes in crazy quilts, album quilts, and pre-1860 antiques as well as American woven coverlets. "Very few people are interested in much more than what matches their wallpaper out here, but you should still only settle for the best you can afford. Just because it's cheap is not a reason to buy."

"The more you know, the luckier you get," advised Cavigga. "Keep your ears open and your mouth shut. I'd rather buy one good quilt than three average ones." Cavigga has taken quilts to Japan on nine different trips and launched three major shows there. She notes that the most popular quilts among first-time buyers in her area are in pink or blue color schemes. She agrees with Fisher that business is good, not flat.

There is actually a trend away from buying quilts simply because of their age. At one time, the older the quilt the higher the price, hence an older quilt was a better investment. But the age of a quilt is no longer the sole determination of value. (Except, of course, if a hitherto undiscovered sixteenth- or seventeenth-century example suddenly shows up on the market!) Other factors, such as design, workmanship, condition, and pattern, always included in determining the value of a quilt, at times supersede age as the prime reason a quilt is collectible or valuable. The truly unique quilt, even if as new as 1930, may be as valuable as one from 1830. And rarity, no matter the age, adds to value.

Pat Schuman of Pat Schuman Country Stuff participates in antiques shows all over the country and finds that California is a big market for quilts. She noted that West Coast collectors appreciated the more sophisticated quilts and were more knowledgeable about quilts in general than buyers in New England. California buyers more often than not hang their quilts on walls instead of using them on beds and prefer a bold geometric design or a unique pictorial over traditional quilt patterns and styles. This is also a trend among the more knowledgeable collectors no matter where they live. Veteran collectors specialize in the unique and unusual or in a certain time period rather than concentrating on traditional.

Preferences for traditional quilts aren't confined to New England, however. What sells the quickest in Oregon, according to Ginnie Christie, are all-pastels, Grandmother's Flower Gardens and Double Wedding Rings. Christie prefers less busy quilts. Her favorite patterns are the North Carolina Lily and the Princess Feather. Her least favorite is the Lone Star, but she's quick to point out that's because she doesn't have a wall in her home big enough to hang one.

"It always seems like the customers want quilts I don't want to carry," said Christie. She echoed the comments of other quilt dealers who said that what sells are Grandmother's Flower Garden, Dresden Plate, and Double Wedding Ring quilts. Those are the three most frequently found twentieth-century quilts, hence the most affordable. Since most were made with soft pastel-colored fabrics, they appeal to the beginning collector or one-quilt buyer because of their decorative qualities. These quilts match almost any decor in any color scheme. Another reason these three patterns don't appeal to dealers and the serious collector is that some were made from precut, predesigned kits. With so much of the work already done for the quiltmaker, a lot of the mystique of a quilt is lost. The proliferation of quilts from kits also means they aren't unique. A quiltmaker would have to have brought something truly of herself to the kit quilt to increase its value today.

Pictorial quilts, rarely done in anything except appliqué, are always popular and are usually priced higher than other quilts. Pictorials include commemorative family quilts, commemorative event quilts, political quilts, some friendship quilts, and album quilts. The most valued pictorial, as we've already noted, is the Baltimore Album quilt. Old pictorial quilts are rare. As we noted in chapter 2, appliqué was expensive to do and required the kind of leisure time only available to the wealthy. There are much fewer appliqué quilts than pieced, and fewer still pictorials.

Geometric designs with good color balance, such as the Ocean Waves patterns of the 1890s, appeal to collectors because of their optical illusion qualities. Indicative of the Victorian period, they are an alternative to the elaborate, sometimes overly fussy stitching of crazy quilts of the same date.

Silk and satin crazy quilts are showing a slight trend away from collectibility. They'll always be popular but they haven't held up well and deterioration will gradually weaken their value. Crazies of the same period in velvet and wool will become more collectible as the silk and satin crazy quilts continue to fray and wear away. Because the wool and velvet hold up better over time, these quilts are still in excellent condition and will stay that way longer, increasing their value.

Amish quilts, geometric and boldly colored, will probably always be collectible. They have become so valuable, in fact, that there are fakes on the market. Worn Amish quilts are being cut, used together with artificially aged new fabric and passed off as antique. Some of the fakes are so good that only an expert checking the binding and backing can tell for sure. Make sure you have an Amish quilt appraised by an expert or buy only from a dealer you trust.

African-American quilts just may be the new quilt-collecting item. A new appreciation for the design sense of African-American quiltmakers (see chapter 15), combined with the scarcity of these quilts in the marketplace, might result in the fastest increase in value among all quilts today.

Crib quilts are among the most collectible, but are very rare. They're so rare, in fact, that fakes are being discovered in this category, too. Larger quilts, cutters, are being cut down to crib size and passed off as original designs. One tip-off of a fake crib quilt is the size of the pattern blocks. A crib quilt, smaller than a bed quilt, would have a scaled-down version of a quilt block pattern. If the crib quilt you're considering has, say, twelve-inch individual blocks, it might have been cut from a larger quilt. Again, establish a relationship with a reputable dealer whom you trust and you won't be tempted by a fake. Question the seller closely about a crib quilt before you buy it.

Documentation adds to the value of a quilt today. Knowing the maker's name, an accurate date, or the history of a quilt can increase the price by anywhere from a third to double its value based on other criteria.. One quilt we saw was not particularly colorful or well done. But the fact that it had been finished on the same day as the battle of the Alamo by women whose male relatives died there made it a unique, and therefore valuable, quilt. Another quilt included embroidered coffins and the names and death dates of the maker's relatives. Other quilts have been made from military uniforms, nursing uniforms, wedding gowns, and christening outfits. Quilts that are both dated and signed by the maker also increase in value because their history is known.

Another trend is to overlook fair or poor condition. Ideally, to be of optimum value, a quilt should be in excellent condition, with no wear, a good binding, and no stains or deteriorated fabric. But if the quilt appropriately represents a certain time period, is visually pleasing and of excellent design, or has an interesting history, condition considerations should be secondary. If the quilt is in really poor condition—one step up from a cutter, let's say—that should be reflected in its price. It's probably a quilt that should be preserved but not at prime price.

At one time any quilt with machine quilting or appliqué was considered of much less value than those done completely by hand. But sewing machines became popular after the Civil War and sewers took great pride in using them. The early machines were capable of sewing tiny stitches and their owners used them to assemble, stitch down appliqué pieces, and quilt the finished tops. So enamored were they with the machines that they even appliquéd their pieces using contrasting thread so the machine stitches would show easily. So don't pass up that obviously machine-made quilt. If you can date it to the period after the Civil War, the quilt can be a valuable example of the advent of a new technology and its use in the home.

The only other trend in the market concerns the art, or innovative, quilt (see chapter 14). Michael James, noted quilt artist, has a price range of $3,000 for smaller works up to $16,000 for large commissioned works.

"I don't overprice my work," he said. "In fact, I was told recently by a highly placed dealer in the craft art world that my prices are too low. Some corporate buyers wouldn't even consider my work because the prices are so far under their art budget. My prices might seem high because they're at the high end of the contemporary quilt market. Those will start at $1,500 to $3,000 for a small piece, then up to $10,000." Price aside, James sees a conservative trend in art quilt buying.

"Times are tough," he said. "Even people with money aren't buying art. Buying art has become ostentatious."

What's collectible and what sells, what appeals to a dealer or a collector and what appeals to the first-time buyer, may never be the same. Just because a dealer recognizes the value of the unique quilt doesn't mean that quilt is easy to sell.

"I like the solid two-color quilts, or quilts that are different," said Christie. "Customers like them, too, but they're not willing to pay what they're worth." Christie adds red-and-white and green-and-white appliqué quilts to her collection and has started buying red-and-white embroidered quilts.

"They're not too expensive right now," she said. Christie also looks for cutter quilts. It's from cutter quilts that stuffed animals, pillows, purses, clothing, and small wall hangings are made. The salvaged pieces are also used to repair other antique quilts of the same age so that only authentic fabric is used.

"People here are willing to pay big bucks for a cutter," said Christie. "Raspberry and blue and white seem to be the preferred colors. I can get $125 to $130 for a cutter." Christie also sells some tops, but her supply is limited by her market.

"Customers only want to pay, maybe, $75 for a top," she explained. "I can't find them that cheap." Christie has the same problem with squares. Her market only wants squares under $2 each and she can't find many at a cheap-enough price to sell them that low. Her customers use squares primarily as a stockpile of antique fabrics for use in repairing quilts.

Christie gets her quilts from pickers.

"That's what they're called, but they're really my friends," she said. "Most of the quilts come from the Midwest, although the early quilts come from New England." Her picker friends regularly send her quilts to view. She selects what she wants and returns the rest. One picker from Illinois, whom Christie has dealt with for years but never met, sends a box that arrives every Thursday.

"Just like clockwork!" said Christie. "The box comes and there's one or two quilts in it every week, and I buy what I want and mail her back what's left." Christie attends the huge antiques show in Brimfield, Massachusetts, twice a year, selling her quilts and hunting for more. Christie noted that all quilt dealers search diligently for quilts.

Christie doesn't have a showroom, preferring to work out of her home. She attends many shows, concentrating on antiques shows held in shopping malls. For the past year the shows have been busy but sales slow.

"We're really bombarding ourselves with shows," she said. "But there are less and less dealers coming. There's plenty of customers coming to look but they just haven't been buying. It is picking up though."

Christie carries the most popular quilts even though they aren't necessarily what she likes or wants to collect.

"I keep the ones I like," she said. Christie, like most dealers, is well educated on the history, patterns, and technical aspects of quilts—so educated, in fact, that she's specialized her collection around her favorites. Many customers are buying their first quilts and respond to the colorful appeal of the traditional patterns such as Grandmother's Flower Garden and Double Wedding Ring. Although she doesn't prefer those patterns, she carries them for her customers, always keeping her eyes open for a quilt to add to her collection.

"Sometimes I'll smell a quilt," she said, "just smell it, and I picture the lady working on it, at night, after everyone's asleep in the house. And I wonder about her, about what made her make that quilt."

It's that curiosity, that wonder, in the heart and mind of the quilt buyer, that really determines the value and sale of a quilt. Even with poor workmanship, shoddy fabrics and poor condition, the truly unique quilt with a story to tell will always be valuable.

Price
Listings

CHAPTER NINE

HOW TO USE THIS GUIDE

The previous chapters have provided invaluable information to the quilt collector. You should read them through thoroughly and then use them as a reference in order to develop your own knowledge of quilts. The next three chapters (chapters 10, 11, and 12) are for reference also, as they list nearly 750 quilts, quilt tops, and related items with their associated prices.

Over the course of six months, a review of the marketplace found these antique quilts for sale; there are certainly many thousands of others available. These quilts were found all over the country at antiques stores, in quilt shops, at flea markets, and at auctions. Since many factors (quality of materials, age, skill of the creator, condition of the quilt, situation of the seller, part of the country) influence the way a quilt is priced, the prices listed are not hard-and-fast rules for pricing a particular quilt. They are guidelines for the buyer and, along with the information gleaned from the previous chapters, should be used to ask informed questions about a desired quilt.

Pieced quilts are listed in chapter 10, and appliqué quilts in chapter 11. Chapter 12 lists various other quilts that we found, such as trapunto, and also blocks and fabric. In each chapter, quilts are grouped under alphabetically arranged headings such as "Amish," "Crazy Quilts," "Dresden Plate," and so on. Within each heading the quilts are also listed alphabetically by pattern name. Quilt tops are listed last in each chapter. Following each quilt name is a brief description of that quilt. In order to avoid clutter in the listings, we have listed just that information that deviates from a standard, "average" antique quilt. So, unless otherwise noted, the following is true of the quilts listed:

The *pattern name* is the most common name for the pattern of the quilt. If the quilt pattern is a variation of a common pattern, we will so note. Many quilters varied standard patterns slightly; we try to give you the most common name that fits the deviation.

The *age* or *date* of the quilt is given by the seller. If we have any reason to think the date may be incorrect, we will say so in the listing.

The *color* listed is the predominant color, that which the quilt seems most to be. There may be other colors on the quilt, in fact, there usually are. If there is just no way to separate the predominant color, then the quilt may be listed as multicolored, or with more than one color if several stand out. The colors may be in solids or prints; if one or the other stands out, that will be noted.

The *condition* of the quilt is good, meaning there are no tears, the binding and backing are intact, and the colors are fairly true. Unless otherwise noted, quilts will have been used and washed some number of times, softening the fabric, removing the stiffness of new fabric. Deviations, toward better condition or worse, are noted in the listing.

Quilt *materials* are cottons, wools, or other natural fibers. Some quilts made after the early 1900s, when synthetics became available, may have some fabrics that are blends or are completely synthetic. When known this will be noted in the listing.

The *work quality* is reasonable, meaning that seams lie flat and are not puckered, the preponderance of points or junctions of the pieces match. Quilting of six to eight stitches per inch is standard, eight to ten is very good, ten or more is excellent; variations will be mentioned. An average amount of quilting on the piece is more than just the minimum required to hold the quilt together; minimal quilting or excessive quilting will be noted. Appliqué stitches are small and even, and barely visible. Variations are noted in the listing.

Quilting means stitches that go through all layers of the quilt from top to backing. All quilting is by hand unless otherwise noted.

Assembly (putting the pieces and the blocks together) is primarily by hand but may be partially or completely done by machine.

Stitching means embroidery, appliqué stitches, or other surface stitches.

From means that the quilt was made in that place, and that this fact can be substantiated. *Found in* means the quilt was found there but most likely was made somewhere else. Most quilts will have no origin listed, as they might have changed hands, or come from a seller who did not know the origin.

Maker known means that the seller has substantial evidence of who actually made the quilt. The quilt may be signed, or the quilt may have come directly from a family member or the maker herself. If there is any question as to the identity of the maker, the term *maker known* is not listed.

Other *information* known about the quilt is listed.

Price is that asked by the seller. All of the quilts listed are or have recently been for sale. Quilts that are in museums, private collections, or are otherwise not available for purchase are not listed.

These price and identification listings should be used as guidelines, for as you have learned in the previous chapters, many factors affect the value of a quilt. Where many of one type of quilt are listed you can establish two facts.

Since we found a goodly number, you probably will, too. And the prices listed will form a nice range for your comparison.

As a further help, turn to Sources and Resources for shops, dealers, and quiltmakers where you can go for both quilts and assistance. Good luck in your search; we are certain you will find the perfect quilt to warm your heart.

CHAPTER TEN

ANTIQUE PIECED QUILTS

Most quilts, except for whole-cloth quilts, are created by assembling smaller pieces of cloth together to form a top. The process of combining fabric together to make a quilt is called patchwork. When these smaller pieces are put together by seaming them to each other, usually in geometric patterns, often creating optical illusions, it is called piecing. The quilt that results is, therefore, a pieced quilt.

There are hundreds of different pieced patterns, some of which date back to when block-style quilting first became popular. In *Clues in the Calico,* Barbara Brackman documented almost four hundred patterns before stopping her search. Eighty-six of these dated from before 1825.

If there are hundreds of pieced block patterns, then there are surely thousands of names for them. Ruth Finley, in *Old Patchwork Quilts,* documented almost twenty different names for a single block pattern. Every time a quiltmaker made even the slightest variation to a pattern, she gave it a new name. Patterns were often renamed when made in a different region of the country. Pioneer quiltmakers gave new names to favorite blocks as another record of their journey west. Sometimes a pattern was given a name for sentimental reasons, for instance, putting a family member's name in the title. Pattern names were changed because the original name held connotations the quiltmaker didn't want connected to her quilt. In this way, Drunkard's Path became Pumpkin Vine and Wandering Foot changed to Turkey Tracks. Sometimes simply changing a color scheme or reversing the use of lights and darks in a pattern earned it a new name.

In the 1890s magazines included patterns and instructions in their issues to attract buyers currently enthralled with that period's quiltmaking craze. Naturally, they wanted their patterns to be original. They might have added a slight variation to the pattern, but even if they didn't, they often gave the block a new name.

Quilt block names often have strong sentimental values, or historical or regional ties. It's often fruitless to argue over a pattern you know is a Bear's Paw but someone else calls by a different name. Make a note of the different name and add it to your growing store of knowledge about quilts.

Because geometric pieced patterns often created an optical illusion when assembled, it's sometimes difficult to find the repeat pattern in a quilt top. Look carefully for the basic block. Although quiltmakers have used all sizes of pieced blocks, the most common are 10, 12, and 16 inches. If the optical illusion overwhelms you, try using a ruler. Move the ruler around the quilt top looking for, say, a 12-inch repeat of a pattern. Usually close inspection of a quilt will show you the horizontal and vertical seam lines of the basic block, but if it doesn't, try to find a repeat by measuring with a ruler. The illustrations on pages 133–135, based on a four-patch block, illustrate how difficult it can be to find a basic block in an optical illusion quilt. Also note the different pattern names given this pattern when the assembly of the basic block is changed slightly.

Another hurdle to finding the basic pattern in a quilt is the set. A quilt set on point, with the blocks placed like diamonds across it, makes a different kind of optical illusion that seems to defy discovery of what pattern was used in it. Some patterns, the Irish Chain in particular, only look like they're set on point, which confuses us further!

All quilts have names. We'll never know what eighteenth-century quiltmakers actually called their blocks, or what name a block was originally given. But varying and naming a pattern was, and remains, one of the ways a quiltmaker added her soul to her quilts. Even though the many names for a single block are confusing to us today, pattern names add to the mystery of a quilt, pique our interest, and make the quilt quest that much more exciting!

The following prices are for antique pieced quilts. Review chapter 9, "How to Use This Guide," before you browse the lists.

Amish Quilts

Amish quilts are among the most prized of antique quilts. Their fascination lies in their use of pure colors: magentas, blues, greens, reds, and purples. Also, the Amish quiltmakers used black as a color, a practice unique to these quilts—with the marked exception of the crazy quilts of the Victorian era.

Like all quiltmakers, the Amish used fabrics left over from other home needlework to created their beautiful quilts. Because their lifestyle and religion prohibited adornment of either their bodies or their homes, plain colored fabrics were all they bought. When we think of the Amish, we think of plain black fabrics, but although they were prohibited from using printed fabrics, because they were thought objects of adornment, the Amish still used bright, clear colors for their clothing and household furnishings. It is these colors, combined

BASIC QUILT BLOCK ASSEMBLY

Old Maid's Puzzle

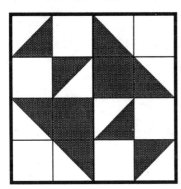

Crosses and Losses

Double Cross

Many different looks can be created with just minor changes to the basic quilt block. Two sections of triangles make the Old Maid's Puzzle block. Just a small change causes the block to become Crosses and Losses. One little twist makes yet another block, Double Cross.

The larger scale assembly of the blocks into a complete quilt affects the look as well. The original Old Maid's Puzzle blocks simply assembled, one after another, with sashing in between and corner squares, leaves the basic block easy to pick out.

with the basic black, that make the Amish quilt so visually startling. Amish quilts were made in three predominant styles. One is reminiscent of the old English-style medallion quilts. These incorporated a central diamond bordered by strips and triangles of alternating black and colored fabric. Strip and Bar

BASIC QUILT BLOCK ASSEMBLY

Take out the sashing and corner squares, give some of the blocks a twist. A totally different quilt appears, and the basic block practically disappears into the overall pattern.

quilts are also common. Another distinctly Amish design is the Trip Around the World, or Sunshine and Shadows quilt. Gradations and varieties of colors radiate in diamondlike strips out from a central square. Although this pattern looks difficult to piece, these quilts were made from prearranged grids showing where each color should be placed in a strip. Then the strips were sewn together to form the radiating diamond illusion.

Another distinctly Amish trait is the way in which colors were combined in their quilts. Colors that seem inappropriate together when we are told about them create wonderful movement and appeal when placed in close proximity in the Amish quilt. These combinations of magenta with blue, or red with purple, actually work exceptionally well together in the hands of the expert Amish quiltmaker. Add in the elaborate quilting done on these quilts and you'll know why they're so valuable.

Because antique Amish quilts are so valuable, fakes have appeared on the market. They're difficult to spot. Unlike scrap bag quilts, in which we can find colors and prints that indicate a specific time period in fabric manufacture, Amish quilts of natural fibers were made into the 1940s. Similar fabric in the same bright colors can be bought today, aged, then assembled into a brand-new Amish quilt with an antique look. Educate yourself to spot the real thing by viewing as many authentic quilts as you can at museums. A reputable and experienced dealer should be able to spot a fake Amish quilt.

Although many other quilts we saw had an Amish look or were purported to be Amish, we have only listed those that could be authenticated as such.

BRICK STEPS: 1920–1940; brown, green, taupe on one side; orange, brown on the other side; reversible quilt, made that way; Midwest Amish; small quilting stitches, clamshell quilting; 82 × 86 $750

CHURN DASH: 1930s; black, blue, burgundy; Ohio Amish crib quilt, set on point with black sets; triple rainbow quilting, straight-line quilting in squares; 36 × 36 $145

FOUR-PATCH BARS: 1930s; black, blue; Ohio Amish crib quilt, excellent condition, excellent assembly and quilting, petal and curved quilting; 36 × 36 $145

FRIENDSHIP DOUBLE IRISH CHAIN: 1915; darks, black; red embroidery signed, feather ring quilting, Holmes County Ohio Amish; 68 × 80 $5,500

NINE-PATCH CHAIN: 1900–1920; black, blue; one black border, one blue border, all polished cottons, Ohio Amish; slight spot fade, small quilting stitches, waffle quilting; 70 × 78 $2,200

OHIO STAR: 1910; darks, blue, brown; Amish, minimal use; 35 × 45 $275

PLAIN QUILT: 1930; solid blue; Amish, minimal use, very small stitches; 60 × 73 $1,295

SAW TOOTH DIAMOND IN SQUARES: 1935; burgundy, black, lavender; all rayon fabrics, lavender border and edge, light green cotton gingham backing, Pennsylvania Amish; very good condition, unused, no wear, some small stains, few spots of color loss; excellent assembly, very small quilting stitches; feather, flower, and leaf quilting; 76 × 76 **$1,100**

SQUARES AND TRIANGLES: 1940s; black, teal, yellow; Indiana Amish, minimal use, recently washed, straight-line quilting; 64 × 80 **$495**

T-SQUARES AND BARS: 1945; blues, greens, gray; Amish, blue chambray edge; double border, one blue, one gray; never used, smells musty; large cable quilting on edge, smaller cable on first border, even smaller cable on second border; 80 × 110 **$1,250**

ZIGZAG: 1930s; black, blue, rust; Ohio Amish, half or lap quilt; excellent condition, unused, unwashed; minimal quilting in zigzags and curves; 80 × 60 **$475**

Crazy Quilts

The crazy quilt style of bed covering is among the oldest known in America. Originally this method of assembly was completely utilitarian and efficient as it used up the leftover fabric from other home needlework required to clothe a family and furnish a home. These leftovers were fitted together to make a piece of fabric big enough to cover a bed. These were the comfortables, or comforters, because the three layers were tied with yarn, thread, or string instead of stitched together.

It wasn't until the mid to late 1800s, especially the Victorian era of the mid 1800s, that crazy quilts became preferred, embellished, and uneconomical. During this time, quiltmakers bought fabric specifically for the quilts instead of using scraps from the home. Preferred fabrics were silks, satins, brocades, and velvets—expensive goods! The fabric was carefully cut and stitched to achieve a randomly placed look that was anything but random. Then the fabric was heavily adorned with embroidery stitching to outline the patches and to add the maker's own history, hobbies, family, and whimsy. Some of these quilts even include small paintings of birds, flowers, and animals. Crazy quilts of the period are fanciful, elaborate, and bright. Unfortunately, the combination of inferior dyes and fragile fabrics has taken its toll on these quilts. It's difficult to find one that survives today that doesn't show some fabric deterioration.

These highly embroidered, flashy crazy quilts were the province of the well-to-do and middle class. They were both examples of expert needlework and statements of financial security if not of wealth. Crazy quilts from this period were the ultimate examples of "keeping up with the Joneses." Because

With wool challis pointed edges, this crazy quilt shows many of the components typical of this style. The fabrics are mostly silks, with some brocades, velvets, and ribbons, too. Embroidery and topstitching abounds. The quilt is over one hundred years old.
Quilt courtesy of Helen Warner

Looking closer at this crazy quilt, we can see some unique little items: the embroidered ribbon celebrating Christmas and the tiny tulips embroidered along one block.
Quilt courtesy of Helen Warner

they were prized they were well cared for, so some are available today. But if they hadn't been made of such highly fragile fabric, more of them would have survived. Toward the turn of the century, crazy quilts tended to be made of wool. Embroidery was confined to covering the seam using a simple feather or buttonhole stitch. One historian attributed this toning down of crazy quilts to a rejection of the gaudiness and overindulgence of the Victorian era.

Crazy quilts—the fancy silk, satin, and velvet ones—provide hours of entertainment. Examining the embroidery and finding clues to the makers' beliefs, opinions, family life, and historic period are fascinating. Many such quilts incorporated ribbons and commemorative fabrics that reveal occupations, leisure activities, political persuasions, and historic events. The addition of one of these interesting and entertaining quilts to your collection is a treasure.

CRAZY QUILT: 1880; red, brown; slight fading overall; 60 × 76 $295

CRAZY QUILT: 1880; blues, reds, beige; all cottons, red border, lavender border, fair to good condition, few small repairs, overall fade, multiple washings, worn top, few tears; minimal straight-line quilting; 70 × 74 $385

CRAZY QUILT: 1880s; darks and light; embroidered brocade, some fabric with raised patterns, silks, some fabric deterioration; fair work, feather topstitching; 58 × 58 $375

CRAZY QUILT: 1880s; darks and lights; brocades, embroidered satins, silks, velvets; very good condition, no fabric loss, feather topstitching carefully done, not excessive in detail; 40 × 40 $1,200

CRAZY QUILT: 1880s; blues, reds, burgundy; satins, corduroy, velvets, medallion center block with embroidered flowers, burgundy satin border, some fabric loss; from New York State, very good work, multicolored topstitching; 68 × 68 $1,500

One type of crazy quilt, very rare and hard to find, is not pieced but appliquéd, and looks like stained glass. Using black ground or foundation fabrics, the quiltmaker appliquéd irregular patches, leaving a 1/4- to 1/2-inch border of black fabric showing to represent the lead solder used in assembling stained-glass window pieces.

CRAZY QUILT: 1880s; darks, jewel tones; some printed fabric, silks, satins, velvets, fans with ribbons, silk thread embroidered flowers, birds, teakettle, shoes, kittens; excellent condition, dated; excellent work; 72 × 72 $3,800

CRAZY QUILT: 1884; multicolors; silks, velvets, satins, painted pieces, embroidered pieces, chenille embroidery on some, very elegant, burgundy velvet border, gold rope on edge, some fabric splits and loss; lots of topstitching, very good work, purchased machine "quilted" taffeta backing; 68 × 68 $1,200

CRAZY QUILT: 1887; burgundy, black; primarily wools with pigs, dogs, pelicans, cats, and other animal shapes; blocks run together, looks very unplanned; dated, signed, slight wear on top, solid piece backing of red and cream; 90 × 110 $4,200

CRAZY QUILT: late 1800s; blacks, gold, green, blues; velvets, satins, some shapes like circles, some areas with embroidery; some fabric loss, minimal yellow feather stitching; 68 × 68 $750

CRAZY QUILT: late 1800s; dark colors; velvets, ribbons, very decorative; slight fabric deterioration in stiffer fabrics, some pieces missing; fans and embroidery in corners, biblical symbols elsewhere, pagoda shape in center, black border; found in California; 69 × 69 $1,000

CRAZY QUILT: 1883; darks; velvets, silks with embroidered pictures, lace edge, yellow-and-red border, fabrics in excellent condition, dated; excellent work, very artistic, tiny glass beads sewn onto feather topstitching, very good topstitching; 60 × 60 $15,000

CRAZY QUILT OF FANS: 1893; blacks, darks; wool challis with wool embroidery of owls, birds, other symbols; dated; fans like quarter of Dresden Plates, some fabric loss in a few areas, some loose embroidery and assembly stitches; 72 × 60 $650

CRAZY QUILT: 1890s; multicolored; two-sided quilt, silks and velvets on one side, cottons on back, few fabric splits; no binding, buttonhole stitching on edge, yellow feather topstitching; 80 × 88 $1,250

CRAZY QUILT: early 1900s; multicolored; maker known, reverses to medallion with winter scene and cheater cloth borders; 60 × 72 $125

CRAZY QUILT: early 1900s; browns; pinwheel and other designs of stitching, wide variety of fabrics; 72 × 88 $295

CRAZY QUILT: early 1900s; brown, blue, multicolored; velvets, silks, satins, yellow feather stitching on block joints and elsewhere; some fabric loss, some wear in spots; 70 × 68 $350

CRAZY QUILT: early 1900s; darks; velvets, satins, large and small pieces; some fabric loss and deterioration, uneven feather stitching overall; 78 × 80 $450

This Snowball quilt is done in the Victorian style, with silk and satins, and yellow feather topstitching. Done around the turn of the century, it has, as one would expect, quite a bit of spot fabric loss.
Quilt courtesy of Betty Wilson

CRAZY QUILT: early 1900s; darks, blues; velvets, satins, ribbons; some fabric loss, back torn in two places; tiny yellow feather stitching overall; 72 × 80 $500

CRAZY QUILT: 1910; multicolored; child size, much fabric deterioration and wear; 30 × 60 $95

CRAZY QUILT: 1916; black, brown, gray; wools, slits in back where money was hidden on westward journey; post-Victorian minimalist style, tied, no quilting; 36 × 42 $250

> *A collector purchased a crazy quilt dated 1916. When she inspected it, she found slits cut in the fabric backing. She did some research and found that the original owner and her family had hidden money in the quilt when they moved west.*

CRAZY QUILT: 1920s; multicolored; all silks, purple backing and edging; no batting, minimal use; 74 × 54 $250

CRAZY QUILT: 1940s; multicolored; overall stains, some fabric loss; herringbone topstitching with some threads missing; 54 × 72 $60

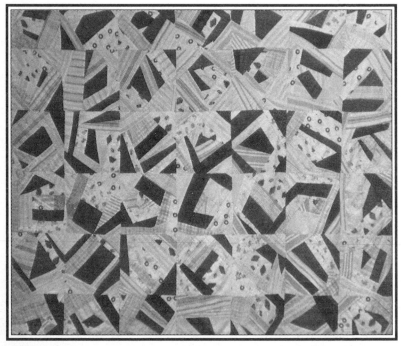

A 1930s version of a crazy quilt, this piece shows a variety of flannel fabrics and the simple style possible with this type of quilt. The darks and the lights balance for an interesting look.
Quilt courtesy of Laura Caro

Double Wedding Ring

The Double Wedding Ring pattern dates from the 1920s and the beginning of a trend away from the traditional straight lines of pieced geometric quilting and toward curved designs. It is a variation of the Pickle Dish pattern. The Double Wedding Ring is a moderately difficult pieced pattern that uses scrap bag fabrics with a white background fabric. The open, white areas of the quilt are usually elaborately quilted with wreaths, feathers, or a crosshatch pattern. Its association with wedded bliss, direct from its name, still makes the Double Wedding Ring the perfect gift quilt.

So popular was the Double Wedding ring pattern that, along with the Dresden Plate, it was offered extensively as a kit in the 1930s. Although many first-time collectors as well as decorators are attracted to the Double Wedding Ring, many dealers and experienced collectors avoid them. There were so many made, and so many are available on the market today, that they are not very valuable. Many collectors also avoid them because they might have been made from kits and are, therefore, less original. Although some dealers won't carry them on a regular basis, if you've developed a relationship with a dealer and you want a Double Wedding Ring, say so. Most dealers can find them for you easily.

DOUBLE WEDDING RING: 1920s; pink, white, multiprints; scalloped edge with pink binding, pink backing; minimal use, outline quilting, floral quilting inside rings; 68 × 82   **$475**

DOUBLE WEDDING RING: 1920s; green, pinks, pastels; scalloped edge, overall fade, very worn binding on one side; outline quilting, circle quilting inside rings; 60 × 70   **$500**

DOUBLE WEDDING RING: 1920s; multicolored pastels; scalloped edge, faded overall, few age spots, straight-line quilting; 76 × 78   **$500**

DOUBLE WEDDING RING: 1920s; yellows, pinks; scalloped edge, unused, unwashed; very good assembly, all junctions match, small quilting stitches, feather wreath quilting in rings; 70 × 78   **$600**

DOUBLE WEDDING RING: 1925; green, yellow; scalloped edge, some over-all wear; 76 × 88   **$475**

DOUBLE WEDDING RING: 1925; pink and blue; scalloped edge; 76 × 76   **$550**

DOUBLE WEDDING RING: 1930s; red, blue, yellow, green; very bright, all solids; poor condition, very faded overall, much fabric loss, damage in places, many stains; 90 × 78   **$150**

This is a beautiful example of the traditional assembly of the Double Wedding Ring, made in the 1930s of many printed fabrics. It has solid patches at the junctions of the rings, curved and pointed edges, and marvelous quilting.

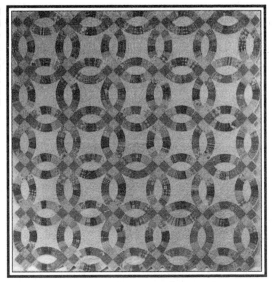

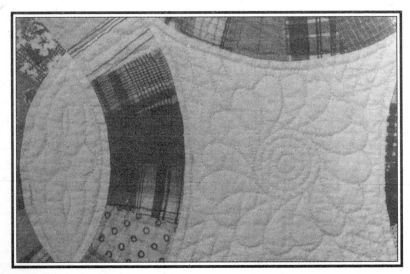

Looking closer at a block from the same quilt, the excellent assembly and lovely print fabrics can be seen. The quilting is excellent, with feather rings, diamond grids, and medallions, as well as the traditional outline quilting on the blocks. Quilting lines can be seen, attesting to the unwashed and unused condition of this classic quilt.

Throughout the world, the Double Wedding Ring is the most well known curved quilt pattern. Even this much loved and heavily used pattern is not without its variations, however. When the ring pieces are enlarged and the center is decreased, the pattern becomes the Pickle Dish. Another variation fills in the ring and is called Pincushion. Not very romantic.

DOUBLE WEDDING RING: 1930s; pastel prints; overall fade; 78 × 96
$375

DOUBLE WEDDING RING: 1930; light yellow, light blue, pastels; slight overall fade, torn binding, little wear otherwise; large quilting stitches, lots of straight-line quilting; 62 × 76
$390

DOUBLE WEDDING RING: 1930s; yellows, golds, blues; scalloped edge on two long sides, yellow back and binding; slight overall fade, worn binding, well used, multiple washings; large daisy flowers in center of rings, outline quilting on rings; 76 × 80
$400

DOUBLE WEDDING RING: 1930; pale green; 60 × 75
$445

DOUBLE WEDDING RING: 1930s; pink, multiprints; scalloped edge with pink binding, slight overall wear; excellent assembly and quilting, very small quilting stitches, scroll and feather quilting; 66 × 80
$450

DOUBLE WEDDING RING: 1930; multipastels; 70 × 80
$475

DOUBLE WEDDING RING: 1930s; pink, green, multiprints, solids; scalloped edge, white border, minimal use, unwashed; very small quilting stitches, lots of quilting, cable quilting on border, straight-line quilting on rings, detailed quilting in rings; 88 × 73
$500

DOUBLE WEDDING RING: 1930s; pink; scalloped edge, worn back, excellent quilting, small stitches; 72 × 72
$500

DOUBLE WEDDING RING: 1930s; yellow; scalloped edge; 45 × 80 $550

DOUBLE WEDDING RING: 1930s; pink, lavender, multiprints; scalloped edge with pink binding; excellent assembly and quilting, very small quilting stitches, detailed quilting in center of rings, diagonal quilting overall; 88 × 88
$550

DOUBLE WEDDING RING: 1930s; various pastels; minimal use; 82 × 80
$650

DOUBLE WEDDING RING: 1930s; pastels; from Maryland, one corner faded, few small stains, worn binding; 72 × 80   **$650**

DOUBLE WEDDING RING: 1930s; red-orange, light blue, solids and prints; small rings, eight inches in diameter; slight overall wear; very even quilting stitches, lots of diamond quilting overall; 76 × 62   **$575**

DOUBLE WEDDING RING: 1930s; peach, sky blue; few age spots, flower and leaf quilting, smaller leaves between rings; 63 × 78   **$895**

DOUBLE WEDDING RING: 1930s; yellow, peach; scalloped border, unused, 114 × 80   **$1,200**

DOUBLE WEDDING RING: 1940s: light blue, navy; straight edge, very little quilting, big stitches, poorly done; 86 × 92   **$290**

DOUBLE WEDDING RING: 1940s; pastels; some overall fade, overall wear, some stains; 70 × 84   **$325**

Romance abounds in quiltmaking in bridal quilts and blocks with names like Cupid's Arrow, Eternal Triangle, Bridal Stairway, and, of course, the Double Wedding Ring.

DOUBLE WEDDING RING VARIATION: 1940; red, white, blue; five-point stars in center of rings; black quilting thread on blue, white elsewhere, very dramatic; 92 × 72   **$5,500**

Drunkard's Path

The Drunkard's Path is a two-patch design that is a square with a quarter circle in one corner. Because it involves curved piecing, this pattern is another challenge to the quiltmaker. Usually the Drunkard's Path is made from only two colors, with half the blocks having the quarter circle in one color and the rest of the block in the second color, while the other half of the blocks have the quarter circle in the second color and the rest of the block in the first color. This pattern is also known as one of the Robbing Peter to Pay Paul variations because, when finished, it looks as if the quarter circle from one square was sewn to the balance of another. We did see one Drunkard's Path quilt made with white fabrics and scrap bag pieces instead of the two-color combination (see photograph, page 151).

Like the Log Cabin, the Drunkard's Path can be assembled in many ways. The illustrations show three ways this two-patch can be put together to achieve different optical effects. The three shown are the traditional assembly, also called World Without End; the Falling Timbers, which is much the same as the Log Cabin's Straight Furrows; and the Love or Lone Rings, which is reminiscent of the Barn Raising style for the Log Cabin.

Other assembly variations include Steeplechase, Mill Wheel, Fool's Puzzle, and Baseball. An excellent source for the assembly variations of the Drunkard's Path can be found in Marguerite Ickis's *The Standard Book of Quilt Making and Collecting*, listed in the bibliography.

Drunkard's Path is also known as World's Puzzle, Solomon's Puzzle, and Rocky Road to Kansas. So that they could continue using this popular pattern, teetotalers and Women's Christian Temperance Union members renamed it the Pumpkin Vine.

DRUNKARD'S PATH: 1880; red, white, blue; pointed edge, edge faded and worn, some stains; chain stitch quilting in paths; 74 × 74 $750

DRUNKARD'S PATH: 1880s; red on white; red back and binding, assembly fair, many junctions don't match, outline quilting; 74 × 82 $400

DRUNKARD'S PATH: 1890s; red on white; two reds, one stable with color intact, one unstable faded to pale peach pink; very unusual look with some squares faded, others not; fair condition, overall fade, overall stains, straight-line quilting; 54 × 70 $138

DRUNKARD'S PATH: 1890–1910; brown on white print, white leaf print on red; minimal use, excellent assembly, good quilting; 72 × 80 $285

DRUNKARD'S PATH: early 1900s; pink on solid white; 72 × 80 $395

DRUNKARD'S PATH: early 1900s; red and white; red backing and edging; slight overall fade; 70 × 78 $425

DRUNKARD'S PATH: early 1900s; pink; patterned pink background, unused; 74 × 78 $550

DRUNKARD'S PATH: 1900–1910; cornflower blue; set with white squares; from Pennsylvania; overall fade, few tiny stains, excellent petal quilting overall with tiny quilting stitches; 64 × 78 $850

DRUNKARD'S PATH: 1910s; red on light blue; excellent condition, unused; very graphic, flower quilting in blue squares, straight-line echo and outline quilting in paths; 70 × 80 $650

DRUNKARD'S PATH: 1920s; lavender and white; overall fade, slightly worn binding, few small stains; 70 × 74 $550

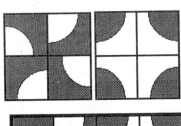

DRUNKARD'S PATH BLOCK ASSEMBLY

The traditional Drunkard's Path is assembled from four mirror-image blocks which are each assembled in two different groups of four. When these bigger blocks are then alternately joined, they present the visual representation of a horrible trial (or trail) for the inebriated.

DRUNKARD'S PATH BLOCK ASSEMBLY FALLING TIMBERS VARIATION

Take two each of the mirror-image blocks and assemble them into a simple four-block group. Then join multiples of that four-block group and the result is the Falling Timbers variation of the Drunkard's Path block. Perhaps more appealing to the visual sense, this pattern is similar to the Log Cabin Straight Furrows variation.

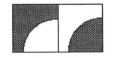

DRUNKARD'S PATH BLOCK ASSEMBLY
LOVE RING VARIATION

Change the mirror-image blocks yet again and assemble them outward from the center. The result is the Love Ring variation of the Drunkard's Path block assembly, a pattern related to the Log Cabin Barn Raising variation.

A true scrap bag quilt, this unusual Drunkard's Path was made in the 1930s and has only two colors per square. Its multicolored floral prints and polka dots give it a wonderful look, even with an overall fade—a sign of much use and many washings.

DRUNKARD'S PATH: 1920s; indigo blue on white; excellent condition, unused, unwashed; minimal straight-line quilting; 78 × 84 **$575**

DRUNKARD'S PATH: 1920s; red print on white; same red print backing and edge; from Ohio; unused, unwashed; excellent assembly, scroll quilting in white blocks; 70 × 82 **$650**

DRUNKARD'S PATH: 1920s; blue and white; blue double border and binding, fair condition, very faded overall, overall soiling, worn binding; excellent assembly, very good quilting, small stitches, straight-line and outline quilting, small flower quilting where white squares' corners meet; 70 × 80 **$750**

DRUNKARD'S PATH: 1930; lavender on white; minimal use; 76 × 84

$270

DRUNKARD'S PATH: 1930; lavender prints; overall fade, binding worn; 68 × 90 **$475**

DRUNKARD'S PATH: 1930s; green and white; 72 × 76 **$295**

DRUNKARD'S PATH: 1930; multicolored; all floral prints, slightly faded overall; 72 × 84 **$700**

Friendship, Album, Sampler, and Signature Quilts

The turn away from whole-cloth to block-style quilts that began in the mid-1700s made these highly collectible quilts possible. Friendship quilts were group projects with each block made or signed by a different person. They developed along the eastern seaboard in the 1840s and are believed to have originated from the concept of the album books that were popular at the time. Guests to a home signed the album book, often including lines of verse or a small drawing. The leap to doing the same thing with quilt blocks was a short one. Early friendship quilts have blocks with long poems or quotes from Scripture. Later versions have only the signature of the maker or a friend. Most often these quilts were multiple blocks of the same pattern, but some were assembled of different patterned blocks. The quilts were made two ways. In the first, a group of quiltmakers chose a pattern, each one made a block, and the group then assembled the quilt and gave it away. The other option was for a quiltmaker to do all the blocks herself and then ask her friends to sign the blocks.

From the friendship style came the album quilt. These quilts were most often done in appliqué and each block had some meaning to the maker. They were carefully thought out and expertly worked. The most famous of these are the Baltimore Album quilts, made for approximately a twenty-year period around the Centennial. There are more than two hundred of these quilts recorded, but it is believed that there are more tucked away in family attics. The highest price ever paid for a quilt at an auction was $176,000, and it was for a Baltimore Album quilt.

The friendship or album-style quilt, made by a group of women who each chose an individual pattern of piecing or appliqué, led to the sampler quilts that were also popular around the time of the Bicentennial. Sampler quilts were made before that time, too. They are a way of learning quilting techniques without making twenty or thirty different quilts. Instead, various quilt block patterns were attempted, ranging from simple to complex, to give the maker experience with various piecing, appliqué, embroidery, and quilting techniques. Older sampler quilts are made from scrap bag fabrics while the ones dating from the Bicentennial are made from three or four coordinating fabrics, each fabric found in each sampler block.

Signature quilts were usually fund-raisers. These quilts were most popular in the last half of the nineteenth century and into the beginning of the twentieth. A small fee was charged for having your name embroidered on the quilt, which, when it was covered with names, was then given away or raffled off. The money raised was used for church additions, abolitionist activities, Civil War gunboats, library books, or the like. Fund-raiser quilts are still made today to raise money for similar causes.

These quilts, the album style particularly, are rare. Pieced friendship quilts are more common, and signature quilts are even more available on the market. According to Larry Zingale, just because a quilt has signatures on it doesn't make it more valuable to collector. That might be true, but to romantic souls like us, a signature quilt, though the people who go with the names will never be known, is a treasure. Because some collectors and dealers don't agree that signatures add much in the way of value to a quilt, you might find some bargains in this style. If you have your heart, and enough money, set on the top of this line, a Baltimore Album quilt, be prepared to wait a good long while and to pay dearly. That one segment of this group is composed of rare, exquisite examples of expert needlework, and they are therefore quite valuable.

ALBUM QUILT: 1870s; indigo, light blue, white; 25 different simple patterns, including Floral Basket, Bow Ties; on point with blue sets, some fade, some color bleed; assembly fair to good, not all junctions match, some stitches visible, feed bag back; 84 × 86 $2,200

ALBUM QUILT: 1880s; deep blue prints on white; from Missouri; 63 × 76
$1,000

CHIMNEY SWEEP ALBUM QUILT: late 1800s; multicolored; friendship quilt, signed by many; 76 × 76 $375

CHIMNEY SWEEP ALBUM QUILT: 1920s; blue and white; five borders, each narrower, alternate blue and white; very good condition, minimal washing, lots of straight-line quilting, four lines of wave quilting in white border; 86 × 60
$560

EIGHT-POINT STARS: late 1800s; browns, blues, multicolors; signature quilt with signature in center octagon of each star, edge is tiny "pinked" scallops, from Vermont church group; some overall fade, some fabric loss in a few areas; inconsistent workmanship square to square, not all junctions match, minimal quilting; 90 × 90 $1,600

FRIENDSHIP CRAZY QUILT: 1880; multicolored; signed with full names in embroidery; 66 × 79 $300

FRIENDSHIP CRAZY QUILT: 1892; muted multicolors; signed by members of church group, some overall wear, from Connecticut; 72 × 86 $450

FRIENDSHIP DOUBLE IRISH CHAIN: 1915; darks, black; red embroidery signed, feather ring quilting; Holmes County, Ohio, Amish; 68 × 80 $5,500

FRIENDSHIP NINE-PATCH DIAMOND: 1867; green, brown, pink, rust; top only; 48 legible names and sayings, stamped and written, from New Hampshire; one square from Maine; many geometric prints, some stains, all points and junctions match, four-poster cutout; 82 × 85 $285

FRIENDSHIP QUILT: 1908; pastels; from Kentucky via California, signed; 64 × 84   **$395**

LONE STAR SAMPLER: 1880s; brown, indigo, red; large center star with three outer sampler borders, madder-dyed reds, unused, unwashed; diamond and feather quilting; from North Carolina; 105 × 105   **$5,700**

NAIVE SAMPLER: late 1880s and 1930s; reds, blues; some nineteenth-century blocks with others pieced and added in the 1930s; 83 × 83   **$1,400**

SAMPLER QUILT: early 1900s; multicolored; silk, brocade, ribbons; fair condition, feather topstitching; 68 × 78   **$300**

SAMPLER QUILT: 1915; blues; outstanding work, from Texas; 66 × 72

$850

SAILBOAT PATCH: 1939; sea-green, blue; green sashing, white sets; fundraising quilt, dated and signed in embroidery; slight wear on binding, some overall fade, excellent assembly and quilting, straight-line quilting overall; 72 × 88   **$625**

STAR AND CROSS VARIATION: 1880s; multicolored; top only, album quilt, from Vermont, signed in center squares, not in indelible ink; excellent condition, although a few signatures have run, excellent assembly; 80 × 80   **$160**

Log Cabin Quilts

Log Cabin blocks are made to resemble the pioneer homes that inspired them. The most common of the Log Cabins is the basic block, which starts with a square in the middle to which are added strips of increasing length until a square is formed of the right dimensions so that enough of the blocks will cover a bed. The center square is traditionally of red fabric to represent the central hearth of the home. The remaining strips are the "logs." As they're placed, these strips seem to overlap and look like the corners of their namesake. Each square is divided on the diagonal by placing only light-colored fabric strips on two sides of the central square and dark-colored strips on the two remaining sides. The Log Cabin is quick to assemble since the strip are placed around the central square. Simply turning the block a quarter turn gets the block ready for the next strip. The illustrations on pages 156–161 demonstrate how Log Cabin piecing is done.

Once the squares are completed there are many different ways to put them together, each achieving a different optical effect. Barn Raising places the light and dark sides of the blocks so that diamond-shaped rings rise from the center. The Streak O' Lightning format places the light and dark diagonal halves in jagged rows. Straight Furrows creates diagonal lines of light and dark across the quilt top. The Light and Dark variation, also called Sunshine and Shadow, places four light sides together, creating a large, light-colored diamond. As other blocks are placed, dark-colored diamonds are also created. The optical illusion of this assembly sometimes makes the dark diamonds seem dominant, while at other times the light diamonds seem to catch our eye.

There are two other variations of the Log Cabin block. Each uses the strip method of assembly but not the same order as the traditional block. Courthouse Steps, instead of adding the strips in a circular way around the central block, adds strips to the opposite sides. This block is more time-consuming to make since it doesn't work in a circle. The symbolism in the Courthouse Steps is also different. Here the central square represents the building while the horizontal strips are the steps leading to it and the vertical strips are the columns supporting it.

The second variation is the Pineapple or Windmill Blades style. Here the central square is set on a point and the strips are added around the outside. This block requires difficult and precise piecing as each strip added is a different size and must be shaped with pointed ends. This is the most dynamic and unusual of the Log Cabin variations. When the blocks are assembled with the lights meeting the lights and the darks meeting the darks on opposite corners, the quilt looks like spinning windmill blades.

The Log Cabin block actually began as a border motif and was used to finish the edges of quilts from approximately 1840 to 1865. After that, the Log Cabin became so popular as a pattern for quilt tops that country fairs honored them with a prize category all their own.

Log Cabin blocks are usually made by placing the red square in the center of a piece of ground fabric and sewing the strips around it to the ground. The ground serves to stabilize the "logs" and let the assembly go fairly quickly. Enough of the ground fabric squares, cut in 10-, 12-, or 16-inch squares, were made to form the quilt top.

Sometimes newspaper was used instead of ground fabric to stabilize the block during assembly. When the quilt was completed, the newspaper was torn away. We saw one quilt top that still had the newspapers on the back.

Log Cabins of silk and satin were used as summer quilts and were rarely quilted with batting inside. Wool and velvet Log Cabins were most often tied because they were too heavy and thick to be quilted. A quilted Log Cabin is rare.

When the light and dark fabrics are properly chosen to create a good contrast, the Log Cabin quilt is a striking reminder of our pioneer heritage.

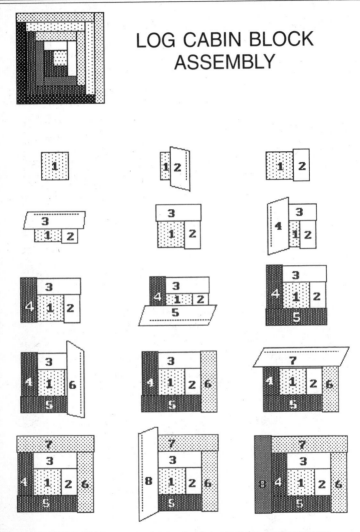

LOG CABIN BLOCK ASSEMBLY

All Log Cabin blocks are made up of strips around a center square. Traditionally, the blocks are dark colors diagonally on one side, light on the other, although the variations are innumerable. The most common assembly method involves starting with a center square on a foundation fabric and adding strips to each side in order, taking care to put the light colors on the same two sides each time.

LOG CABIN BLOCK ASSEMBLY SUNSHINE AND SHADOWS VARIATION

When the blocks are complete, they may be assembled in various ways. Shown is a Sunshine and Shadows variation.

BARN RAISING LOG CABIN: 1900; black, red; all silks, very small "logs," homespun back, few small repairs but otherwise excellent condition, found in Colorado; 76 × 66   **$2,500**

BARN RAISING LOG CABIN: 1900; brown, green, yellow, white, green print edge, brown print back, no batting; overall fade, overall wear, minimal straight-line quilting; 80 × 84   **$775**

LOG CABIN BLOCK ASSEMBLY BARN RAISING VARIATION

Simply change the arrangement of the blocks and the pattern becomes the favorite Barn Raising.

BARN RAISING LOG CABIN VARIATION: 1800s; forest green, unused, simple quilting, pieced backing; wide "logs" rather than strips, not all junctions match, from Pennsylvania; 86 × 86 **$1,000**

COURTHOUSE STEPS LOG CABIN: 1830–1840; blacks, browns, reds, greens; wool challis, striped border, print backing; fair condition, many moth holes, torn top, worn binding, no quilting; Mennonite; 68 × 72 **$650**

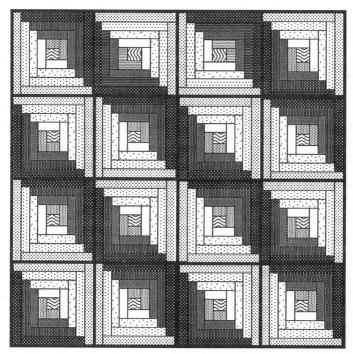

LOG CABIN BLOCK ASSEMBLY STRAIGHT FURROWS VARIATION

Alter the block arrangement yet again, and the quilt pattern becomes Straight Furrows. The possibilities are endless.

COURTHOUSE STEPS LOG CABIN: 1900; multicolored; wool, flannel, challis, cotton, excellent condition; tied, no quilting; 76 × 78   **$500**

COURTHOUSE STEPS LOG CABIN: early 1900s; brown, pink on pink; salvaged section of larger damaged quilt, new binding, still some fabric splits, fabric deterioration in brown, some rub wear overall; some shirting fabrics, some unusual prints, excellent assembly; 40 × 60   **$95**

LOG CABIN BLOCK ASSEMBLY COURTHOUSE STEPS VARIATION

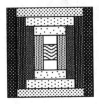

Change the position of the light and dark logs, and the order in which they are added, and the block takes on the completely different look of Courthouse Steps.

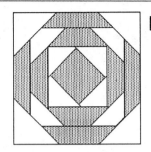

PINEAPPLE LOG CABIN BLOCK ASSEMBLY

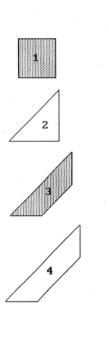

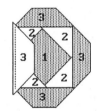

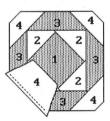

Although still basically made up of strips around a center square, the Pineapple Log Cabin is made a little differently. The center is set on the foundation fabric on point, then alternating rows of light and dark hexagonal strips are added.

This all-cotton Courthouse Steps Log Cabin contains some very interesting print fabrics, including some chintzes. From the early 1900s, this quilt has much wear and fabric disintegration.

COURTHOUSE STEPS LOG CABIN: 1906; green, blue, pink, white; unused pristine whites, makers known, Iowa State Fair 1st prize winner, ribbon attached; 79 × 86 $900

LOG CABIN: 1850s–1880s; multicolored; cotton, silk backing, poor to fair condition, worn top, worn backing, worn binding, overall fade; 62 × 85

$300

LOG CABIN: 1880s; multicolored; wools, few velvets, satins, corduroy, brown print backing, very heavy batting; fair to good condition, some tears on top, some fabric deterioration, few small repairs with embroidery, minimal straight line quilting; 88 × 76 $225

LOG CABIN: late 1880s; brown, tan; large center square of cheater cloth showing *Pickwick Papers*, sashing, added skirt; torn and worn binding, fair condition overall; 80 × 80 $395

LOG CABIN: late 1800s; browns, beiges; dark velvets, lighter wools, red satin centers, narrow black wool sashing; some tears, some fabric loss, tied, no quilting; 70 × 80 $800

LOG CABIN: 1890s; multicolored; all wools, fair to good condition, some areas of fabric loss and wear, good assembly; 50 × 60 $425

LOG CABIN: 1890–1910; black, deep red, blue; all velvets, small areas of repairs; from Pennsylvania; 55 × 58 $1,100

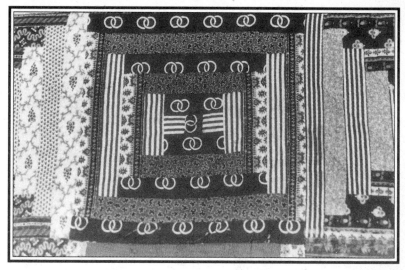

With typical early-1900s prints, this same quilt shows dark and light blues, browns, and pink on pink, among other colors. Some fabric splits can be seen.

LOG CABIN: 1900; black and red; Mennonite crib quilt, Streak O' Lightning assembly variation; small hole in top; 40 × 50 — **$495**

LOG CABIN: early 1900s; multicolored; all wools, no batting, assembly and quilting only fair; 72 × 72 — **$348**

LOG CABIN: early 1900s; dark and light multicolored; overall wear; 64 × 74 — **$450**

LOG CABIN: early 1900s; browns, blues, reds; all cotton ginghams, slight overall fade, slight overall wear; minimal quilting; 80 × 72 — **$595**

LOG CABIN: 1910; blues; overall fade; 76 × 60 — **$450**

LOG CABIN: 1920s; darks, reds; all wools, red sashing and binding; some small tears, holes, some loose assembly stitches; many junctions don't match; 72 × 80 — **$600**

LOG CABIN: 1920s; green, brown, light purple, egg yolk yellow, all solids; yellow and green border; Mennonite; excellent condition, unused, unwashed, one tiny stain on back; 70 × 78 — **$750**

LOG CABIN STRAIGHT FURROWS: late 1800s; greens, tans; chintz fabrics, green faded to mustard, pink backing; some fabric loss and tears, some stains, printed polka dots deteriorating fabric, worn binding; tied, no quilting; 54 × 77 — **$125**

This beautiful wall hanging shows the traditional Pineapple assembly of the Log Cabin style. Done in silks, the light and dark sides of each square, placed the way they are, create the Fan Blade look, just as they should.

LOG CABIN STRAIGHT FURROWS: 1910; blue, pink; all ginghams, blue print backing; six borders, alternate pink and white; excellent condition, unused, unwashed, minimal outline quilting; 70 × 78 $585

LOG CABIN STRAIGHT FURROWS: 1920; red, blue, beige; floral backing, vertical stripe border; excellent condition, unused, unwashed, no quilting; 70 × 78 $875

LOG CABIN VARIATION: 1930s; burgundy, yellows; from Pennsylvania; few small holes, outline and straight-line quilting; 60 × 76 $550

LOG CABIN VARIATION: early 1900s; multiple blues; very wide logs, wide blue border, calicoes and ginghams; lattice quilting on border, otherwise just tied; 60 × 80 $645

PINEAPPLE LOG CABIN: 1900; purple, red, other brights; wools, twills, silks, black velvet center blocks, plaid border; minimal use, some fabric deterioration; 78 × 84 $950

One-patch Designs

One-patch is just that, a pattern comprised of only one piece cut repeatedly from the fabric. The most recognizable one-patch design is Grandmother's Flower Garden, which is made using a hexagon shape. Other one-patch designs are Tumbler, Thousand Pyramids (made from triangles), Postage Stamp (composed of tiny squares), and Bar (made of rectangles). The Hit and Miss and Roman Stripes patterns were among the earliest of one-patch designs when quiltmakers first experimented with piecing.

Although predominantly scrap bag quilts, some one-patch designs have traditional color or light and dark arrangements. In Roman Stripes, strips of dark fabric pieces were sewed together. These were alternated with strips of light fabric. The Tumbler, Thousand Pyramids, Brick Wall, and Postage Stamp patterns alternated light and dark fabrics within the strips. In Brick Wall, for an added visual treat, the strips were joined together in an offset way, with the seams of each block not matching, so the final result looked like a brick wall with no two "bricks" evenly placed together.

Traditionally, the center hexagon of a Grandmother's Flower Garden is yellow, with anywhere from three to five rings of hexagons added around it. The blocks thus created are assembled, using green diamond shapes to make the "paths" or "walkways" between the flower beds. The blocks may also be assembled with a strip made of plain white or muslin hexagons. The rings of the flowers could alternate light and dark, or be made of gradations of tones of the same color.

One-patch designs, except the hexagon used in Grandmother's Flower Garden, were popular as charm quilts, where no two pieces of fabric were the same. Charm quilts were especially popular during the miniaturization period, when, for a short time, the number of pieces in the quilt top became the standard for quilting expertise.

Flower Garden quilts have been popular since 1800, reaching a peak in 1925 and still going strong today. In the early 1800s, the hexagons were pieced using the English or template method, where fabric was pressed around a template cut to the right size. The pieces were then sewed together using an overcast stitch and the paper templates were removed. It's rare, but you can sometimes find one of these quilt tops with the paper templates still in place. This and the evidence of overcast stitching are good clues that the quilt was made in the 1800s. In this century, the hexagon pieces were stitched together, without templates, using a running stitch.

The one-patch design is called an all-over set, for there's only one way to put the pieces together, after all. Their beauty and originality come in the choices the quiltmaker made in selecting which light piece went next to which dark one, which print went next to which solid.

Charm quilts tell their own story, though they are harder to interpret than an album quilt or a crazy quilt. Because they contain hundreds of different fabrics, they are a record, not only of the quiltmaker's family but of her friends, neighbors, and extended family as well, for in order to get enough pieces without repeating any, she must have traded scrap bag fabrics with her peers. From these quilts we get a record of what fabrics a quiltmaker had on hand, but we can only speculate what she made originally from that fabric. The charm of charm quilts lies in our own imagination.

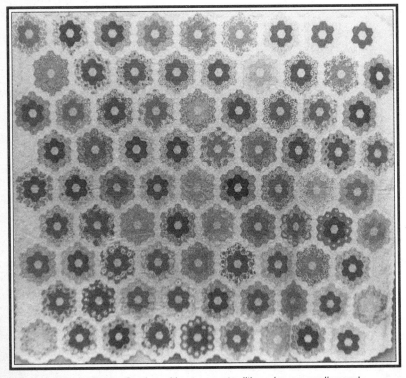

A Grandmother's Flower Garden without some traditions (no green diamond pathways), this quilt from the 1930s still shows the same color centers and has the scrap bag look.
Quilt courtesy of Helen Warner

BABY BLOCKS: 1800s; blues, pinks, reds; from Midwest; excellent assembly, all junctions match, outline quilting; 70 × 80   **$500**

BABY BLOCKS: early 1900s; browns, white; some white blocks in piqué weave, some stains, worn binding; very good assembly, nearly all junctions match, straight-line quilting; 78 × 73   **$425**

BABY BLOCKS: 1930s; blues; overall stains, worn binding, outline quilting of blocks; 36 × 45   **$125**

> *When the Grandmother's Flower Garden is assembled into a diamond shape rather than a circle, the pattern is called Diamond Field, Field of Diamonds, or Rainbow Tiles.*

DIAMOND FIELD: 1929; bright reds; from Oklahoma via Colorado; maker known, excellent work; 74 × 78   **$675**

DIAMOND PATCHES: 1900; blues, white; blue triple border, set on point with white sets, overall fade; straight-line echo quilting; 75 × 80   **$795**

FIRECRACKER: 1890s; reds, blues, beige, gold; diagonal-style Roman Bars, all satins, red border, satin backing, excellent condition, unused; excellent assembly and topstitching, feather topstitching on block junctions; 70 × 74   **$1,250**

FLYING GEESE: late 1800s; pastels; overall fade; 30 × 50   **$175**

GRANDMOTHER'S FLOWER GARDEN: 1915; pale green; scalloped border, minimal use; 78 × 80   **$600**

GRANDMOTHER'S FLOWER GARDEN: 1920s; red, purple, blue; 70 × 90   **$450**

> *The hexagon is the basis of one of the most popular and often-created patterns for quilts: Grandmother's Flower Garden. The hexagon shape is found in the oldest mosaic tile floors and this is most likely the inspiration for its use in quilts.*

GRANDMOTHER'S FLOWER GARDEN: 1920s; green, pink, yellow; wavy edge, green path between gardens; very faded, well washed, uneven assembly, many junctions don't match, outline quilting; 78 × 80   **$500**

GRANDMOTHER'S FLOWER GARDEN: 1920s; green, pinks; 84 × 70   **$750**

GRANDMOTHER'S FLOWER GARDEN: 1920s; lavender, green; scalloped edges on two sides, minimal use; 88 × 101   **$750**

GRANDMOTHER'S FLOWER GARDEN: 1925; pastels, solids, cream; green pathways between flowers, scalloped edge; excellent condition, unused, unwashed, straight-line quilting around flowers; 78 × 82   **$385**

GRANDMOTHER'S FLOWER GARDEN: 1930s; yellow, multicolored solids; two straight sides, two pointed; white binding; 64 × 76   **$350**

GRANDMOTHER'S FLOWER GARDEN: 1930s; pastels, all solids; scalloped edge, two borders; good assembly, fair quilting, large stitches, outline quilting; 82 × 78   **$385**

GRANDMOTHER'S FLOWER GARDEN: 1930s; green, yellow, blue; wavy edge, green paths between gardens; overall fade, very good assembly, outline quilting; 78 × 84   **$400**

GRANDMOTHER'S FLOWER GARDEN: 1930s; yellow, green, multiprints; green path between flowers, two edges pointed, two edges straight, yellow backing and binding; unwashed, unused, excellent assembly, outline quilting; 90 × 77   **$425**

GRANDMOTHER'S FLOWER GARDEN: 1930s; yellow, multiprints; two edges straight, two edges pointed; excellent condition, minimal use, unwashed, few spots, straight-line quilting, outline quilting in hexagons; 110 x 70   **$425**

GRANDMOTHER'S FLOWER GARDEN: 1930s; yellow, green, brights; green border and backing; excellent condition, unwashed, unused; star quilting in center of flowers, outline and grid quilting overall; 84 × 89   **$425**

GRANDMOTHER'S FLOWER GARDEN: 1930s; green, yellow, blue, pink pastels; scalloped edge, light green backing and binding; excellent condition, unwashed, unused, fair assembly, some puckers on junctions, outline quilting; 70 × 78   **$450**

GRANDMOTHER'S FLOWER GARDEN: 1930s; multipastels and prints; scalloped edges with blue binding, very small pieces, unused, unwashed; very small quilting stitches, straight-line quilting; 92 × 76   **$525**

GRANDMOTHER'S FLOWER GARDEN: 1930s; multicolored pastels; scalloped border; 60 × 90   **$750**

JOSEPH'S COAT VARIATION: 1890; rainbow colors, brights, blue on white; vertical Roman stripe like three rainbows, blue-on-white print sashing between

This is a beautiful example of the traditional assembly of the Grandmother's Flower Garden. The pointed edge, same-color centers, and green diamond pathways between the gardens are classic, as are the solid-colored second rings, print third and white fourth rings.

Looking closer at a block from the same Grandmother's Flower Garden, the excellent assembly and lovely print fabrics can be seen. The traditional outline quilting is there. This quilt was made in the 1960s and demonstrates that expert quiltmaking has come down through time unchanged.

The One-patch Grandmother's Flower Garden block is taken to its limits to make this Trip Around the World–style hexagonal throw. This 1930s piece shows alternating light and dark rows, and is very visual, in browns, reds, and almost every other color imaginable.
Quilt courtesy of Lois Belden

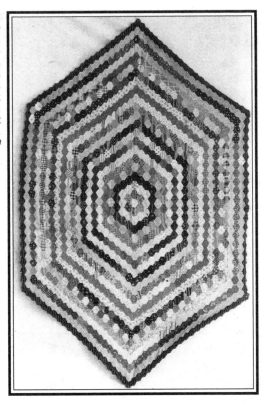

stripes and on border and edges; very good condition, minimal use, few washings, excellent assembly, very good quilting, small quilting stitches, straight-line and grid; 78 × 80 $950

MEDALLION QUILT: late 1800s; blue on white; blue border with feather quilting, straight-line quilting elsewhere, some wear on top, some tears, badly worn and torn binding; 56 × 56 $275

MEDALLION QUILT: 1900; red and white; large squares, few stains, overall fade; 82 × 82 $750

MOSAIC QUILT: 1850; Prussian blue and jewel tones; all silks, 10-inch border; from North Carolina; some fabric splits in border, small flowers embroidered in border; 78 × 88 $8,000

POSTAGE STAMP: 1880s; various blues; lap quilt; found in New Mexico; 42 × 49 $395

A close-up of the same quilt reveals the tiny prints of the fabrics and minimal
straight-line quilting.
Quilt courtesy of Lois Belden

POSTAGE STAMP: 1910; reds, blues; new backing, excellent condition, unwashed, unused, possibly quilted very recently; minimal straight-line quilting; 66 × 78   **$425**

POSTAGE STAMP: 1920s; blues; from Ohio; 64 × 72   **$395**

POSTAGE STAMP: early 1930s; multicolored; 79 × 88   **$725**

POSTAGE STAMP: 1930s; deep blue and multicolors; 4,452 1-inch square pieces, striped fabric on outer rows looks like a border; from Oklahoma; 60 × 68   **$880**

POSTAGE STAMP: early 1950s; diagonal pieces, blocks set on point, no batting, straight-line quilting overall; 96 × 80   **$325**

POSTAGE STAMP PATCHES: 1880–1890; gray, red, beige; 25 × 25 squares in each block, floral backing, green sashing; fair to good condition, overall soiling, overall discoloration, straight-line quilting; 70 x 82   **$185**

ROMAN STRIPES: 1890s; green, cranberry, tan; strips on diagonal within the squares, wools and cottons, Prairie Point edge; some wear on points and overall, fair-to-good assembly, minimal quilting; 48 × 66   **$425**

ROMAN STRIPES: 1910; multicolored; maker known; minimal use; 65 × 77 **$550**

ROMAN STRIPES: 1910; black, red, grays; very bold colors, all silk, delicate, few minor repairs done with pre-1900 fabrics; found in Colorado; 75 × 65 **$650**

ROMAN STRIPES ZIGZAG: early 1800s; teal, beige, rust; English print chintz fabrics; lots of wear, some tears, some stains, badly worn binding; echo quilting on Zigzags; 84 × 84 **$800**

RAINBOW AROUND THE WORLD: 1930s; multipastels with red, black, white; all miniprints, triple border of black, white, red; excellent condition, minimal use, very good assembly, lots of straight-line quilting; 78 x 80 **$550**

SAWTOOTH BARS: 1880–1890s; red and white; very good condition, unwashed, minimal use; clamshell quilting; 78 × 79 **$450**

SAWTOOTH DIAMONDS IN SQUARES: 1880s; red, white; very good condition, minimal use; very good assembly, nearly all junctions match, straight-line and clamshell quilting; 84 × 84 **$1,200**

SPLIT STRIPE: 1890s; red, white; very good condition, minimal use, some loose stitches, slight overall fade; very good quilting, small stitches, grid quilting between stripes, outline quilting on stripes; 80 × 77 **$250**

STRIP PATTERN WITH SQUARES: 1939; green, gold, white; pair of matching quilts, unique strip pattern, blocks set on point with white sets; slight overall fade; 80 × 64 (price per pair) **$1,250**

STRIPES: 1880–1890s; red and white; Split Bar variation, three 1-inch stripes with 4-inch stripe between, overall fade; very good assembly, small even quilting stitches, feather and curved line quilting; 78 × 74 **$650**

THOUSAND PYRAMIDS: 1820; red, indigo; 1-inch triangle pyramids, chintz border in red and green, some damage to border, some age spots; 106 × 112 **$3,800**

TRIANGLES: early 1900s; yellow, red, brown; small pieces around white center square, set on point; possibly multigenerational quilt, not all junctions match; some soiling, fabric deterioration, color loss; straight-line quilting in diamonds; replacement binding, machine applied; 60 × 72 **$220**

TRIANGLES AND DIAMONDS: 1930; pastels, white; white border, pink edging, minimal use; wreath and grid quilting in center, diamond quilting on border; 72 × 72 **$545**

TRIANGLES AND DIAMONDS IN SQUARES: 1880s; red, white; red sashing, red border on two sides, overall fade, overall soiling and stains; very good quilting, small stitches, some loose stitches, straight-line quilting, grid quilting on sashing; 72 × 84 **$550**

TRIANGLES IN TRIANGLES: 1920; blues; contains nearly every color; from Missouri; 72 × 82   **$800**

TRIANGLES MAKE DIAMONDS: 1920s; blues, pinks, lights, darks; pink triangle border, pink binding, unwashed, unused, quilting lines remain, few soiled spots; very good assembly, very small quilting stitches, outline quilting; 88 × 67
$470

The Trip Around the World pattern, with its ever widening rows of colored squares, is also called Sunshine and Shadows, which is also the name of a particular assembly of blocks in Log Cabin quilts.

TRIP AROUND THE WORLD: 1920s; blues, greens; slight overall fade, cross quilting in blocks; 70 × 68   **$475**

TRIP AROUND THE WORLD: 1930s; pastels, prints, solids; crib quilt, lavender binding, 1-inch squares; overall wear, overall fade, new binding, outline quilting; 42 × 44   **$125**

TRIP AROUND THE WORLD: 1930; blues; Postage Stamp style; from Colorado via Oklahoma; 69 × 77   **$550**

TRIP AROUND THE WORLD IN DIAMONDS: 1920s; blues, reds; excellent assembly, all junctions match; overall fade, few small stains, worn binding; 68 × 78   **$550**

TRIP AROUND THE WORLD, POSTAGE STAMP: 1920s; multicolored; hundreds of pieces, dozens of fabrics, overall fade, worn binding, well used, multiple washings; lots of ties, no quilting; 68 × 70   **$500**

The Tumbling Blocks pattern is also called Baby Blocks, Stair Steps, and Illusion.

TUMBLING BLOCKS: 1870s; blues; some burgundies, from Indiana, close straight-line quilting; 73 × 80   **$1,395**

TRIP AROUND THE WORLD ASSEMBLY

The expanding diamond optical illusion created by Trip Around the World is made by stitching small blocks into strips, then stitching the strips together. This simple One-patch pattern depends on the clever and skillful use of fabric colors to create a dramatic look.

TUMBLING BLOCKS: late 1880s; red, white, blue; overall faded and worn, few small tears; 73 × 78 $750

TUMBLING BLOCKS: 1890; red, white, blue; from Ohio; diagonal quilting in blocks; 68 × 82 $1,200

TUMBLING BLOCKS: 1890s; red, black, gold, brown; all wool challis, gray striped wool backing, sawtooth border of black and red; Ohio Amish; few moth and other holes, otherwise very good condition, clear colors; excellent assembly, very heavy batting, no quilting; 72 × 60   **$2,500**

TUMBLING BLOCKS AND STARS: 1860s; browns, blues, pinks; floral edge, print back; from Pennsylvania; some overall wear, outline quilting on blocks; 100 × 85   **$1,850**

TUMBLING BLOCKS/OHIO STAR VARIATION: 1930; light blue, pink, yellow; all stars solid colors, six blocks around each star; some wear overall, flower quilting; 67 × 83   **$535**

TUMBLING STAR: 1930; pink, white, black; Baby Blocks and four-point stars, African-American quilt; from New Jersey; maker known; excellent assembly, outline and cross quilting in squares; 69 × 80   **$475**

WILD GOOSE CHASE: 1928; cornflower blue; dated; 80 × 86   **$500**

Patriotic, Political, and Commemorative Quilts

Patriotic, political, and commemorative material has long been incorporated into the creation of quilts. Printed fabrics showing popular and interesting events and figures can be found on quilts. Political party ribbons have found their way into crazy quilt designs.

In times of national fervor, when feelings of patriotism run high, all sorts of patriotic material shows up on quilts. There are instances of quilts being made to look like flags, and of flags being pieced together to make quilts. We even heard a story of a Southern family, Union supporters, who cut the American flag into squares and pieced it together to make a quilt so they could display it in defiance of Confederate soldiers.

Because they are unique, one-of-a-kind pieces, such quilts can be very valuable. (See chapter 11, "Antique Appliqué Quilts," for more information.)

CIGAR FLANNELS: 1930s; reds, blues; date may be later, American and Zionist flags, sewed to be hung; 72 × 76   **$2,800**

FLAG QUILT: 1915; blue; stars and stripes in one corner, poorly assembled and executed, made of vegetable-dyed sugar sacks; from Mississippi; uneven, poorly done wave quilting, unique piece; 76 × 84   **$7,000**

GARFIELD MONUMENT: 1881; beige, brown, gold; top only, excellent condition; Brickyard variation, top of monument appliqued, some hand assembly, some machine, edging all machine applied; 68 × 84   **$185**

The Garfield's Monument pattern was named for the president, and is actually a brickwork variation. Done in 1881, this quilt top is beiges and browns in color, and has both hand and machine assembly stitches. The top block of the monument is appliquéd.

PATRIOTIC FANS: 1880; red and white on blue; wool and cotton twills, red-and-white fans on blue background; faded overall, slight overall wear, edge very faded; 66 × 60   **$2,600**

WHIG'S DEFEAT: 1930–1940; multicolored; overall fade, some stains, some loose seams, heavy use and washings; 72 × 79   **$295**

Seven-patch, Five-patch, and Others

The number of squares on the side of the quilt block determines into which category it falls. Sometimes. Seven-patch blocks have seven pieces on a side, while a five-patch block has five. Divide the five into twenty-five and it's still a five-patch block. As quiltmakers began to experiment with different block patterns, they certainly tried any number of combinations and sizes of block pieces.

And they even went beyond the standard block completely, creating blocks that don't easily fall into any categories at all. Imagine the first enterprising quiltmaker who created School House blocks with windows and chimneys, and Alphabet blocks with all of the letters of the alphabet created out of pieces.

A close-up of a Whig's Defeat block shows the difficulty of piecing curved and straight pieces. This 1930s quilt has seen much use and wear and has some loose stitches and seams from that.

The popular Bear's Paw is a seven-patch block. Jack in the Box is a five-patch, as are Cakestand and Star and Cross. The Mariner's Compass, which is really a variation of a star, is made of long, thin diamondlike patches radiating from a center patch. Orange Peel is curved pieces and triangles that form— well, sort of—hexagons. Bunting looks like fans. It can be great fun and very challenging to figure out what kind of block you are looking at, and think about who first had the idea to make such a block.

ALPHABET: 1916; yellow, green; signed; from Pennsylvania; unused, pencil lines for quilting remain, very small stitches, junctions match, each letter framed with border, lots of chain and line quilting; 80 x 100   **$9,500**

ALPHABET: 1930s; pink; crib quilt, embroidery on letters; 35 × 50   **$395**

BEAR'S PAW: 1890s; red and white; very good assembly; 78 × 82   **$475**

BEAR'S PAW: late 1800s; pink, white, green; faded on one side of top; 78 × 105   **$175**

BEAR'S PAW: late 1800s; blue, red, darks; printed backing; 70 × 82   **$425**

BEAR'S PAW: late 1880s; indigo; wide binding; 80 × 84   **$550**

In moving around the country, quilt patterns were often renamed by quiltmakers for something with which they were more familiar. The Bear's Paw pattern of the East became the Crow's Foot pattern of Illinois, the Duck's Foot on Long Island, and the Hand of Friendship to the Philadelphia Quakers.

BEAR'S PAW: 1910s; red and white; slightly faded overall, slightly worn binding; 70 × 80 $475

BEAR'S PAW: 1910; indigo blue on white; indigo border, minimal use, excellent condition; very small quilting stitches, lots of quilting on border; 70 × 78 $750

BEAR'S PAW: 1920s; red, white, pink; slight overall fade, feather quilting; 70 × 82 $350

BEAR'S PAW: 1920s; red and white; slight overall fade, few stains, very yellowed white backing; clamshell quilting overall with grid quilting between some squares; 68 × 78 $400

BEAR'S PAW: 1920s; pink, green; from Kansas; scalloped edge; 85 × 66 $475

BEAR'S PAW: 1930s; green, rose; all points match, some wear on binding; 72 × 84 $125

BUNTING: 1890s; red and white; white border all around, red border on two sides, minimal use; very good assembly, nearly all junctions match, simple straight-line quilting overall; 64 × 72 $685

BUNTING: 1930s; pastels, purples; solids and calicos, excellent color balance, excellent condition, unused, unwashed; excellent assembly, all junctions match, outline quilting, decorative quilting in corners, one small corner unquilted; 78 × 80 $845

CAKESTAND: 1880; orange, brown; very faded overall; 75 × 100 $295

CAKESTAND: early 1900s; pastels; 48 × 72 $175

CROSSROADS TO TEXAS: 1880s; blue, white; white sashing, overall fade, some stains; straight-line quilting; 66 × 83 $595

DAHLIA: 1940; yellow, teal, blue; three-dimensional inner petals, white sets; excellent condition, very slight soiling overall; only fair assembly; 82 × 82 $190

> *Political, military, territorial, and migration events in American history are commemorated with quilt blocks such as 54-40 or Fight (after the division of the Pacific Northwest between the United States and Canada), Burgoyne Surrounded, Free Trade, Underground Railroad, Rocky Road to California, Lincoln's Platform, and Crossroads to Texas.*

DOE AND DART: 1930s; pale yellow; binding replaced; 78 × 78　　**$430**

FOX AND GEESE: 1840s; indigo on white; wide double sawtooth border, unused; feather plates and plumes quilting overall; from Pennsylvania; 96 × 98
　　$3,500

GARDEN MAZE LATTICE: 1870s; indigo and white; minimal use and wear, overall fade; straight-line echo quilting overall; 62 × 74　　**$395**

GOOSE TRACKS: 1930; pink on white; few small stains, amateurish straight-line quilting overall, crib quilt; 44 × 50　　**$215**

GOOSE TRACKS: 1930s; pale pink; old top, new back, machine quilted; 68 × 90　　**$260**

GOOSE TRACKS VARIATION: late 1940s; blues; from Ohio; 83 × 78　**$440**

HANDS ALL AROUND: 1880–1900; red on white; Bear's Paw variation; from Pennsylvania; very good condition, unwashed, unused, straight-line quilting overall, inconsistent workmanship; 81 × 82　　**$850**

INDIAN MEADOWS: 1900; multiprints; cotton batting, some fabric deterioration and loss, overall fade; excellent quilting, straight-line and crisscross; 65 × 72　　**$345**

JACK IN THE BOX: 1890–1900; multicolored; Postage Stamp pieces, overall fade; 81 × 83　　**$1,500**

MARINER'S COMPASS: 1850; red on white; scalloped edge with half Compasses, 12-inch border with swags and bows; from Indiana; some disintegration of reds, double-stitched flower quilting overall, triple-stitched diagonal straight-line quilting on border; 78 × 88　　**$2,900**

MARINER'S COMPASS: 1900; light blue, cranberry, camel; unused, circle quilting, extra heavy batting; from Connecticut; 80 × 84　　**$695**

MARINER'S COMPASS/FEATHERED STAR: 1870; green, blue, yellow; overall fade, unusual combination and look; 82 × 76　　**$3,800**

This close-up shows part of an Indian Meadows quilt, with good color balance within the blocks and excellent quilting. Use and washing, since its creation in 1900, have caused some color loss, but the quilt still has a very appealing look.

MARINER'S COMPASS/ORANGE PEEL: 1930s; red and white; optical illusion quilt, sawtooth border; 70 × 76 $550

MELON PATCH: 1870; green, black, pink; date may be later, machine assembled, bold green print on black ground; melon corners mitered, all junctions match, some stains, some loose stitches; 78 × 78 $130

ORANGE PEEL: 1920s; red and white; excellent condition, unused, unwashed; excellent assembly, minimal quilting; 68 × 76 $700

ORANGE PEEL: 1930s; multiprints and white; Prairie Point edge, some small stains, one large stain, some loose seam stitches; outline quilting; 78 × 84 $300

Quilt block names have been inspired by both the unusual and the commonplace. Names based on everyday things in nature include: Tulip, American Beauty Rose, Flying Swallows, Tobacco Leaf, Mountain Laurel, Corn and Beans, and Melon Patch.

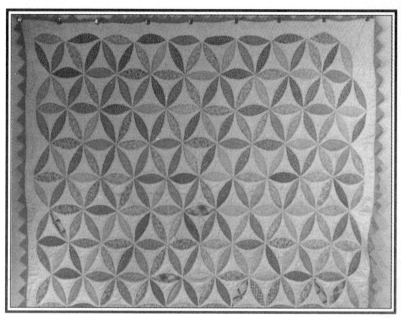

Made in the 1930s, this marvelously eye-catching Orange Peel quilt is done in multiple prints and pastels. The Prairie Points edge and excellent assembly make this a great find, even with a few loose stitches and some stains in spots.

A closer look at the Orange Peel quilt shows excellent assembly, with all points matching, neat outline quilting, and the softening of the fabric that comes from many washings.

> *The Rising Sun pattern looks similar to the Mariner's Compass except that some of the rays don't start in the center. One example of this pattern had 185 triangles comprising the sun. Because this pattern was extremely hard to piece, it is rare, valuable, and desirable.*

RISING SUN: early 1900s; blues, whites, rose, reds; set with white blocks, navy calico binding; some overall fade, washed and used; 60 × 84   **$550**

ROB PETER TO PAY PAUL: 1875; red and white on navy; walnut-dyed backing, signed; made in Texas, moved to Tennessee; unwashed, few age spots; fan quilting overall; large, awkward quilting stitches; 78 × 80   **$430**

SCHOOL HOUSE: 1870s; brown on white; 40 blocks, green sashing and border, from Kentucky, Ocean Waves quilting; 80 × 80   **$2,700**

SCHOOL HOUSE: 1890; indigo blue; all blocks face the same way, blue border, minimal use; 82 × 91   **$1,800**

SCHOOL HOUSE: early 1900s; grays, blues, white; excellent condition, unwashed, unused, quilting lines remain; diagonal straight-line quilting; 70 × 80   **$325**

SCHOOL HOUSE: 1910s; reds, blues, grays; white sashing, unwashed, unused, few small stains; straight-line and outline quilting on houses, grid quilting on sashing; 72 × 88   **$400**

SCHOOL HOUSE: 1914; red, brown, pink; overall faded and worn; 78 × 100   **$895**

SCHOOL HOUSE: early 1930s; blue, red; blue sashing, red edge; overall fade, slightly worn binding; 72 × 80   **$750**

SEVEN SISTERS: 1880s; purple, browns, indigo, orange, tan; tan sets, some calicoes, plaid binding, tan border, some wear on binding; very good assembly, nearly all junctions match, well-balanced colors in very busy and graphic quilt, diagonal quilting in stars, diamond quilting elsewhere; 72 × 84   **$1,400**

SNOW CRYSTALS: 1920s; multiprints; pink sashing, never washed, unused; straight-line quilting, detail quilting corners; 89 × 66   **$275**

STAR AND CROSS: 1890s; reds; set on point with chevron sashing, some color loss and fade, chevron straight-line quilting; 72 × 64   **$425**

ZIGZAG: 1900; red with light blue on white print; diagonal quilting, fair quality assembly, amateur quilting; 74 × 82   **$675**

The embroidery over the door says "Church of God" on this variation of the School House block. Several other names, and the date 1948, are embroidered elsewhere on the quilt. The sashing is green, the rooftops bright red, the sky is blue, and the churches are white with pale yellow windows and doors. A unique look.

Photograph courtesy of Susan Parrish

Besides the Star and Cross patterns, religious beliefs and stories inspired quilt blocks with such names as Jacob's Ladder, Job's Tears, World Without End, Three Crosses, Star of Bethlehem, The Cross and the Crown, Hosanna, King David's Crown, Golgotha, Cross Upon Cross, Palm Leaves, and Delectable Mountains
(from Pilgrims Progress*).*

Single, Double, and Triple Irish Chain

It's been said that the Irish Chain is the most universally recognized pieced quilting pattern known today. We think the Double Wedding Ring, Dresden Plate, and crazy quilt share that honor, but there's no doubt that the Irish Chain continues to appeal to collectors and contemporary quiltmakers.

The appeal of the Irish Chain is its optical illusion effect. Whether set straight or on point, the Irish Chain is one of those quilts that seem to defy our senses. Only by looking carefully and closely can we determine that the stunning optical effect of the single Irish Chain is created by using the simple Nine-patch block. These Nine-patches are assembled with squares of plain fabric that have one-piece squares the color of the chain appliquéd to each corner. It is this added element, those appliquéd corners, that causes the Nine-patch to escape our searching eye. Once we know this, it's easy to spot the basic blocks of the chain and recognize that they are simply Nine-patches sewed to a plain square.

The Double Irish Chain is created the same way except instead of a Nine-patch and a single color, a Twenty-five-patch and two colors are used. Worked in a five-by-five grid, the Double Irish Chain uses a dark and a light fabric, either two shades of the same color or two coordinating colors. The darker of the two colors is the fabric used for the appliquéd squares in the corners of the plain blocks.

For the Triple Irish Chain, another color is added, making three in the cabin, and the basic block is now a Forty-nine patch. The three colors are alternated carefully with the seven-by-seven-square block, and the darkest of the three is again appliquéd to the corners of the plain blocks.

Normally the plain blocks in an Irish Chain are left plain except for quilting. Quilting patterns can be as simple as straight lines extended from the small squares in the pattern or as elaborate as feather or wreath patterns. Some Irish Chains have appliquéd designs in the plain blocks, or use fabric with animal, floral, or fruit designs instead of solid colors.

Irish Chain quilts are valued for their optical illusion effect and because current trends in quilt collecting lean toward the two- or three-color coordinated style. The clean, ordered look of the two-color quilt and the simplicity of the design with its complex look, make Irish Chain quilts much sought after.

SINGLE IRISH CHAIN: 1846; indigo on white; some wear in white, tiny half-moon and star quilting inspired by the great comet of 1846; 75 x 80
$2,500

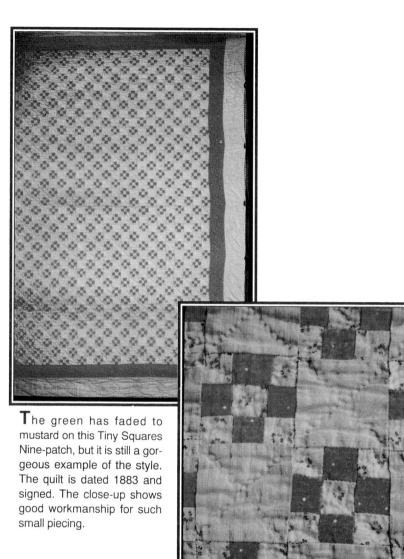

The green has faded to mustard on this Tiny Squares Nine-patch, but it is still a gorgeous example of the style. The quilt is dated 1883 and signed. The close-up shows good workmanship for such small piecing.

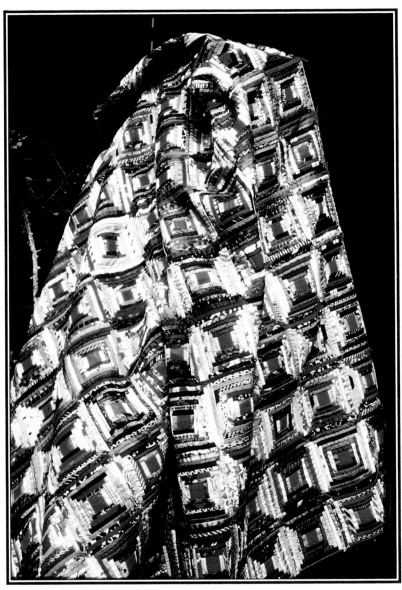

This Courthouse Steps variation of the Log Cabin shows the traditional red center square of this pattern. The tiny strips of the blocks make this a vibrant, lively quilt.

Photograph courtesy of Susan Parrish

In typical Amish style, the reds and blues in this quilt enhance each other, creating a stunning look. It has outstanding feather-ring quilting and dates from 1915.

This pieced and appliquéd sampler is representative of the album-style quilt popular in the late 1800s. The colors are bright, the patterns intricate, and the workmanship excellent.

Photograph courtesy of Susan Parrish

A wonderful example of the style, this Hawaiian appliqué has echo quilting and a stunning, graphic look. There is something regal about this quilt, and the pattern is intriguing.

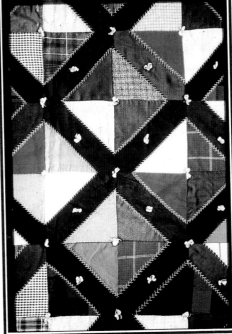

Quilt courtesy of Betty Wilson

Made in the early 1800s, this Triangles Makes Diamonds quilt is a lovely example of a wool quilt that has held its color and condition. The blue/black sashing sets up the colors, and the black feather topstitching enhances the whole look. The close-up looks in greater detail at this attractive quilt.

Quilt courtesy of Helen Warner

An excellent example of a crazy quilt, this silk, satin, and velvet piece has wool challis pointed edges and lots of embroidery and topstitching. The close-up shows interesting little features that also typify the style. A Christmas ribbon can be seen on this hundred-year-old quilt, along with some tiny tulips embroidered along one block.

Photograph by David Caras, courtesy of Michael James

This is a Michael James original named Shadowbox (copyright 1988). It is machine-pieced cotton and silk, and a perfect example of the innovation quilt artists are adding to the technique and creation of quilts.

DOUBLE IRISH CHAIN ASSEMBLY

The Double Irish Chain is actually a simple Five-patch block set with plain blocks that have small squares appliquéd in the corners. The final assembly gives the crossing parallel lines effect.

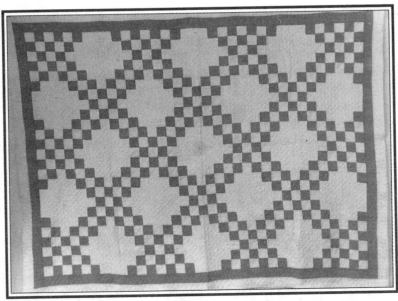

Even with a few rust spots and stains, this early-1900s Double Irish Chain is a good find. Lavender on white, this quilt shows very good assembly and balance, even into the corners. A simple border frames this piece nicely, making for a pleasing look.

A close-up of the same quilt shows both appliquéd corners and pieced corners, all perfectly matched, along with some echo line quilting.

SINGLE IRISH CHAIN: early 1900s; blue and white; worn binding, much use and washing, very faded overall; very good assembly, all junctions match, small quilting stitches, outline quilting, straight-line quilting across blocks; 80 × 80   **$450**

SINGLE IRISH CHAIN: early 1900s; red, white; Postage Stamp style; Flying Geese border, some stains; 75 × 75   **$2,400**

SINGLE IRISH CHAIN: 1920; red and white; slight overall fade, straight-line quilting; 80 × 78   **$600**

SINGLE IRISH CHAIN: 1920; pink and white; 83 × 68   **$750**

> *The Single Irish Chain, when set straight in vertical and horizontal rows rather than on the diagonal, is also called Kitty in the Corner.*

SINGLE IRISH CHAIN: 1930; cornflower blue on white; blue edging; from Pennsylvania; straight-line quilting; 79 × 79   **$795**

SINGLE IRISH CHAIN: 1930s; red and white; unused; 64 × 76   **$695**

SINGLE IRISH CHAIN AND NINE-PATCH VARIATION: 1940; yellow on white; excellent condition, probably unused, straight-line quilting overall; 76 × 77   **$375**

DOUBLE IRISH CHAIN: 1820; brown, Turkey red, teal; chintz fabrics, unused, unwashed; for four-poster bed, some minor fabric disintegration in browns; from Maine; family genealogy back to 1600s in India ink in one block; diagonal straight-line quilting overall; 78 × 86   **$3,000**

DOUBLE IRISH CHAIN: 1840–1850; soft salmon red; maker known; from West Virginia via Colorado; unused; 74 × 82   **$1,200**

DOUBLE IRISH CHAIN: 1870; browns, greens, blues, white; dozens of different fabrics, some stains, overall use and wear; very good assembly, nearly all junctions match, small appliqué stitches, straight-line quilting overall; 70 × 94   **$495**

DOUBLE IRISH CHAIN: 1890; blue and white; unusual look, center of chain dark blue, two outside chains medium blue, very graphic; junctions match, very good work; few stains; 70 × 70   **$795**

DOUBLE IRISH CHAIN: 1890s; blue and white; double Sawtooth border on two sides, single Sawtooth border on two sides; from Ohio; maker known; few age spots, minimal use, feather wreath quilting in white blocks; 70 × 80   **$1,150**

DOUBLE IRISH CHAIN: early 1900s; lavender and white; small rust stains, water stains overall; excellent quilting, tiny stitches, diamond and double line quilting; 60 × 80   **$295**

DOUBLE IRISH CHAIN: early 1900s; red, green, white; red binding on two sides, green binding on two sides, unwashed; from West Virginia, crisscross quilting overall; 65 × 84   **$500**

DOUBLE IRISH CHAIN: early 1900s; red on white; overall fade, flowers quilted in white squares; 70 × 76   **$575**

DOUBLE IRISH CHAIN: early 1900s; pinks on pink; from New Hampshire; 72 × 76   **$650**

DOUBLE IRISH CHAIN: 1920s; blue and white; outline and straight-line quilting; 78 × 80   **$375**

DOUBLE IRISH CHAIN: 1920s; red and white; overall fade, worn binding, outline quilting; 68 × 74   **$375**

DOUBLE IRISH CHAIN: 1930; lavender; from Pennsylvania; minimal use; 86 × 77   **$400**

DOUBLE IRISH CHAIN: 1930s; blue on cream; early machine quilting; 66 × 78   **$250**

DOUBLE IRISH CHAIN: 1930; pink, green, white; from Nebraska; unwashed, unused, quilting lines remain; excellent assembly, junctions match, tiny appliqué stitches, straight-line echo quilting; 72 × 77   **$575**

TRIPLE IRISH CHAIN: 1880s; green, rust, white; minimal use and washing; excellent assembly, minimal quilting; 72 × 80   **$285**

TRIPLE IRISH CHAIN: 1890s; green, white; green binding and backing, overall fade, worn binding; corner appliqué squares slightly misshapen, minimal outline quilting; 72 × 78   **$300**

TRIPLE IRISH CHAIN: 1930s; multiprints and pastels; printed binding, white border, unwashed, unused; diagonal quilting on squares, cable quilting on border; 88 × 87   **$500**

Stars

Since Colonial times, stars have been among the most popular of quilt patterns. The square, rectangle, and diamond are the three basic geometric shapes used by quilters. Of these, the diamond is the most difficult to piece, as the angles left around are odd, and must be filled with more diamond, square, and triangle pieces. The eight-point star is among the earliest pieced designs, its use traced back to 1750. Star patterns were often reserved for best quilts, and since the best quilts were more carefully preserved, many star quilts survived when others of the same age did not.

Use of diamond patches in decorative work did not start with quilting. Diamond patches were used in medieval times, and the shape in quilts probably came from ancient tilework.

The LeMoyne Star, sometimes called the Lemon Star in a mispronunciation of its real name, is the basis for many star patterns, most notably the Star of Bethlehem or Lone Star, which are still popular with quiltmakers today. From the early to mid-nineteenth century, Star of Bethlehem quilts were assembled block-style, composed of as many as twelve or sixteen separate, intricately pieced stars. It wasn't until the late nineteenth and early twentieth centuries that such quilts were made with one large star radiating from the middle. The photograph below shows a block-style Star of Bethlehem quilt.

In shades of gold and orange, with lavender accents, this wonderful example of the traditional set and arrangement of the Star of Bethlehem was made in the 1920s. It is in pristine condition, having been handed down within a family.
Quilt courtesy of Miriam Zimmer

The same Star of Bethlehem quilt, seen in close-up, shows the nonjunction of some of the points and squares, and some very nice flower petal and straight-line quilting. The overall look of this quilt makes up for any minor shortcomings in assembly.
Quilt courtesy of Miriam Zimmer

The diamond shape and star patterns also led to the development of lily, peony, and tulip designs. Further variation of the star pattern led to the Feathered Star, which added a strip of Sawtooth along the outside edges of the star pattern and was popular from 1890 to the present. Diamond patterns as stars or flowers can be pieced or appliquéd, sometimes with stems and leaves also pieced or appliquéd in such a star-based floral quilt.

To create her star from diamonds, the quiltmaker used a template that was often handed down to her from her quiltmaking ancestors or was loaned by a good friend or neighbor. If no template was available, there was a sophisticated method of folding and cutting fabric to make the diamonds that bypassed the ignorance of geometry required to create a template from scratch. A good discussion of these fascinating folding methods, along with diagrams, is included in Ruth Finley's *Old Patchwork Quilts*.

Variations on the star pattern abounded, leading to four-point, five-point, and six-point stars, as well as the Variable Star and the Ohio Star. Since many quiltmakers renamed their pattern to reflect their own lifestyle, region, or family, there are also a plethora of names used to describe the same pattern. Some denote the same design done in different patterns of lights and darks, or simply the change in optical illusion created by setting a star pattern on point.

It is the challenge and versatility of the diamond patch and star pattern that have intrigued quiltmakers for three centuries and produced a multitude of patterns still being used today.

BROKEN STAR: 1890; red, green, yellow; yellow bleeds/runs, plaid blanket as batting, some few stains; possibly new binding, straight-line quilting; 80 × 84 $295

BROKEN STAR: 1920s; reds, blues, white; blue backing, excellent condition, unwashed, unused, quilting lines remain; excellent assembly, small quilting stitches, medallion quilting in white between star pieces; 80 × 84 $750

BROKEN STAR: 1920; pink, red, medium blue, white; very good condition, slight overall fade, few tiny stains; excellent assembly, all junctions match, very good quilting, close straight-line quilting, outline quilting on diamond pieces of stars; 70 × 78 $975

BROKEN STAR: 1930s; red, green, blue, gold; double border on two sides, triple border on two sides, never washed, minimal use; diamond quilting, zig-zag quilting on borders; 72 × 69 $500

BROKEN STAR: 1930; blue, yellow, lavender, green, pastels, white; from the Midwest; some tears on top, worn binding; very good assembly, all junctions match, small quilting stitches, straight-line and outline quilting; 80 × 82 $675

DOUBLE STAR: 1880s; pink, brown; set on white blocks, pink sashing, slight overall fade, straight-line quilting overall; 80 × 84 $725

EIGHT-POINT STAR: 1940s; yellow, blue, pink; crib quilt, pink sashing, fair-to-poor condition, very worn top, much use and washing; fair work, amateurish quilting, large stitches, possibly done by a child; 36 × 36 $150

FEATHERED STAR: 1830s; red, white, green; 40 stars in red on white with green sashing, from North Carolina; some small fabric disintegration in green with blue showing through; 78 × 84 $3,900

FEATHERED STAR: 1845–1850; rose on white; linen backing, overall fade, few stains; exceptional quilting, tiny stitches; 84 × 80 $2,200

FEATHERED STAR: 1880; teal, red; four blocks square, Sawtooth edge and border, red sashing; feather quilting on border, pineapple quilting in sashing and on edge, diagonal quilting on star; from Ohio; some slight repairs; 82 × 84
$2,400

FEATHERED STAR: 1890s; brown, blue, white; pieced back, same fabrics as front; minimal use, very good assembly, small quilting stitches, clamshell and scroll quilting; 68 × 68   **$850**

FEATHERED STAR: 1890s; blue, white; blue double border, minimal use, few discolored spots; excellent assembly and quilting, feather wreath quilting; 72 × 78   **$1,000**

FEATHERED STAR: 1890s; red on white; feather wreath and diamond quilting, double crisscross quilting on border; minimal use, quilting lines remain; 78 × 90   **$2,200**

FEATHERED STAR: 1900s; blues, pinks, white; few stains, minimal use, very good assembly; small quilting stitches, outline and straight-line quilting; 72 × 78   **$550**

FEATHERED STAR: 1930s; rose, gold; rose binding, gold border, few small spots, minimal use, never washed; straight-line quilting, crisscross quilting between stars; 90 × 85   **$475**

FEATHERED AND OHIO STARS: 1940; blue, yellow, gray, gold; four central Feathered Stars with Ohio Stars on border; very good assembly, most junctions match, straight-line quilting; 67 × 69   **$375**

FIVE STARS: 1880; red, navy, burgundy; all prints, very thin batting; 91 × 23   **$795**

> *When the westward migration began, quilt block names often changed. The Ship's Wheel, a popular pattern in New England, became the Harvest Sun. An obscure pattern called Harpoons was adapted and renamed the Wheat pattern. Both changes reflected the new locations and the living conditions of the quiltmakers rather than any major change in the patterns.*

HARVEST SUN: 1860; pumpkin yellow, white; very good condition, minimal use, some small stains; very good assembly, nearly all junctions match, grid quilting overall; 70 × 78   **$485**

HARVEST SUN: 1860s; yellow, green, blue, red; some overall color loss, feather and diamond quilting around stars, echo quilting on stars; from Rhode Island; 96 × 80   **$770**

This classic LeMoyne Star quilt from the late 1900s shows excellent color balance overall and in the stars, using scrap bag fabrics. The stars are set on point with white sashing, and the quilt has an extra border on the chin edge.
Quilt courtesy of Doris Dean

LEMOYNE STAR: 1880s; red, white; few spots on back, unwashed, minimal use; very good assembly, most junctions match, small quilting stitches; 68 × 78
$750

LEMOYNE STAR: 1890s; blue, green, white; some old repairs, overall fade, worn binding; 68 × 74
$350

LEMOYNE STAR: early 1900s; blue on white; blue double border; overall fade, few stains; 68 × 80
$600

LEMOYNE STAR: 1910s; blue, red, white; slightly worn binding, overall fade, red border; outline quilting, grid quilting on border; 68 × 72
$525

LEMOYNE STAR: 1910; blue; from Pennsylvania; 74 × 108
$650

LEMOYNE STAR: 1920s; multicolored brights; from Missouri; minimal use; 64 × 76
$475

LEMOYNE STAR: 1920s; browns, red; red border; from Pennsylvania; one corner discolored/stained, cable quilting on border, lattice quilting elsewhere; 72 × 78
$750

One of the stars from this same LeMoyne Star quilt, seen in close-up, shows that the maker had a little trouble with the center assembly. The rest of the assembly, including the sashes, is beautiful, as is the leaf-and-vine and the straight-line quilting.
Quilt courtesy of Doris Dean

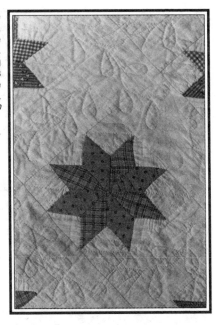

The most common use of the diamond patch in piecework is in the LeMoyne Star. Named after the LeMoyne brothers, who settled in Louisiana in 1699, the pattern is very old and is the basis for many other blocks, including the Pieced Lily variations, the Lone Star, and the Golden Glow, with its gathered petals within the star. The LeMoyne Star is always eight-pointed. Most knowledgeable dealers will not make this mistake, but many quiltmakers and others will call the eight-point star a Lemon Star. Some quilt historians believe that this name change occurred because of mispronunciations of the name LeMoyne. Lemon Star and LeMoyne Star are the same pattern.

LEMOYNE STAR: 1920–1930; multicolored prints; 60 × 90 $750
LEMOYNE STAR: 1930s; red, blue, yellow; very bright yellows, nine stars;
89 × 76 $675

Most Pieced Lily blocks are variations of the LeMoyne Star pattern. By leaving off two, three, or four of the eight points of the LeMoyne Star, or making two, three, or four of the eight points in green as leaves, a geometric depiction of the lily is achieved. Stems and other leaves may be appliquéd or pieced onto the block. The lily pattern has eight different names, according to the variety of lily common to the area where the quiltmaker lived. In the Northeast the pattern would be called Meadow Lily; in the South, the Carolina Lily; in Pennsylvania, the Tiger Lily; in Kentucky and in Tennessee, the Mountain Lily; in Ohio, Indiana, and Illinois, the Fire Lily; west of the Mississippi, the Prairie Lily; and beyond the Great Divide, the Mariposa Lily.

LILY: 1930s; salmon pink, green, yellow; all cotton sateens, diamond edge and border; spiderweb quilting overall, minimal use; 78 × 84   **$395**

LONE STAR/STAR OF BETHLEHEM: 1915; purple, pink; from Texas; 60 × 75   **$550**

One of the best-known, best-liked, and most-used patterns has two just-as-well-known names. In the East it is called the Star of Bethlehem, in the West, the Lone Star. It has also been called Joseph's Coat. The pattern is based on the eight-point LeMoyne Star. Each of the large diamonds in the pattern is made of smaller diamonds. Colors are selected to form bands of color that match in each of the eight large diamonds and radiate out from the center. Not always made as one large star filling the center of the quilt, the Lone Star/Star of Bethlehem can also be made of twelve 18-inch blocks, each with its own star.

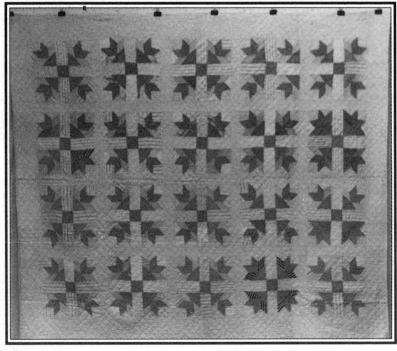

This beautiful lily variation was made in Iowa in the 1880s of fabric scraps
that included apron ties and shirttails. With white sashing and border, the
quilt is a balanced delight.
Quilt courtesy of Miriam Zimmer

LONE STAR/STAR OF BETHLEHEM: 1920; multicolored pastels; zigzag border, some overall fade, binding frayed; excellent assembly, junctions match, minimal quilting in large daisy design; 78 × 80 $125

LONE STAR/STAR OF BETHLEHEM: 1920; red, white, blue, pink; from Kansas; overall fade, some fabric deterioration, especially in blue, some loose stitches; fair-to-poor assembly and quilting; rainbow and straight-line quilting overall; 64 × 64 $195

LONE STAR/STAR OF BETHLEHEM: 1920; greens, browns; excellent condition, unused; excellent assembly, outline quilting; 68 × 78 $525

LONE STAR/STAR OF BETHLEHEM: 1920; multicolored, lots of medallion quilting; 66 × 80 $700

LONE STAR/STAR OF BETHLEHEM: 1920; burgundy, blue; lots of quilting 50 × 82 $750

A close-up reveals the quilt's excellent assembly and lovely colors. The ginghams are black and white that have faded to a pleasant shade; the rest of the colors are pinks, light blues, and reds. Lovely grid quilting covers the entire quilt. A rare find.
Quilt courtesy of Miriam Zimmer

LONE STAR/STAR OF BETHLEHEM: 1920; pink, rose, blues, green; green border, very good condition, minimal use; very good assembly, nearly all junctions match, small quilting stitches, feather wreath quilting, grid quilting on border; 100 × 100   **$1,150**

LONE STAR/STAR OF BETHLEHEM: 1920s; blues, pinks; blue border, edge, and backing; overall fade, some stains, very good assembly, small quilting stitches, outline quilting; 60 × 70   **$450**

LONE STAR/STAR OF BETHLEHEM: 1920s; all pastels; from Michigan; 67 × 76   **$595**

LONE STAR/STAR OF BETHLEHEM: 1920s; blue, red, green, yellow: bold colors, minimal use; 66 × 80   **$625**

LONE STAR/STAR OF BETHLEHEM: 1920s; green, gold, blue; very good assembly, feather and straight-line quilting; 68 × 78   **$675**

LONE STAR/STAR OF BETHLEHEM: 1930s; red, gold; some wear overall, some fabric loss, feather quilting; 72 × 83   **$195**

LONE STAR/STAR OF BETHLEHEM: 1930s; rose, green; pink border, green binding, colors alternate in rows to form star, unwashed, unused; lots of quilting, diamond quilting in each diamond, stars quilted around edge of star, cable quilting on border; 88 × 82   **$350**

LONE STAR/STAR OF BETHLEHEM: 1930s; red, white, blue; soiled overall, some stains, unwashed, unused; star quilting; 78 × 80   **$600**

LONE STAR/STAR OF BETHLEHEM: 1930s; red, white, navy blue; bright colors, slight overall fade; grid and outline quilting; 70 × 80   **$650**

LONE STAR/STAR OF BETHLEHEM: 1930; yellow; 74 × 86   **$400**

LONE STAR/STAR OF BETHLEHEM: 1930; blue, red; 64 × 80   **$550**

LONE STAR/STAR OF BETHLEHEM: 1930; multi-greens; from New England; 70 × 80   **$400**

LONE STAR/STAR OF BETHLEHEM: 1940s; tan, beige, golds; all solid colors, excellent assembly, very good quilting, lots of quilting; straight-line on star, medallion and circular elsewhere; 84 × 80   **$950**

LONE STAR/STAR OF BETHLEHEM: 1940; orange, blue, yellow; old top, quilted in 1989, unused, from Oklahoma via Colorado; 70 × 79   **$1,200**

NINE LONE STARS: 1860–1880; red, yellow, green; three narrow borders, one of each color; minimal use, few small spots, straight-line quilting; 86 × 87   **$950**

STAR: 1920s; peach, light green; 64 × 76   **$325**

STAR OF BETHLEHEM VARIATION: late 1920s; deep blue and yellow on ivory; excellent condition, unwashed; 78 × 84   **$650**

STARS AND STRIPES: 1920; red, white, blue; from Arkansas; very graphic; 76 × 76   **$775**

SUNBURST: 1890s; reds; poor condition, overall wear, fade, much fabric deterioration; very strong country look, very good quilting, outline quilting overall; 90 × 70   **$225**

SUNBURST: early 1900s; red, mustard-yellow; fair condition, overall wear and fade, some tears, stains, fabric loss; straight-line quilting overall; 72 × 71   **$175**

TEXAS LONE STAR: 1910; greens, browns; possibly vegetable dyed, pair of quilts; 84 × 86 (price per pair)   **$1,250**

TOUCHING STARS: 1830–1840; multicolored; slight fabric deterioration in places; few stains; from Pennsylvania; tape binding, probably recent replacement; 92 × 92   **$2,400**

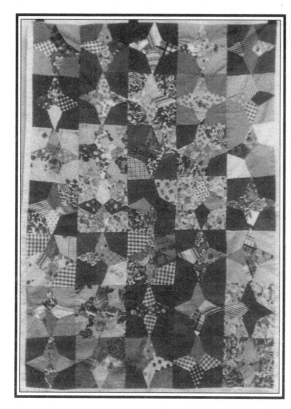

A good example of a basic Four-point Star pattern, this crib or lap quilt was made in the 1940s of scrap bag fabrics. As a summer coverlet, it is tied and not quilted.
Quilt courtesy of Lois Belden

Two-patch, Four-patch, Nine-patch

When early quiltmakers first experimented with piecing geometric shapes together, they did so by simple divisions of the square. Folding a square in half and cutting it along the diagonal formed two triangles, the first Two-patch design. By cutting a light-colored square and a dark-colored square the same way and attaching one light triangle to one dark one, a new look emerged, and form met tone and color. Sewing many of these simple Two-patch squares together resulted in the Sawtooth pattern. By turning each stitched square a quarter turn yet another design was created. As quiltmakers added their own color sense and artistic eye to the Two-patch design, hundreds of variations came to be.

From the Two-patch came the Four-patch. The quilt pattern we used at the beginning of this chapter to illustrate how to find the basic block in a geometric quilt is a Four-patch design. Each of the four squares within the

The plaid fabric in this early-1900s Barrister's Block variation is a striking black-and-red flannel. Unfortunately, it points out, rather than hides, a less-than-perfect assembly.

Four-patch is itself a Two-patch, except where a full square is used. From the illustrations (pp. 133–135) we see just three of the ways in which these pieces can be assembled, an indication of the variation attainable from a simple square.

From the Four-patch, the quiltmaker turned to the Nine-patch. Once again the square was divided into smaller geometric forms and assembled together in three rows of three blocks each. So endless is the variation on the basic block that half of all pieced quilt patterns are based on either the Four-patch or the Nine-patch arrangement.

From the early 1800s to the present, the simple Nine-patch has been the chosen pattern for teaching anyone to quilt. At its most basic, it is simply nine squares joined together, three rows of three squares. Here again, it is the choice of color, tone, and proximity that creates the artistry of the basic Nine-patch quilt. From the basic block, variations continue, each more and more complex, by further divisions of each of the blocks in a Nine-patch into smaller geometric divisions of triangles, rectangles, and diamonds. From there, quiltmakers have graduated to such intricate patterns as Storm at Sea, Ohio Star, or Turkey Tracks.

It is also with the division of the squares into two, four, and nine parts that pieced quilts achieve their optical illusion qualities. When we add the individual quiltmaker's choice of color, tone, and texture to these geometric forms, its easy to see why no two quilts are ever alike—even when made from the same basic pattern.

For the ease of the reader, and because there are so many of each of these types of quilts, we have kept the subgroupings of Four-patch and Nine-patch quilts separate in the following list.

Four-patch Quilts

BARRISTER'S BLOCK: early 1900s; Buffalo red plaid, blue; some stains; 61 × 81 $650

BARRISTER'S BLOCK: 1910; pink, green, red, blue; striped back, pink and green sashing; very good condition, minimal use, straight-line quilting overall; 80 × 82 $575

BIG DIPPER: early 1900s; blue and white; excellent condition, unwashed, unused; excellent assembly, feather wreath and straight-line quilting; 70 × 78 $750

BLAZING STARS: 1870s; gold, green, chocolate brown, white; narrow sashing, Streak O' Lightning border; from Ohio; very good condition, minimal use; very good assembly, nearly all junctions match, straight-line quilting; 72 × 78 $1,200

BLAZING STARS: 1900s; green, yellow, red, blue; set on point with yellow sashing diagonally, LeMoyne Stars in sashing junctions, excellent condition, unused, unwashed; very good assembly, nearly all junctions match, outline quilting; 70 × 78 $1,200

BORROW AND RETURN: 1928; bright pink on white; maker known; minimal use, lots of quilting; 72 × 76 $750

BORROW AND RETURN: 1930s; pink gingham check and white; from Oklahoma; overall fade; amateurish line quilting; 63 × 71 $445

BOW TIE: 1890s; blue, gray, red; slight overall fade; 50 × 58 $400

BOW TIE: 1890s; reds, browns, blues; red sashing, fair-to-good condition, slight overall fade, overall soiling, worn binding, few tears on back; cable quilting on sashing, outline quilting on ties; 68 × 78 $450

BOW TIE: 1890; red, gray; 61 × 72 $395

BOW TIE: early 1900s; excellent assembly, small quilting stitches, curved and straight-line quilting; 72 × 78 $450

BOW TIE: 1920s; red and white; red border, overall fade; 66 × 78 $475

BOW TIE: early 1900s; reds, pinks, grays; overall fade, few stains, multiple washings; 78 × 68 **$400**

BOW TIE: 1930s; red, blues, pink; Bow Ties small, set on point with pink-on-pink sets; few stains, some color loss, diamond quilting overall, uneven stitches, machine-applied binding; 54 × 72 **$265**

BOW TIE: 1940s; multicolored; octagonal centers, large quilting stitches, half-circle quilting; 80 × 72 **$125**

BROKEN DISHES: 1880; dusty blue and pink; very good assembly, unused; 80 × 90 **$595**

BROKEN DISHES: 1890s; blue and white; blue border, overall fade; cable quilting on border, straight-line quilting elsewhere; 72 × 76 **$485**

BROKEN DISHES: 1890s; blues, reds, white; double border, unused, unwashed, quilting lines remain; very good assembly, small quilting stitches, feather wreath quilting, lattice quilting on border; 70 × 78 **$600**

BROKEN DISHES: early 1900s; red on white; red border and edge, few small stains; 73 × 73 **$600**

BROKEN DISHES: early 1900s; browns, other darks; tweedlike backing and edge, unused; 73 × 73 **$795**

CARPENTER'S WHEEL: 1910s; maroons, browns, grays; very busy pattern, very good condition, minimal use; outline quilting; 72 × 80 **$550**

CHIMNEY SWEEP: 1880; blues, white; blue border, two illegible signatures in one block, few stains; grid quilting overall; 74 × 58 **$450**

CHIMNEY SWEEP: 1920s; pink and white; pink sashing and border, overall fade; leaf quilting in sashing, grid quilting on blocks; 77 × 63 **$575**

The Corn and Beans quilt block was inspired by the practice of planting pole beans between rows of sweet corn in the family garden.

CORN AND BEANS: 1880–1890; black, reds; black with tiny floral print, several red prints on white, homespun backing, semicircular curved quilting; from Texas; 68 × 74 **$1,000**

CORN AND BEANS: 1890s; green, gold, blue; excellent assembly, all junctions match, circle and straight-line quilting; 72 × 78 **$600**

CROSSES AND LOSSES: 1860s; blue and white; blue strip border, very good condition, minimal use; very small quilting stitches, feather wreath quilting; 70 × 78
$750

DOUBLE FOUR-PATCH: 1930s; multicolored darks; print block sets same as backing fabric, machine applied binding; summer comforter, no batting, tied, no quilting; 72 × 80
$125

DOUBLE Z: 1880; blue, tan; blue sashing and edge; from northern New York State; minimal use, straight-line quilting overall; 87 × 76
$1,095

The Doves in the Window pattern was named for the custom of having a special window near the rafters of a barn for pet pigeons to enter and roost.

DOVES IN THE WINDOW: 1920s; blue, white; overall wear, worn binding, overall fade; fair assembly, many junctions don't match, minimal quilting; 76 × 70
$585

DOVES IN THE WINDOW: 1930s; kelly green; overall wear; 72 × 86
$400

FOUR-PATCH: 1890s; pink on pink, browns; set on point in bars, some stains, straight-line chevron quilting; 77 × 92
$275

FOUR-POINT STARS: 1900; reds, blues; from Iowa; slightly faded overall; outline quilting; 76 × 67
$585

HOVERING HAWKS: 1920s; lavender and white; white sets, lavender border, some stains; very small quilting stitches, circular flower quilting on white sets, straight-line quilting on squares, chain quilting on border; 80 × 90
$395

HOVERING HAWKS VARIATION: 1930s; nile green, black; large and small triangles, Sawtooth and Half-cube border, very graphic; unused, few small stains, excellent assembly, junctions match, tiny quilting stitches; 72 × 82
$650

INDIANA PUZZLE/SNAIL'S TRAIL: 1930s; light pink, white; excellent condition, unused, unwashed; very good assembly, flower quilting in center of blocks; 76 × 76
$475

INDIANA PUZZLE VARIATION: 1910; blue, white; very unusual interpretation of pattern; from Texas; 70 × 80
$2,500

> *As an example of how easy it is to create a new pattern and a new name for the long list of quilt blocks, consider the Jacob's Ladder block. This pre–Revolutionary War pattern uses only two colors, a dark and a light. If a quiltmaker reverses the placement of the dark and light and adds a third color, the pattern becomes Stepping Stone.*

JACOB'S LADDER: 1900; blue and white; slightly worn binding; straight-line quilting; 78 × 80 $435

JACOB'S LADDER: 1920s; blue on cream; some overall wear; 72 × 108 $350

JACOB'S LADDER: 1920s; pink and white; pink border, unused, unwashed; good quilting, fair assembly, not all junctions match, minimal quilting; 70 × 80 $450

> *During the Civil War, the Jacob's Ladder pattern was renamed the Underground Railroad and the Job's Tears block became known as the Slave Cabin.*

JACOB'S LADDER: 1920s; pink; floral print with green leaves, excellent condition; 72 × 84 $575

JACOB'S LADDER: 1930s; dark and light multiprints; set on point with pink sets, pink binding; unwashed, unused, straight-line quilting overall; 76 × 88 $350

JACOB'S LADDER: early 1930s; black, red, blue, gray; 64 × 84 $400

JACOB'S LADDER: 1933; red and white; initialed and dated; from Vermont; 73 × 86 $335

JACOB'S LADDER VARIATION: 1910; pink, blue, yellow; Tail of Benjamin's Kite, light blue print sashing, dark blue border, African-American; from family in Missouri; slightly faded overall, some stains, straight-line quilting overall; 72 × 78 $245

An unusual variation of the Indiana Puzzle, this dark-blue-and-white quilt was made in Texas in 1910. Was the block cleverly planned this way or was it the product of an inexperienced quiltmaker?

Stepping Stones, a Jacob's Ladder variation, was called the Tail of Benjamin's Kite in Pennsylvania, Underground Railroad in the Western Reserve, and Wagon Tracks or the Trail of the Covered Wagon in Mississippi and prairie country.

KING'S CROSS VARIATION: 1880s; blues, roses, white; rose print sets, machine applied binding, unused, unwashed, few stains on back; double diagonal straight-line quilting, feed sack backing; 70 × 78 $425

This close-up shows the arrangement of the pieces on the blue-and-white quilt more distinctly, along with some rather large, uneven quilt stitches. An inexperienced quiltmaker, perhaps, but a stunning quilt nonetheless.

LOVER'S KNOT: 1880s; indigo on white; excellent condition, unused; from Pennsylvania; triple-line echo and feather quilting; 81 × 70   **$895**

OCEAN WAVES: 1870; red with black; overall fade, black splatter fabric, chain quilting on border; 80 × 80   **$1,200**

OCEAN WAVES: 1880; teal, pink, brown; overall fade, some stains; 64 x 70   **$595**

OCEAN WAVES: 1890; blues, reds, white; Flying Geese border, white sets, excellent condition, unused, unwashed, quilting lines remain; very good quilting, aster flowers quilting in white sets, grid quilting overall; 80 × 82   **$1,200**

OCEAN WAVES: 1890–1900; pink, tan, blue; no batting, minimal straight-line quilting, pink on pink at block intersections; 72 × 84   **$195**

OCEAN WAVES: 1900; black and white gingham; excellent condition, minimal use; 66 × 77   **$410**

OCEAN WAVES: 1920; lime green, lavender, pink, multicolors; set with green blocks, green border, few stains; straight-line quilting overall; 84 × 76   **$450**

OCEAN WAVES: 1920; green and white; from Indiana; 84 × 91   **$525**

OCEAN WAVES: 1920; blue, greens, white; excellent condition, unused, unwashed; excellent assembly, all junctions match; 60 × 72   **$600**

OCEAN WAVES: 1930s; blue, red, multicolored; minimal use; outline quilting; 70 × 80   **$750**

OCEAN WAVES: 1944; yellow and multicolored; from Kansas; dated, maker known; minimal use; 66 × 82   **$850**

OCEAN WAVES VARIATION: 1930s; multicolored; optical illusion quilt, hand pieced, straight-line machine quilting, printed backing; 72 × 72   **$225**

OLD MAID'S PUZZLE: 1880s; burgundy, blue; from Colorado; 62 × 80

$750

OLD MAID'S PUZZLE: 1920s; pink on white; pink border, washed many times, overall fade, very worn binding; straight-line and outline quilting; 72 × 80   **$550**

PIERCED STAR: 1870s; gold, browns; sashing of unusual brown fabric printed with gold cherries, excellent condition, unused, unwashed; diamond quilting overall; 78 × 80   **$385**

Actually considered a good luck symbol, the swastika form is found in almost every ancient and primitive culture, including North American Indian Art. It was a popular quilt block pattern, especially in traditional Pennsylvania/German folk art. When it was taken as the symbol of Hitler's Third Reich, it quickly fell out of favor as a quilt block; thus quilts with this symbol must have been made before the 1940s. Pieces already made and quilt blocks resembling the swastika were renamed Pinwheel, Twist and Turn, Crazy Ann, Follow the Leader, Flyfoot, and Devils' Puzzle.

PINWHEEL: early 1900s; blue, white; overall fade, minimal use; straight-line and circle quilting; 78 × 84   **$750**

PINWHEEL: 1920s; pink on pink, reds; set on point with pink on pink blocks, some stains; cable quilting on border; 80 × 78   **$625**

PINWHEEL: 1925; yellow on white; set with white blocks; from Midwest; worn binding, chin edge cut down and rebound, overall wear; very good assembly, junctions match, diamond quilting; 82 × 64   **$195**

PINWHEEL: 1930s; pink on white; various shades and tones of pink, worn binding; fair-to-good assembly, lots of quilting in straight lines and curves; 90 × 72 $225

PINWHEEL: 1930s; pink, blue, red; pink on pink border and sashing; some few stains, zigzag quilting, large stitches; 72 × 72 $320

PINWHEEL: 1940s; yellow, green, black, pink; pink border, floral print backing, very good condition, minimal use; very good assembly, nearly all junctions match, straight-line quilting; 70 × 70 $185

PINWHEEL VARIATION: 1880s; blue on white; blue border, fair condition, very faded overall, many rust spots, heavily used, worn binding; clamshell quilting on border, straight-line quilting on blocks; 70 × 78 $550

ROCKY ROAD TO OKLAHOMA: 1930s; orange, black; large and small pointed leaves in quilting, diagonal quilting on border, minimal use; 74 × 80
                                                                                                                        $295

ROLLING STAR: 1920s; multicolored; excellent condition, never washed, unused, straight-line quilting; 62 × 75 $200

ROLLING STAR: 1920s; reds, browns; red sashing and border, overall faded, overall wear; lattice quilting in sashing, outline quilting on star; 70 × 84 $400

ROLLING STAR: 1930s; red, green; set with white blocks, fair condition, frayed binding, overall fade and wear; excellent assembly, close diamond quilting, straight-line quilting on border; 84 × 92 $325

ROLLING STAR: 1930s; yellow, soft green; from Missouri, excellent quilting; 64 × 77 $550

SAWTOOTH SQUARES: early 1900s; browns; elongated hexagons as sashing, feather quilting in hexagons, double straight-line quilting in squares; some fabric loss and deterioration, overall stains and soiling, frayed binding; 88 × 78
                                                                                                                        $375

SIXTEEN-PATCH: 1900; blues; set with blue blocks, very heavy batting; overall and spot fade, some tears and fabric loss, fair-to-poor condition, poor-quality straight-line quilting overall; 40 × 60 $225

SIXTEEN-PATCH: 1920s; light blues; all shirting fabric, blue sashing; minimal use, very good assembly, junctions match, outline and echo quilting; 62 × 72 $275

STARS, FIVE FOUR-POINT: 1940s; reds, multicolored prints; machine quilted in scroll pattern, yellow backing; 72 × 80 $195

TREE OF LIFE: 1920s; green on white; from Pennsylvania; maker known; excellent condition, unused, chevron and grid quilting overall; 82 x 70 $1,150

TREE OF LIFE: 1870s; rust print, black on white print, white; excellent condition, few tiny stains on one area, unused, minimal washing; excellent assembly, all junctions match, very good quilting, very small stitches, grid quilting overall; 85 × 75   **$1,500**

TREE OF LIFE: 1930s; peach and white; from Iowa; 75 × 60   **$450**

WINDMILL: 1890s; indigo blue and white; navy blue border; 76 × 80
$495

WINDMILL: 1890s; indigo blue and white; double border, overall fade, slightly worn binding, some loose and broken quilting stitches, feather quilting; 74 × 78   **$500**

Nine-patch Quilts

ATTIC WINDOWS: 1940s; red, white; wool crib quilt; looks Amish, is not; wools frayed, worn, new binding, no quilting, no batting, machine appliqués in circles; 30 × 40   **$215**

AUNT SUKEY'S CHOICE: 1920s; yellow, blue; blue sashing and binding, unwashed, unused; straight-line quilting overall, cable quilting on sashing; 96 × 83   **$350**

> *Basket blocks, popular in quilting, are among the few quilt patterns*
> *that combine piecework and appliqué in the same block. The basket*
> *is pieced from triangles, then the butterflies, flowers, bees, and/or*
> *handles are appliquéd to the block. Other, less exacting, examples of*
> *piecework and appliqué in a single block are Fan, Dresden Plate, and*
> *some lily and tulip variation blocks.*

BASKET: 1840–1850; red and green; all prints, appliqué handles, outstanding quilting in heart designs; 69 × 75   **$1,200**

BASKET: 1860–1880; red on white; signed in ink; some overall wear, from Maine; 73 × 84   **$950**

BASKET: 1870; pink, green; appliqué handles on baskets, diamond set, Sawtooth border; some color loss overall and in spots, some stains; excellent assembly and quilting; 70 × 60   **$300**

BASKET: 1880s; greens, blues; appliqué handles, slight overall fade; very good assembly, small appliqué stitches, small quilting stitches, vine and cable quilting; 70 × 78   **$127**

BASKET: 1880s; purple, red, white; red border, appliqué and machine applied handles, slight overall fade, worn binding; grid quilting, straight-line quilting on border; 72 × 82   **$650**

BASKET: 1880s; rose-red on white; appliqué handles on baskets, small area of restoration, minimal use; 81 × 81   **$900**

BASKET: 1890s; blue on white; appliqué handles, very worn binding, much overall fade, much use and washing; 76 × 72   **$450**

BASKET: late 1800s; blue on white; no handles on baskets, few slight stains, minimal quilting in straight lines, diamond quilting on border; 78 × 82   **$525**

BASKET: 1890s; browns, pinks; no handles on baskets, every basket different, slightly worn overall, browns slightly faded; 72 × 78   **$325**

BASKET: 1890s; pink, brown, light blue; appliqué handles, overall fade, well washed; straight-line quilting; 70 × 78   **$400**

BASKET: 1890s; red and white; appliqué handles, red border, good-to-excellent condition, minimal use; fair assembly, hand quilting on baskets and blocks, machine quilting on border; 76 × 88   **$725**

BASKET: early 1900s; pinks, blues; appliqué handles; overall fade, uneven appliqué stitches, outline quilting; 70 × 76   **$400**

BASKET: 1920s; rose-pink, white; no handles, blocks on point with white sets, overall fade, some use; feather ring quilting in white sets, grid quilting on baskets and overall; 68 × 74   **$435**

BASKET: 1920s; browns, greens; no handles, faded overall, well washed and used; 78 × 80   **$500**

BASKET: 1930; greens; no handles on baskets; from Ohio; 84 × 78   **$450**

CACTUS BASKET: late 1800s; reds, browns; tied, no quilting; print backing, some stains; 72 × 80   **$195**

CACTUS BASKET: 1890s; red and white; three-inch-tall baskets arranged in two rows, one white border, one red-and-white diamond border; excellent condition, unused, washed once, very small quilting stitches in wreaths and straight lines, excellent assembly; 70 × 64   **$1,000**

CACTUS BASKET: 1930s; red, yellow, blue, green; red sashing, overall fade, minimal quilting, straight-line quilting in sashing; 80 × 78   **$375**

CACTUS BASKET: 1930s; pink and peach; 62 × 78   **$375**

CACTUS BASKET: 1930s; red, brown; 63 × 85   **$395**

CACTUS BASKET: 1930s; green, red, blue; 85 × 75 $425

CACTUS BASKET: 1930s; pink on white; some yellowing of white, multiple washings; 78 × 82 $425

CACTUS BASKET VARIATION: late 1930s; multicolored; set on point, lavender print backing, some stains, overall fabric aging and yellowing, little wear; no quilting, tied; 66 × 82 $95

CAT AND MICE: 1900; red; unused; 65 × 72 $700

A very popular pattern, Churn Dash is just one of the common tools, occupations, household items, and clothing for which quilt blocks are named. Others are Reel (for a spool used for wool), the Dresden Plate, Pickle Dish, Chips and Whetstone, Broken Dishes, and Fan.

CHURN DASH: 1880; red, brown; few stains; 78 × 82 $550

CHURN DASH: 1885–1890; navy blue, pink, white; minimal use, few age spots; lots of chain and straight-line quilting; 80 × 80 $425

CHURN DASH: 1890s; red, green, brown, white; worn binding, some fabric deterioration in browns, some mildew spots; straight-line and scallop quilting; 64 × 80 $500

CHURN DASH: 1890s; red and white; slight overall fade; 70 × 68 $525

CHURN DASH: late 1800s; red, blue, pink, white; pink border, stained back, overall fade, well used, washed; very good assembly, nearly all junctions match; straight-line quilting; 64 × 76 $450

CHURN DASH: early 1900s; reds, rose, maroon, white; rose sets, some overall wear, fabric deterioration in reds, worn binding; fair-quality quilting, outline; 70 × 75 $275

CHURN DASH: 1920; indigos; indigo binding, minimal use, minimal wash, small quilting stitches, feather and wreath quilting; 74 × 84 $895

CHURN DASH: 1930; multicolored; zigzag sashing, some feed bag fabrics, excellent condition; excellent assembly, good quilting in Fan designs; 73 × 74 $225

DELECTABLE MOUNTAINS: 1875–1885; multicolored; green chevron border, green edge; signed, maker known; fair condition, many rust stains, much fabric loss, outline and fan quilting; 70 × 84 $450

Names for quilt blocks came from any number of sources.
The Delectable Mountains block was named for a line in the
popular book Pilgrim's Progress.

DELECTABLE MOUNTAINS: 1880–1890; red on white; cut-out corners for four-poster bed; overall soiling and yellowing, some stains; excellent assembly, lots of straight-line and outline quilting; 92 × 80 $595

DELECTABLE MOUNTAINS: 1890s; red and white; very faded overall, some small stains, worn binding, multiple sashings; outline quilting, very good assembly; 70 × 78 $750

DELECTABLE MOUNTAINS: 1890; blue prints, white; slight overall fade, some stains; blue sashing with square quilting; 72 × 84 $1,500

DELECTABLE MOUNTAINS: 1930s; dark green, white; excellent condition, unused, unwashed; straight-line echo quilting; 68 × 78 $700

DELECTABLE MOUNTAINS: 1930s; pale green; unused, circle and star quilting; 70 × 86 $850

DOUBLE NINE-PATCH: 1920s; black, rose, maroon, cream; minimal use, small quilting stitches, straight-line quilting overall; 84 × 70 $295

FLOWER BASKET: late 1930s; pinks and greens; kit quilt, vine and leaf quilting with some small areas of trapunto and some crewel work; 78 × 96
          $1,250

GARDEN MAZE: 1920s; yellow, gold, pink, brown; minimal use, straight-line quilting overall; 63 × 80 $395

GRANDMOTHER'S BASKET: 1800; green and red; slight overall fade, lots of medallion quilting; 69 × 74 $975

H BLOCK: 1930s; light green on white; four H's per square, squares set on point with white sets, green double border; slight overall fade; 82 × 90 $675

MAPLE LEAF: 1920s; multiprints and solids; triple border on two sides, pink binding; diagonal straight-line quilting overall; 86 × 57 $250

MONKEY WRENCH: 1880s; deep salmon red; slight overall fade; found in Colorado; 63 × 77 $600

MONKEY WRENCH: early 1890s; black and white; some patched spots, fair-to-good condition, overall fade; excellent assembly, minimally quilted; 45 × 72 $495

The Wrench or Monkey Wrench block is just one of many quilt blocks inspired by common household tools and work. Others include Anvil, Ship's Wheel, Water Mill, Sawtooth, and Carpenter's Wheel.

MONKEY WRENCH: 1890s; blues, browns, white; set on point with white blocks, slight overall fade, minimal use; feather wreath quilting in white sets, very good assembly, 78 × 82 — $500

MONKEY WRENCH: 1890s; blue and white; feather quilting; 72 × 78 — $650

MONKEY WRENCH: late 1800s; soft pink on white; excellent quilting; 64 × 76 — $695

NINE-PATCH: 1800; brown, cheddar, red; all homespun wools, madder-dyed reds, some fabric loss; signed, from South Carolina; 72 × 78 — $3,200

NINE-PATCH: late 1800s; red and navy on white; unused, excellent condition, vivid reds; 72 × 78 — $895

NINE-PATCH: 1850; browns; some burgundy and indigo fabrics look home dyed; from Texas, makers known; 80 × 62 — $2,700

NINE-PATCH: 1880s; indigo; slight overall fade and soiling; simple straight-line quilting; 82 × 80 — $650

NINE-PATCH: 1890–1900; red and white; flower sack backing with printing; from Missouri; 83 × 62 — $500

NINE-PATCH: late 1800s; dark red, blue, tan; minimal use; 75 × 67 — $525

NINE-PATCH: late 1800s; red, medium blue; some faded areas; from Pennsylvania; 78 × 82 — $575

The use of light and dark fabrics set in the Barn Raising style is not limited to Log Cabin quilts. One quiltmaker used a Nine-patch pattern with the block half dark fabrics and half light to get the same telescoping optical illusion.

Made in the early 1900s in black and white, this Snail's Trail variation of the Wrench pattern shows how graphic and interesting a simple pattern in two colors can be. Even though this quilt has a few repairs, some small spots, and is faded overall, it is a good find.

NINE-PATCH: early 1900s; browns, pinks, multicolored; very worn overall, worn binding, 78 × 60 $300

NINE-PATCH: early 1900s; black, navy, red; worn binding, faded overall; 78 × 88 $330

NINE-PATCH: early 1900s; reds, blues, greens, rose; set on point with green calico sashing, border on two sides; unwashed, unused, few spots, straight-line diagonal quilting; 79 × 69 $450

NINE-PATCH: early 1900s; pink on pink and white; white sets, overall fade, some stains; very good assembly, small quilting stitches, star quilting in white sets, chevron quilting in Nine-patch blocks; 84 x 66 $495

NINE-PATCH: 1900; red and white; few small stains, unused, unwashed; straight-line and cable quilting; 70 × 76 $775

NINE-PATCH: 1910s; green, blue, pinks; green print sashing, one side faded, well used, worn binding; curved and clamshell quilting, very good assembly; 70 × 80 $350

Made of scrap bag fabrics in shades of browns, some of which look berry-dyed, this Nine-patch was completed in 1850 in Texas. The quilting is well done, but the color balance and assembly could be better.

NINE-PATCH: 1910s; red and white; slight overall fade, minimal use, red border; concentric circle quilting, cable quilting on border; 72 × 78 $650

NINE-PATCH: 1920s; red, blues, white; set on point with white sets, overall fade and wear, worn binding; concentric circle quilting; 80 x 72 $400

NINE-PATCH: 1930s; light blue, multicolors; border on two sides, few spots, overall use, well washed; 65 × 82 $125

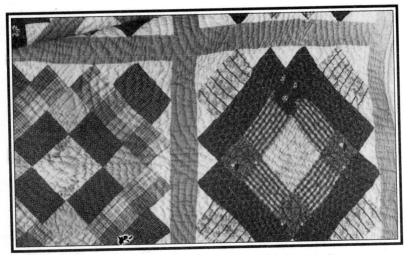

A closer look at the same Nine-patch shows better color balance in the individual squares than in the whole quilt. The less-than-good assembly can also be noted, especially where the sashing is joined.

NINE-PATCH: early 1930s; red, off-white; scalloped edge; 66 × 78 $400

NINE-PATCH: 1930s; pink; overall fade, spots of wear, doll's quilt; 24 × 24 $135

NINE-PATCH: 1930s; blue, pink; overall faded and worn; 70 × 100 $375

NINE-PATCH: 1930s; red, blue; minimal use, minimal quilting; 70 × 100 $495

NINE-PATCH: 1940; reds, yellows, multicolors; white sets, red border, slight overall discoloration; very good assembly, small quilting stitches, cable quilting in border; 78 × 80 $350

NINE-PATCH AND BABY BLOCK VARIATION: 1930s; yellow; print sashing, some overall stains, machine-applied binding; 80 × 72 $145

NINE-PATCH OF TINY SQUARES: 1883; pink, yellow, green (faded to mustard-gold); dated and signed; 2,286 tiny pieces, pink on pink border; slight overall fade and color changes; 60 × 68 $475

NINE-PATCH VARIATION: late 1800s; red on white; one large central square with Nine-patch inside, variation squares in corners, double red border, diamond quilting overall; 72 × 78 $598

NINE-PATCH VARIATION: early 1900s; peach on white; pointed edge; 76 × 82 $335

NINE-PATCH VARIATION: 1930s; aqua-blue; few small tears; 73 × 82 $495

NINE-PATCH WILD GOOSE CHASE: 1830s; mustard, reds, browns; set on point with white sets, fabric loss in aniline browns, mustard may be faded green, overall fade, overall soiling; excellent quilting, floral circle quilting in white sets; 84 × 74   **$450**

OHIO STAR: 1880s; blue on white; blue border, minimal use, minimal washing; straight-line quilting; 72 × 82   **$350**

OHIO STAR: early 1900s; red, white; white sets, some color loss in reds, few slight repairs, straight-line quilting overall; 70 × 76   **$365**

OHIO STAR: 1920s; blues, white; blue border, excellent condition, unwashed, unused; 76 × 78   **$450**

OHIO STAR: 1930s; light blue, white; faded overall; 72 × 82   **$375**

OHIO STAR: 1930s; green on white; some overall and spot stains; minimal quilting, large stitches; 70 × 83   **$390**

The Pine Tree is the most authentically American symbol, and was used on coins in Colonial Massachusetts, on flags during the Revolution, and on quilts to the present day.

PINE TREE: late 1800s; blue on white; blue backing and edge, slight overall fade; 68 × 72   **$500**

PINE TREE: 1870; green on white; green border and sashing with feather quilting; all junctions match, very good quilting; 68 × 84   **$1,250**

Although it's possible to create stunning optical illusions with some different placements of the Pine Tree block, most quiltmakers use the traditional style of setting them on point in rows, so that each tree stands individually. Pine Tree variations include Tree Of Paradise, Tree of Life, Tree of Temptation, and Apple Tree. Add different leaves and get Cherry Tree or Little Beech Tree. Use diamonds and have Lozenge Tree and Live Oak Tree.

Made in 1870, this dark-green-on-white Pine Tree shows well-done grid and feather quilting. The trees are all well assembled and the overall look is quite pleasing.

PINE TREE: 1920s; red on white; very little quilting; 70 × 80   **$225**

PINE TREE: 1920; green, brown; overall fade, worn binding; 78 × 76   **$550**

PINE TREE: 1925; dark rose, cream; dated, maker known; on point with rose sets, excellent condition, unused, unwashed; straight-line quilting overall; 65 × 90   **$550**

PINE TREE: 1930s; seafoam green; alternately scalloped and pointed edges; 74 × 86   **$450**

PINWHEEL NINE-PATCH: 1850; pumpkin, green; set on point with green sets, triple border, very good condition, minimal use and washings; very good assembly, small quilting stitches, feather wreath quilting in green sets, grid quilting in squares; 70 × 80   **$650**

PINWHEEL STAR VARIATION: late 1800s; rose, multicolored prints; overall fade; from Connecticut; 76 × 80   **$325**

ROLLING STONE: 1890s; red on white; set on point with white squares; minimal use, slight overall fade, some fabric loss, white discolored overall; fair-to-poor machine assembly, good hand quilting, feather quilting on white sets, double line on squares; 60 × 54   **$415**

ROLLING STONE: 1900; blues, whites; all tiny prints or polka dots, blue polka dot border; 66 × 79   **$1,050**

SAWTOOTH: 1870s; grays on white; all grays with tiny prints; maker known, from Missouri; 64 × 73   **$850**

SAWTOOTH PATCH: 1920s; red and white; overall fade, straight-line quilting overall; 72 × 80   **$500**

Besides Shoo-Fly, nature has supplied quilters with other names, including Snail's Trail, Sunburst, Swallow, Autumn Leaves, Four Winds, Bird's Nest, Spider Web, Tea Leaf, Dove, Butterfly, Hens and Chickens, Grapevine, and Honeycomb.

SHOO FLY: 1920; blue on white; double border; from Iowa; unwashed, unused, straight-line quilting overall; 78 × 88   **$695**

SHOO FLY MAZE: 1880s; red, white, black; Sawtooth border, fabrics of red calico and white with tiny black polka dots, very unusual and graphic; from Pennsylvania; minimal quilting; 74 × 75   **$875**

SNOWBALL AND PERIWINKLE: 1920; blue; lap quilt; maker known, from Missouri; 50 × 60   **$375**

The Turkey Tracks block was originally called the Wandering Foot. Superstition said that a husband who slept under such a quilt would be taken up by wanderlust and the wife could end up following her husband to the ends of the earth—or, at best, to a lonely cabin on the prairie. In an attempt to end the superstition, the name was changed to Turkey Tracks and the pattern once again became popular.

TURKEY TRACKS: 1890; rusty red, green; yellowed overall, some rust stains; small quilting stitches, all junctions match; from New York; 92 × 79   **$795**

A variation of a Sawtooth Patch block, this 1880s quilt was made in Missouri in the 1880–1890 time period. The colors, on white, are shades of grays and taupe, a very neutral look.

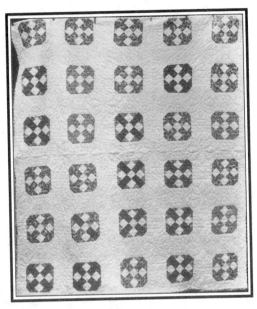

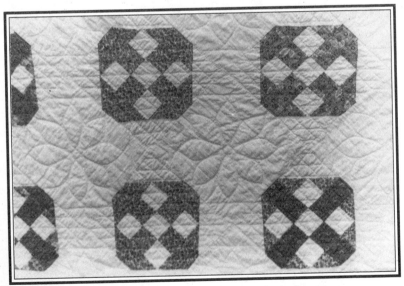

In close-up, the white set can be seen. The quilting, in large daisy shapes and even gridwork, is excellent, as are the assembly and overall balance of the quilt.

TURKEY TRACKS: early 1900s; red, green, white; overall fade, slightly worn binding, multiple washings; 72 × 84   **$650**

VARIABLE STAR: 1930s; green, brown; excellent condition, unwashed; circle quilting; 68 × 72   **$600**

Pieced Quilt Tops

A quilt top is, of course, simply an unfinished quilt. The original quiltmaker put the pieces together, and then, for some unknown reason, never completed it. There are several advantages to collecting quilt tops.

Since they were never completed they were also never used, so most are in very good condition compared to completed quilts of the same age. Since they managed to survive without being turned into dust rags, they probably had some value to someone or were of a unique pattern, so you can have a more difficult patterned piece for less money. They are easier to handle, clean, and hang than completed quilts. You can see the assembly, and better judge the condition of the fabrics without all that batting and backing in the way.

Of course, you don't get any lovely quilting, but you can have the top filled and quilted if you wish. And if you are a quilter, you can have the pleasure of finishing a wonderful quilt yourself, incorporating something of you into an antique that will have even greater value to your grandchildren.

Most quilt dealers carry quilt tops and will look out for them for you if that's the way you want to go. They are treasures waiting to be completed.

BLAZING STAR: 1920s; pink, white, multicolored lights and darks; top only, ginghams, chambrays, solids; 72 × 85   **$80**

BLOCKED STARS: 1930s; red, white, blue; top only, set on point with white sets, eight-point star in center, six-point stars around; some puckers at joints, some loose stitches; 80 × 72   **$75**

BOW TIE: 1920; blue; top only; 78 × 80   **$145**

BOW TIE: 1940; black, taupe; top only, wool crepe and cotton, triple border on one side; 76 × 76   **$125**

BROKEN DISHES: 1930s; pastel prints and solids; top only, pink sets and border; 78 × 82   **$85**

BROKEN STAR AND COURTHOUSE STEPS COMBINATION: 1890s; red, white, gray; top only; few stains, machine assembly in squares; 70 × 80   **$275**

BROKEN STAR: 1930s; yellow, pink, multicolored bold and pastel prints; top only, excellent assembly, junctions match; 108 × 90   **$95**

CACTUS BASKET: 1930; multicolored; top only, set alternately with white blocks, embroidered flowers in baskets, machine assembled; 64 x 74   **$195**

CRAZY QUILT: late 1800s; turquoise-blue, hot pink, orange; top only, very vibrant, all bold colors, all silks; each block different, individual; found in California; 65 × 65   **$595**

CRAZY QUILT: late 1800s; black, burgundy; top only, satins, ribbons; some fabric deterioration, some pieces missing; 54 × 70   **$175**

CRAZY QUILT (FOUR-PATCH, ROMAN WALL VARIATION): 1920–1930; multicolored; top only, newspaper stiffeners on back, black-and-white border; 80 × 72   **$250**

CROWN OF THORNS: early 1900s; rose, red, lights, darks; top only, rose sets, few small age spots; 78 × 67   **$125**

DOUBLE IRISH CHAIN: 1880–1890; rust, green, cream; top only, side border; some stains, soiling, overall fade, color loss in places; 88 × 100   **$250**

DOUBLE T: 1940s; reds; top only, set on point with red blocks; excellent assembly, excellent condition; 54 × 54   **$95**

DOUBLE WEDDING RING: 1940s; pastels; top only, scalloped self-border, machine pieced, some stains; 62 × 84   **$245**

This 1940s Double T quilt top has blocks set on point with red gingham squares. Its excellent condition and assembly would make quilting it a wonderful project for a modern quiltmaker.

> *The Great Depression added its share of quilt block pattern names to a quilter's repertoire. Economy came to be in 1933, Depression in 1937, Thrifty and the Thrifty Wife in 1939. A block called Hard Times was also created during this period.*

ECONOMY: 1890–1910; blues, grays, maroon; top only, gray sets, triple border on two sides, double border on other two sides; 66 × 83   **$125**

ECONOMY: 1930s; bright solids, multiprints; top only, red sashing, machine assembled; 83 × 75   **$75**

FIELD OF STARS: 1930; red, white, blue; top only; 74 × 86   **$245**

GARDEN OF EDEN VARIATION: 1930s; blue on white; top only, some stains, machine pieced; 92 × 94   **$225**

GARFIELD MONUMENT: 1881; beige, brown, gold; top only, excellent condition; Brickyard variation, top of monument appliquéd, some hand assembly, some machine piecing, edging all machine applied; 68 × 84   **$185**

GOOSE IN A POND: 1900; blue, lavender, pink; top only, excellent condition, excellent assembly; 36 × 90   **$75**

GRANDMOTHER'S FAN: early 1900s; darks, multicolored; top only, silks, velvets, wools, double border; fair condition, some fabric deterioration, yellow feather topstitching on all piece edges, crazy quilt style; 78 × 89   **$85**

GRANDMOTHER'S FLOWER BASKET: 1940s; multipastels; top only, set on point, appliqué handles, Brick Bar border, slight fade in one area; 100 × 80   **$188**

GRANDMOTHER'S FLOWER GARDEN: 1920s; peach, solid brights, multiprints; top only, peach centers of flowers; 80 × 90   **$105**

JOSEPH'S COAT: 1930s; yellow, multicolors; top only, scalloped edge, few stains; 70 × 93   **$75**

LEMOYNE STAR: 1870; tan, blues; top only, star blocks alternate with plain blocks of print fabric, some overall fabric deterioration; excellent assembly; 90 × 90   **$295**

LEMOYNE STAR: 1880s; red, white, blue; top only, child's quilt; 40 x 36   **$175**

LEMOYNE STAR: late 1920s; multicolored prints; top only, feather stitch embroidery around stars; 68 × 68   **$75**

LOG CABIN: late 1800s; multicolored; top only, sugar and tea sack fabrics with some satins, very worn, many tears, much fabric deterioration; 82 × 72
$68

LOG CABIN (WINDMILL): 1930; pastels; top only, white chintz background, some age spots on background; 74 × 86 **$285**

LOG CABIN: 1940s; black and white, reds; top only, large logs, distinctive arrangement of colors; 70 × 80 **$45**

LONE STAR: 1940s; red, pinks, pastels; top only, pink background; 74 × 74 **$75**

MEDALLION ROMAN STRIPE: 1870; multicolored; top only, Roman Stripe border; 76 × 72 **$325**

NINE-PATCH: 1930s; rose, gray, blue, white; top only, rose sashing and border; machine pieced; 90 × 73 **$110**

NINE-PATCH: 1940s; blacks, multicolors; top only; 45 × 63 **$29**

NINE-PATCH DIAMOND FRIENDSHIP: 1867; green, brown, pink, rust; top only, 48 legible names and sayings, stamped and written; from New Hampshire, one square from Maine; many geometric prints, some stains, all points and junctions match, four-poster cutout; 82 × 85 **$285**

OCEAN WAVES: early 1900s; green, multicolors; top only, green sets; 74 × 95 **$85**

OCEAN WAVES: 1930s; multicolored prints and solids; top only, unbleached muslin sets; 86 × 70 **$75**

OCEAN WAVES: 1930; multicolored; top only, all prints; hand and machine assembly, puckers around center blocks, many junctions don't match; 70 × 82
$265

PINEAPPLE COURTHOUSE STEPS: late 1930s; multicolored; top only, all silks, some tears, some fabric deterioration, few pieces missing; 72 × 72 **$165**

PINEAPPLE LOG CABIN: 1870s; multicolored; top only, all silk, some fabric loss in some silks, has been rebound, pineapples built on hexagon foundation; from North Carolina; 86 × 90 **$2,900**

PINEAPPLE LOG CABIN: early 1900s; green, gold, red; top only, African-American; from family in Missouri; spot and overall fade, excellent assembly; 88 × 80 **$225**

PYRAMIDS: 1920s; multicolored lights and darks; top only, large Pyramids pieces, one edge damaged; 83 × 80 **$35**

ROLLING STONE: 1920s; reds, blues, grays; top only, set on point, zigzag border; hand and machine pieced; 84 × 70 **$110**

ROMAN STRIPE SQUARES: late 1800s; top only, one square damaged on one side; 76 × 66 **$65**

SCHOOL HOUSE: late 1800s; indigo prints; top only; from New England; 80 × 82 **$450**

SCHOOL HOUSE: 1920s; brown, rust, blues, tan; top only, tan muslin sashing and border; 70 × 84 **$90**

> *Early in this century, many popular women's magazines published quilt patterns. The Skyrocket pattern was first published in* Women's World *magazine in February 1928.*

SKYROCKET: late 1930s; red, blue; top only, purple print sashing, good color balance, fair assembly, excellent condition; 72 × 72 **$155**

STAR AND CROSS VARIATION: 1880s; multicolored; top only, album quilt; from Vermont; signed in center squares, not in indelible ink; excellent condition, although a few signatures have run; excellent assembly; 80 × 80 **$160**

STAR OF BETHLEHEM: 1990; red, yellow, blue, gray; top only, red frame and white border, white sets; lines marked for feather wreath quilting in white sets, outline on star, not all points match, some hand assembly, some machine assembly; 76 × 76 **$285**

TOBACCO SILK FLAGS: 1920s; deep reds; top only; from New Jersey; some embroidery around flags; 70 × 83 **$2,300**

TREE OF LIFE: 1930s; green on white; top only, Sawtooth sash; 72 × 94 **$250**

CHAPTER ELEVEN
ANTIQUE APPLIQUÉ QUILTS

Patchwork quilt tops that are assembled by sewing smaller fabric pieces to a fabric ground are called appliqué. In very early quilts, appliqué was done in the Broderie-Perse method, using the central medallion style. Typical of this is the Tree of Life, a pattern many quiltmakers varied later using conventional appliqué, creating their own branches, leaves, and flowers instead of cutting the design out whole from printed cloth. Broderie-Perse was awkward work because it involved handling large pieces of cloth. Block-style appliqué began in the early 1700s. Originally used on clothing, it soon found its way into quilts.

There are fewer named pattern blocks for appliqué than there are for pieced blocks. This isn't because appliquéers were any less creative but because many appliqué quilts are made from individual designs. There are four basic appliqué designs from which all others are inspired. They are the rose, wreath, leaf cluster, and princess feather. Some appliqué patterns were much copied and so earned names of their own. Whig Rose, Rose of Sharon, Sunbonnet Sue, Oak Leaf, and some Pennsylvania Dutch quilt patterns are among this group.

But most often, since quiltmakers knew appliqué technique so well they could experiment, they created their own designs copying nature, technology, and common and rare items around them. They borrowed designs from India shawls and carpets just as pieced-block creators copied from ancient mosaic floor and wall patterns. In this way, peacocks, pomegranates, "pickle pears," baskets, flowers, animals, and birds were all represented on quilts using appliqué methods. Quiltmakers also incorporated aspects of their lives, drawing on religion, work, family, politics, and social events for appliqué designs.

They drew their designs freehand, traced them from other patterns, even used household objects to trace around, and then cut out the shapes they needed.

Appliqué quilts were almost always considered best quilts. They required fine, exacting work. They were more time-consuming than most pieced blocks. They also used more fabric. For the elaborate Baltimore Album quilts, fabric was bought specifically for the quilt. Appliqué was considered a sign of affluence in Colonial America and in the South. Scraps were rarely used in

An unusual-looking figure, perhaps an attempt at a Pineapple or a Music Lyre, repeats in this red-on-white quilt with white sashing. The figures are surrounded by some lovely feather quilting from the late 1800s.

appliqués made as show or best quilts. Many of them survive today because they were so highly valued by the original makers and recipients.

The price list for appliqué quilts follows. You might want to review chapter 9, "How to Use This Guide," to refresh your memory about the definitions of the terms included in the listings.

ALBUM SAMPLER: 1860; green, red; from Pennsylvania; a few stains, some fabric deterioration, fern border; 78 × 78 $2,600

ANIMALS, BIRDS, DRAGONS: 1884; red on white, signed and dated, muslin backing; 78 × 80 $825

BASKETS: 1930s–1940s; brown; gold sashing in narrow overlay strips, machine appliqué, purchased edging for basket handles, 72 × 90 $345

BLOSSOMS: 1920s; red, yellow, green, on white; pair of quilts, machine appliqué, excellent condition, unused, few tiny stains; tiny quilting stitches, waffle quilting overall, narrow cable quilting on border; 78 × 80 (price for the pair) $1,200

BIRDS ON VINE: 1940s; red, teal; pair of quilts; from Iowa; kit quilts; 74 × 93 (price for both) $1,200

This Pennsylvania Dutch contemporary appliqué of reds and greens is representative of this style of quilt. It could be an appealing addition to a collection.

BRIDE'S QUILT: 1920; red hearts on white; from Texas; unusual pattern; 60 × 72 $325

CARNATION: 1880; red and green; white sets, binding worn, overall fade, fabric deterioration in reds; exquisite tiny appliqué stitches, triple bar quilting overall, four-feather quilting in white sets; 98 × 98 $540

CAROLINA LILY: 1930s; pink; 70 × 78 $435

COCK'S COMB AND VINING: 1840–1860; red, gold, green; from central Ohio; reverse appliqué border, unwashed, mint condition, line quilting overall; 90 × 90 $5,400

CROWNS AND THORNS: 1920s; red, green, yellow; machine-attached red stripe border, chain quilting on border, interlocking circles and echo quilting elsewhere, very faded overall; 72 × 72 $385

DOGWOOD: 1920s; rose-pink, green; triple border, Prairie Point edge, very good condition, minimal use; many dogwood blossoms, very close together, some uneven appliqué stitches; 84 × 70 $650

DOGWOOD: 1930; pinks, greens; from Ohio; 74 × 88 $575

DOUBLE TULIP: 1840; red, green, white; from Pennsylvania; 10-inch border with vines and buds, stippled quilting with wandering feather pattern; 95 × 105   **$3,800**

EIGHT-POINT STARS: 1900; red and white, ten stars on quilt, red border; overall fade and wear; lots of straight-line quilting; 50 × 75   **$375**

FLORAL: 1920s; pink, yellow, green, blue; pink wild roses, green leaves; excellent tiny appliqué stitches, monogram in quilt center; feather, circle, crisscross straight-line quilting; 70 × 80   **$425**

FLORAL: 1930s–1940s; blue and light blue on white; from Ohio; very small appliqué stitches, few tiny tears, unwashed, outline quilting; 76 × 92

$775

FLORAL WITH DAISIES: 1930; pink, green; unwashed, unused, quilting lines remain, machine assembled, quilting of squares and daisies on flowers, quilting in curves on border; 80 × 80   **$1,500**

FLOWER (ONE BLOSSOM): late 1800s; red, green; minimal use, simple overall quilting; found in California; 80 × 80   **$1,000**

The flowers look like thistles in this beautiful red-and-green appliqué from the 1860s. Close triple lines, wreaths, and leaves in the quilting are indicative of the care the maker put into this quilt.

FLOWERS: 1920; pink and green; flowers in five squares set with pink and green squares, pink and green rectangle block border; unwashed, some age spots; 90 × 70   **$285**

FLOWERS: 1930s; pink, orange, yellow; pair of twin quilts; 72 × 56 (price for each)   **$400**

FLOWERS: 1930s; yellow, green; overall fade, few tears, some loose appliqué stitches, outline quilting, feather wreath quilting in center; 72 × 80
$575

FLOWERS: 1930; pastels; 76 × 82   **$595**

FLOWERS: 1930; pink, lavender; 76 × 84   **$595**

FLOWERS AND BUTTERFLY: 1930; pink; 82 × 82   **$550**

FLOWERS AND KITTENS: 1940; pinks; crib quilt from Pennsylvania, embroidery on appliqués; 84 × 82   **$225**

FLOWERS AND LEAVES: 1860; red and green; many mildew stains, cotton debris inside; very tiny stitches; 88 × 88   **$750**

FLOWERS AND FERNS: 1860–1870; red, green on white; some overall soiling and some spots; feather, wreath, and triple-line quilting; 84 × 84   **$1,600**

FLOWERS AND VINES: 1930; reds, greens; from Pennsylvania; 72 x 80
$600

FLOWERS IN BASKETS: 1930; pastels; 72 × 86   **$300**

FLOWERS IN POTS: 1920s; purple, green; flowers look Deco, in blocks set on point, narrow green sashing with white corners, very good condition, slight overall fade; very good work, small appliqué stitches, diamond and outline quilting; 80 × 90   **$750**

FLOWERS IN A POT: 1930s; beige, multicolored prints; scalloped edge; 78 × 86   **$495**

FLOWERS OF SPRING: 1930s; red, lavender, yellow, blue, rose on white; possibly kit quilt, machine applied lavender border, matched color buttonhole stitching on flower edges; unwashed, unused, very good work, small appliqué stitches; 94 × 70   **$595**

FREE-FORM: 1980s; red on white; red edging, white border with diagonal quilting, straight-line quilting overall, some color loss, tiny appliqué stitches; 70 × 70   **$485**

FREE-FORM FLOWERS IN POTS: 1850s; red, green on white; overall fade, some washings, some areas of trapunto work; 72 × 80   **$2,500**

HEXAGONS: 1833; red, white, green; dated and signed; chintz fabric, center frame appliqué in hexagons with diagonal quilting, three chintz borders, clamshell quilting on two outer borders; 104 x 104   **$6,500**

This 1940s whimsical crib quilt has strawberry Ice Cream Cones with tan cones and sashing.

ICE CREAM CONES: 1940s; strawberry, tan, white; crib quilt, very good outline quilting; 30 × 40 **$250**

IRISES: 1920s; lavender, green; swag border with bows, very slight overall fade, minimal use, few washings; mostly very good appliqué, few stitches uneven, grid quilting overall; 76 × 84 **$850**

LEAVES: 1850s; red and green; cotton debris in very thin batting, fair to good condition, slight overall fade, greens fading to khaki, overall soiling; tiny appliqué stitches, some loose; minimal straight-line quilting; 107 × 107 **$875**

LEAVES: 1875; red, white, blue; overall wear and fade; 66 × 89 **$750**

LEAVES: 1880; red on white; originally from Quebec; 66 × 72 **$395**

LEAVES AND STAR FLOWERS: 1880s; rusty red, green; rusty red print sashing, overall and spot stains, some fabric deterioration; minimal straight-line quilting; 76 × 76 **$445**

MEDALLION SAMPLER: 1850s; red, brown, cheddar, teal on white; 40 small medallions surrounding large center one, flowers in pots appliquéd around border; quilting of hearts, hands, and flowers; from Pennsylvania; 84 × 84 **$12,500**

MEXICAN ROSE: late 1800s; pink on white; some fiber loss, diamond quilting on border, shell quilting around roses; 80 × 86 **$385**

MEXICAN ROSE: early 1900s; pink, green, white; tiny appliqué stitches, orange flower centers, minimal use, never washed; feather circle quilting in center, straight-line and zigzag quilting on border; 78 × 78 **$600**

MORNING GLORY: 1920s; blue, green, lavender; scalloped border, overall fade and wear, chin edge cut down and replaced; very small appliqué stitches; 80 × 70 **$165**

MORNING GLORY: 1930s; pastels, gold; salvaged from larger damaged quilt; new binding, excellent appliqué stitches; 65 × 70 **$95**

MUSTARD SUN AND RED HEARTS: late 1800s; mustard-gold, red, and blue; faded overall, blue sashing, tiny appliqué stitches, chevron quilting on sashing; 72 × 68 **$2,350**

The eagle was used extensively in quilts during and shortly after the War of 1812. It resurfaced in popularity in 1846 during the Mexican War and again during the Civil War. The eagle's popularity in quilts has always been tied to times of intense patriotism.

NORTH CAROLINA LILY: 1840s; red and green on white; lilies alternate with eagles and small birds; from North Carolina; double border, circular and medallion quilting; 78 × 88 **$3,400**

NORTH CAROLINA LILY: 1895–1900; beige, red; black-and-white polka dot background, very country look, lilies placed horizontally; some age spots; unwashed; diamond quilting overall; 78 × 80 **$425**

NORTH CAROLINA LILY: 1930s; green, rose; small stitches; 72 x 84

$125

OAK LEAF REEL: 1920; blue on white; wavy edge with blue binding, slight overall fade; fair-to-good work, some appliqué stitches large and/or uneven; 90 × 100 **$695**

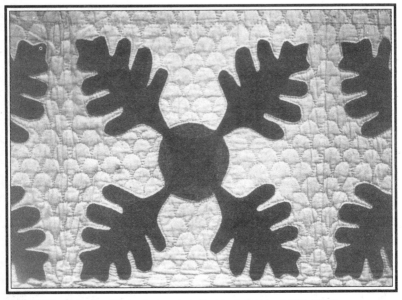

Red fabric with tiny yellow sprigs accents the center circles of this 1850s
Oak Leaf appliqué. The leaves are navy and green.

OAK LEAF REEL: 1930s; pink on white; pink border, matching pillow
sham, some slight stains, minimal use; feather wreath quilting between the
reels, grid quilting overall, feather quilting on border, excellent quilting, very
small stitches; 72 × 72 $450

OAK LEAVES: 1850; navy, green; accents of red print; tiny, even stitches;
clamshell quilting; 76 × 80 $2,220

OAK LEAVES: 1875; beige, white, red; some joints of oak leaves have
appliqué hearts; slightly worn binding, some age spots, overall wear; lots of
excellent quilting in hearts, garlands, and straight lines; 90 × 90 $475

*The Oak Leaf, a popular appliqué design, has also been adapted to
pieced quilt blocks, and is the symbol of strength and virility.*

The overall look of the same quilt, whole, is very graphic with very well done clamshell quilting and a strong border.

OAK LEAVES: 1930s; yellow on white; minimal use, quilting lines remain, tiny stitches in line quilting overall; 72 × 82 $495

OAK LEAVES: 1938; red on white; dated, slight overall fade, appliqué triangles on edge, circle quilting; 86 × 66 $2,000

OAK LEAVES AND ACORN: 1940s; green, gold, yellow on white; kit quilt, green curved edge, unused, excellent oak leaf and acorn quilting; 80 × 92

$750

OHIO ROSE: late 1800s; red, blue, yellow; embroidered stems, 11 stitches per inch, feather and leaf quilting on border, diagonal quilting on blocks; 67 × 80
$975

OHIO ROSE: 1930; red, green; some use, washed, stain in one corner; tiny appliqué stitches, circle and straight-line quilting; 72 × 78 $695

OHIO ROSE: 1930; yellow; 78 × 78 $750

OHIO ROSE: 1930s; hot pink, Depression green; 72 × 86 $570

ORANGES AND ORANGE BLOSSOMS: 1930s; orange, green, yellow; green triangle border, green edging; excellent condition, unused, unwashed; excellent work, small appliqué stitches; tree, leaf, and cable quilting; 79 × 93 $750

PANSIES: 1930s; blues, white; flowers on white block set with blue blocks, blue border, slight overall discoloration, excellent condition, unused, unwashed; very good work; tiny, even appliqué stitches; pansy quilting in blue sets, straight-line quilting overall, grid quilting on border; 74 × 74   **$750**

PARCHEESI BOARD: 1920s; yellow, green, rose, blue, all brights; fans appliquéd in large circles make Parcheesi Board with bars between circles for "pathways," pink topstitching on edges of circles; excellent condition, unwashed, unused, quilting lines remain; fleur-de-lis, scroll, and flower quilting on border; outline quilting on pathway bars and circle fans; 80 × 80   **$1,250**

> *The Pineapple is the symbol of hospitality and a house open to friends and strangers alike. It is still a popular appliqué, pieced, and quilting design today.*

PINEAPPLE AND CRESCENTS: 1870–1880; red, taupe, gold; Amish-made quilt; echo quilting overall; 82 × 82   **$1,900**

> *The Pomegranate is a symbol of fertility, and was often used as an appliqué or quilting pattern in bride quilts. It was also common in hand-painted India chintzes and with Broderie-Perse style appliqué.*

POMEGRANATE: late 1880s; blue, gold, red; overall fade, straight-line quilting; 70 × 80   **$300**

PRINCESS FEATHER: 1870; red and green; feathers in four blocks, star in center, swag border with flowers, some wear in reds, very small appliqué stitches; 60 × 80   **$1,650**

PRINCESS FEATHER: 1890; green, yellow, pink; border added later with machine quilting; 94 × 79 **$650**

PRINCESS FEATHER: 1890s; red, green, blue; blue appliqué triangle border, unwashed, minimal use, straight-line quilting on border, feather quilting elsewhere; 72 × 84 **$700**

PRINCESS FEATHER: 1930s; pinks and greens; from Pennsylvania; wreath and vine quilting; 80 × 83 **$995**

RED POPPY: 1940s; cranberry, red, green; kit quilt, curved edge, unused; from Ohio; very neat appliqué stitches; leaf, poppy, and curved quilting overall; 86 × 100 **$525**

The Rose of Sharon is one of the oldest and most popular appliqué quilt patterns. Traditionally it was a pattern reserved for a bride's quilt.

ROSE OF SHARON: 1884; red and green; minimal use, homemade dyes; excellent wreath, vine, and heart quilting; coordinated double binding; from Missouri, maker known, 16-year-old; 92 × 92 **$1,250**

ROSE OF SHARON: 1890; red, white, green; Masonic symbol in rose, replaced binding, some overall soiling, straight-line quilting; 78 × 80 **$995**

ROSE OF SUMMER: 1930s; red, white, blue; strong colors; from Arkansas, maker known; 64 × 76 **$450**

ROSE (VARIABLE): 1860–1880; teal-blue, Turkey red, orange; very artistic, Turkey red swag border, minimal use, Pennsylvania Dutch, clover/four hearts quilting in center, grid quilting overall; 72 × 74 **$1,900**

ROSE WREATH: 1850s; red and green; maker known; much medallion quilting; 74 × 76 **$2,400**

ROSES: late 1800s; red, pink, white; slight overall fade, unwashed; small appliqué stitches, leaves and roses in quilting; 78 × 84 **$450**

ROSES: 1920s; yellow, green; matching pair of quilts, very good quilting; 67 × 69 (price per pair) **$995**

ROSES: 1940s; pinks, greens; kit quilt, roses and buds, scalloped edges with pink binding; wreath quilting; 73 × 86 **$525**

This beautiful Rose appliqué is done in shades of peach, pink, and green, and shows the delicacy and intricacy that can be achieved by an expert quiltmaker. The grid and straight-line quilting set off the pattern very well.

ROSES AND THORNS: 1930s; pink, rose, gray; some embroidery on stems; 76 × 88 **$495**

SAMPLER: late 1800s; red, green, gold; roses, flowers in pots, wreaths; appliqué swag border with flowerbuds, some loose stitches, overcast-blanket-stitched edges with some stitches missing; straight-line quilting in squares, diagonal quilting on border; from Pennsylvania; 72 × 72 **$1,800**

SAMPLER: 1895; red, cheddar, brown; dated, maker known, 11-year-old girl; 70 sampler blocks, some are of family pets and personal mementos; 12-inch border; from Pennsylvania; 80 × 84 **$6,800**

SAMPLER: 1920s; light blue on white; Moorish and Islamic designs; each block initialed, makers known; work quality varies from block to block; 66 × 77 **$1,500**

Made in the 1920s by students for a teacher, this medium-blue-and-white appliqué sampler is initialed in each block. The quality of work in these Moorish and Islamic-looking circular designs varies from block to block.

SIGNATURE STARS: 1929; yellow; blue embroidered signatures and stars, quilting lines remain, unwashed; 79 × 88 $475

SNOWFLAKES: 1930s; blue on cream; triple border; from Pennsylvania; overall fade, much use and washing, few water stains in one area, slightly worn binding, excellent work, tiny appliqué stitches, outline and straight-line quilting; 90 × 90 $875

THISTLE: 1920; red, green on white; red and green borders, some loose stitches, some loose pieces; heart, circle, curved quilting; 70 × 86 $495

TOUCHING HEARTS: 1940s; multicolored pastels; 64 × 76 $300

TULIPS: 1870s; red with green leaves; from New England; slight oxidation of greens; 98 × 70 $950

TULIPS: 1880s; green and red; binding worn and fraying, many loose stitches, overall fade, few old repairs; tiny appliqué stitches, double-row block and diagonal quilting; 68 × 84 $395

TULIPS: 1880s; yellow, green; quite worn, especially binding; very faded overall, some stains, fair condition; tiny appliqué stitches, feather and wreath quilting; 90 × 78 $475

TULIPS: 1920s; red, green; unused, unwashed, overall yellowing of white background, circle and feather quilting; 72 × 76 $475

TULIPS: 1920s; pink, yellow, red; from Pennsylvania; unused, excellent condition; 73 × 80 $495

TULIPS: 1920s; red and green; 78 × 96 $495

TULIPS: 1920s; pink, lavender, green; pair of quilts, lavender double border, tulips in white blocks set on point with lavender blocks, very good condition, minimal use; very good work, very small appliqué stitches, grid and outline quilting; 50 × 80 (price for the pair) $1,200

TULIPS IN BASKETS: 1930s; red and white; 36 baskets, red border; unwashed, some age spots, small appliqué stitches, oval quilting on border, wreath quilting with double star in center between baskets; 73 × 73 $535

WATER LILY: 1930s; pink and white, French knots in lily centers, feather quilting, tiny appliqué stitches, washed, minimal use; 70 × 80 $650

WILD ROSE: 1930s; pink, pastels; embroidery on roses, French knots in centers; excellent condition, unused, tiny appliqué stitches, excellent straight-line quilting overall; 80 × 78 $575

WINDMILL WITH TULIPS: 1890; apple green and rose; 82 × 86 $500

Dresden Plate

This is one of the rare patterns that combine pieced and appliquéd patchwork. It is probable that this pattern originated by combining four squares of Grandmother's Fan or Japanese Fan patterns to create a circle.

The Dresden Plate is a scrap bag quilt, using various wedge-shaped pieces to form the plate. After all sections of the plate have been stitched together, the resulting circle is appliquéd to a white ground fabric and a circle of plain fabric, often yellow in color, is appliquéd over the center. A variation of the central plain circle is the addition of four diamonds placed at right angles to each other, which gives the plate the appearance of a button. Rarely, black topstitching or black buttonhole stitching is found along the outside border of each plate. The Dresden Plate pattern was sometimes used as a signature quilt by embroidering names in each section of the plate.

This pattern was most popular from approximately 1925 through 1950. It was one of the patterns sold in pre-cut, pre-designed kit form. So many of

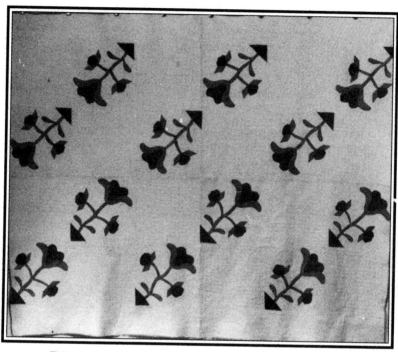

This very worn and frayed 1880s Tulip appliqué in reds and greens shows an interesting look caused by setting the Tulip block with white squares and arranging the blocks facing each other in two opposing rows.

A closer look shows the damage to the greens in this quilt, many parts of which have fabric deterioration and loss. The red print with tiny yellow accents can also be seen, along with some very nice clamshell and close grid quilting.

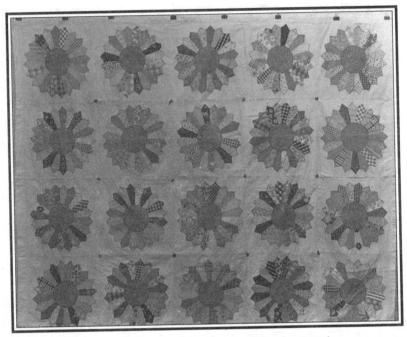

A tied coverlet with no quilting, this 1920s Dresden Plate shows neat centers, all of the same fabric, and pointed plate edges, a nice variation on the traditional curved edges.
Quilt courtesy of Doris Dean

these quilts were made, in fact, that it isn't rare to find them. The problem with this pattern is that too many included the light-colored pastels popular during the second quarter of the twentieth century. Viewed from a distance, some of these lighter fabrics seem to blend in with the white background so that it looks as if pieces of the plate are missing.

There are many Dresden Plate quilts available—too many, in fact, to make them valuable right now. But really distinctive, well-worked, original-looking Dresden Plate can still be a good find. If you like this pattern, hold out until you find one that's truly unique.

DRESDEN PLATE: 1930s; various grays; wavy edge, old machine quilting, much overall wear, some stains; 74 × 90 $240

DRESDEN PLATE: 1930s; pink, multicolored pastels; petal border, scalloped edges, unwashed, minimal use; blanket stitches on edges of plates; 68 × 82
                                                                          $295

A closer look at this quilt reveals black topstitching, a machine-applied binding, and all of the wonderful printed fabrics from the maker's scrap bag.
Quilt courtesy of Doris Dean

DRESDEN PLATE: 1930s; pink, multicolored prints; double center of plates, pointed plate edges, black embroidery on plate edges, appliqué green leaves in corners, green backing and binding; 76 × 66   **$295**

DRESDEN PLATE: 1930s; blue, gray, pinks; curved edge, pointed plates, very small plate centers; some overall fade, binding quite worn, uneven appliqué stitches; 72 × 80   **$300**

DRESDEN PLATE: 1930s; blue, green, darks; scalloped edge, torn back with old repairs, overall fade, some mildew stains; 70 × 72   **$350**

DRESDEN PLATE: 1930s; pastels; quilting lines remain, unwashed, excellent condition; 78 × 90   **$395**

DRESDEN PLATE: 1930s; multipastels; yellow border, pointed plates, chain quilting on border, petal quilting between plates; unused; 65 × 50   **$345**

DRESDEN PLATE: 1930s; lavender, pastels; scalloped edge; 64 x 70   **$650**

DRESDEN PLATE: 1930s; golden yellow, multicolored; yellow centers, yellow border, unused, quilting lines remain; tiny appliqué stitches, minimal decorative quilting; 80 × 84   **$745**

Political, Patriotic, and Commemorative Quilts

Quiltmakers have long recorded history through their art, and all sorts of historical, patriotic, and political materials have found their way onto quilts. Commemorative fabrics were printed very early. In England, fabric depicting George Washington was printed soon after the Revolution. Other presidents, maps, historic buildings, events, and battle scenes were pictured on cloth, and these prints have often been used in quilts. Eagle quilts date from 1807. Pictorial representations of famous people and events were created for the Centennial in 1875, the Chicago World's Fair in 1933, and even for the 199th anniversary of the Statue of Liberty.

Political quilt block patterns developed as well. The appliquéd Whig Rose, a variation of the Rose of Sharon pattern, is attributed to the presidential election of 1828. Although the last election entered by the Whig party was in 1851, the pattern is still popular today. Pieced patterns were named Whig's Defeat, Clay's Choice, Lincoln's Platform, The Little Giant (for Stephen Douglas), Garfield's Monument, and Dolly Madison Star. (See chapter 10 for more information on these quilts.)

Jean B. Hall is curating an exhibit of political quilts at the New England Quilt Museum; the exhibit will include quilts featuring Henry Clay, Chester A. Arthur, Grover Cleveland, and other nineteenth-century politicians. The show will also include several quilts from the FDR era, one for Jimmy Carter, and even one commemorating the Nixon resignation.

Political, patriotic, and commemorative quilts are extremely rare, which explains why we only found two of them. Most of the known ones are already in the hands of private collectors and museums. These are not the types of quilt you find in a quilt shop, for these quilts, when found, go directly to interested collectors without ever seeing a showroom. If these are the kind you want to collect, establishing a relationship with a quilt dealer is essential. Odds are you won't find one of these treasures by searching through quilt dealers' showrooms.

WHIG ROSE: 1860s; green, brown, orange; swag border, pink appliqué centers; slight overall discoloration, tiny appliqué stitches, minimal quilting; 80 × 78 $950

WHIG ROSE (VARIATION): 1860–1870; red, green, gold; patch roses in Whig centers; overall fade, overall soiling, some small stains, binding slightly worn; tiny appliqué stitches, straight-line quilting overall; 80 × 80 $2,500

Reverse Appliqué and Hawaiian Quilting

Soon after the missionary wives arrived in Hawaii in 1820, they introduced quilting to the Hawaiian women. Already in the habit of making decorative bed coverings, the Hawaiians gave quilting their own unique design variations.

Hawaiian-style quilts start with cutting a design out of a paper folded in eighths. After cutting a patterned design along the edge of the paper, the paper was opened up, laid on a piece of cloth, and the cloth was cut in the same design. The large design was then appliquéd onto a ground fabric. The first quilt made this way is attributed to a woman seeing the shadows of breadfruit trees on a white sheet left on the grass to bleach. She immediately cut the shadow pattern she had seen out of Turkey red cloth and appliquéd it to the same sheet. These quilts are usually done in only two colors, one of them always white, and are difficult to make because of the large size of the appliqué. Reds, greens, or blues, combined with white, were the most popular colors for these quilts.

Hawaiian quilt designs were distinctly individual. Quiltmakers created their own patterns, and the woman who copied another woman's patterns had to beg forgiveness for her theft. The designs were inspired by nature's flowers, fruits, and trees.

Another distinctive Hawaiian quilt style is patterned after their flag. The photograph on page 247 illustrates this style.

Hawaiian appliqué is actually a form of reverse appliqué, where the design is cut out of a piece of fabric, which is then stitched down to a ground fabric. In appliqué, however, a piece of fabric shaped in the design is sewn to the ground with the ground showing around the piece. In reverse appliqué, the ground fabric shows through the cut piece of the top fabric, and that ground showing through actually creates the design. Reverse appliqué is more difficult than traditional appliqué because it means working in reverse of the usual way, with more precise cutting and measuring needed.

Hawaiian quilts are valuable because they are unique. Traditionally they were made as gifts, and families have kept close tabs on them. Because they are cut from whole cloth, they're difficult to assemble. The intricacies of cutting the paper require exact and expert work.

Reverse appliqué quilts are also rare, and not usually found in the market-place. Both types will be very expensive to own—if you can find people willing to sell them. We saw at least three others in addition to those we have listed here, and the owners said they knew of a few others. None were for sale.

Made in the 1930s, this light-rose-on-pink reverse appliqué is a good example of the Hawaiian style of quiltmaking, with the dark-on-light colors and the large central fruit tree pattern.

A closer look reveals the fine woven fabric and neatly turned edges of this quilt. Actually a summer spread, it has no filler or quilting.

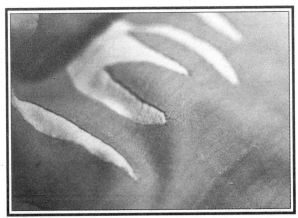

This quilt is made from four Hawaiian flags with a square center appliquéd in gold fabric. It was made in 1900, and is quilted overall with straight-line quilting. The bright clear colors are indicative of a wall hanging, certainly never intended for use as a bed covering. *Photograph courtesy of Susan Parrish*

FLOWERS AND WILDLIFE: 1790–1820; red and blue eagles, wild turkeys, plumes, stars and flowers; center frame quilt with appliqué and reverse appliqué; red and gold floral chintz sashing and border; outline quilting around appliqués, diagonal straight-line quilting overall; 84 × 84   **$7,400**

FLYING GEESE: 1880s; white on white, 80 blocks; bride's quilt from North Carolina; 86 × 90   **$2,700**

PALM TREE: 1930; light rose on pink; Hawaiian appliqué; top only, a few stains, some loose stitches; 88 × 91   **$295**

Sunbonnet Sue and Variations

One of the most endearing of all appliqué designs is the Sunbonnet Sue. These faceless lassies have been worked in fabric appliqué and in embroidery, both outline and filled in, and all of them are characterized by their oversized bonnets. Sunbonnet Sue dates from the early 1900s. In 1912, Marie Webster of the *Ladies' Home Journal* included a quilt in that magazine featuring a version of Sunbonnet Sue, but it wasn't until the 1920s that the pattern achieved widespread popularity among quiltmakers. This popularity continues today. *Quilt World* magazine has included patterns for an embroidered alphabet Sunbonnet Sue in each issue since its August/September 1989 issue. These patterns were taken from a coloring book by Bertha Corbette printed in 1929. According to *Quilt World*, Corbette is one of the claimed originators of the Sunbonnet Sue pattern. Other quilt magazines also regularly feature patterns for various styles of Sunbonnet Sue.

The popularity of Sunbonnet Sue (one pattern was named Colonial Lady) led to a male counterpart. Overall Sam and Overall Bill both use fabric representation of the straw hat for their patterns. These male representations are also faceless and usually viewed from the back. An important element of these designs is the back pocket of the overalls. One Overall Sam quilt we saw had a tiny triangle of handkerchief peeking out of each pocket.

The popularity of the Sunbonnet Sue character also spawned many other similar figures on quilts, some completely original, some from magazine patterns, and even some from kits. They could be of whimsical figures like donkeys, or common things around the house like cats. One of the most interesting and unusual we saw was an original design patterned after the Little Dutch Girl on the household cleanser can.

Sunbonnet Sue is one of those patterns, along with Dresden Plate and Double Wedding Ring, that collectors either love or hate. Some collectors think they're desirable because they're cute. Others think they're too cute, almost sappy. If you love them, take heart. There are many of them around because they were a very popular early twentieth-century quilt pattern.

BUTTERFLIES: 1930s; navy, multicolored; navy print border, set on point, unused, unwashed; straight-line and outline quilting; 76 × 98   **$675**

CATS: 1930s; cobalt blue, red, white; excellent design and color balance, blue cats in center of white squares, red sashing with small green square at junctions, possibly African-American; unused, unwashed, clamshell quilting, large uneven quilting stitches; 72 × 78   **$2,500**

DONKEYS: 1920s; maroon and rose on white; kit quilt, 12 donkeys; unused, mint condition; minimal quilting; 82 × 78   **$300**

LITTLE DUTCH GIRL: 1920s; rose, green, purple, multicolored brights; blocks with figures set with white blocks, pink border, green edge and corner blocks, colored topstitching on edge of figures; excellent condition, minimal use, excellent work, straight-line quilting overall; 80 × 84   **$750**

OVERALL SAM: 1930s–1940s; blue faded to purple; embroidery accents, overcast edges, four-petal daisies embroidered at set corners, minimal quilting, no filler; 72 × 76   **$190**

OVERALL SAM: 1920s; blues, grays, greens; pair of quilts, black topstitching on edge of figures, blue border, overall fade, some few spots; grid quilting overall, cable quilting on border; 50 × 78 (price for the pair)   **$950**

ROOSTERS: 1940; various reds; from Indiana; each rooster slightly different, unusual "folksy" look, binding worn; 72 × 80   **$725**

SCOTTIE DOGS: 1920; pinks, pastels; embroidered noses, eyes, whiskers; appliqué collars; very small appliqué stitches, good detail; recently quilted, diamond quilting, unwashed; 76 × 94   **$675**

SUNBONNET SUE: early 1900s; multicolored; some tears, border very worn; 72 × 88   **$225**

SUNBONNET SUE: 1930s; blue, yellow, pink; one area faded, minimal use; outline quilting of figures, minimal straight-line quilting elsewhere, buttons on front of dresses; 72 × 80   **$475**

SUNBONNET SUE: 1935; yellow; white sets, yellow sashing with Nine-patch blocks, yellow diamond border, embroidery accents, machine assembled, curved and straight-line quilting; overall soiling; 66 x 86   **$245**

SUNBONNET SUE: 1940s; red polka dot; tied, no quilting, machine appliqué with straight stitch embroidery covering, considerable overall fade on top; 90 × 60   **$345**

SUNBONNET SUE/OVERALL SAM: 1930s; red, white, blue; minimal use; 76 × 84   **$500**

SUNBONNET SUE/OVERALL SAM: 1930s; blues, reds; overall fade, many washings; tiny appliqué stitches, some embroidery on dresses and overalls; 70 × 72   **$400**

Appliqué Quilt Tops

As in pieced work, appliqué tops can also be found. They are less common because appliqué was less common. But the advantages of an appliqué top make them excellent pieces to look for. For considerably less money than you would pay for a finished quilt, you can have a stunning wall hanging. And if

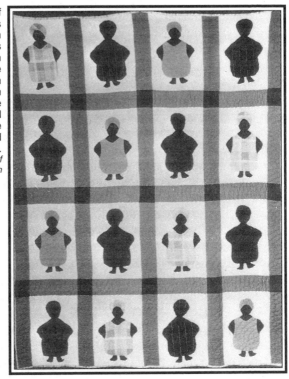

In the style of Sunbonnet Sue, this African-American "Mammies" quilt was made in 1950 in Oklahoma. The sashing is blue with bright red squares in the corners, while the dresses and headdresses are plaid, striped, and solid-colored fabrics. *Photograph courtesy of Susan Parrish*

you want to do the work yourself, or find someone who will assemble and quilt your treasure, you can have a beautiful finished quilt, too.

CARNATIONS: 1940s; red, blue on white; top only, kit quilt, flowers have embroidered accents, quilting marks remain; 80 × 92 $175

COCKSCOMB: late 1800s; red, forest green; top only, diamond set, alternate plain blocks with appliquéd, small diamond sash and border, very small appliqué stitches; Pennsylvania Dutch; price would be $1,500 if finished; 80 × 80 $310

FLOWER POTS IN CIRCLES: 1870s; red, green, gold; top only, faded in spots; amateur attempt at color restoration, would be $200 without this; both machine and hand pieced; 78 × 78 $95

FRUIT BASKET AND BUTTERFLIES: 1940s; red and pink; top only, white muslin background, red stripe around border, buttonhole appliqué; 70 × 80
          $75

The Lobster pattern was especially popular during the War of 1812 as a way of ridiculing the British, who, because of their red coats, were commonly called Lobsterbacks.

LOBSTER: 1940s; polka dot blue on white, white on polka dot blue; tops only, pair of mirror-image quilts; some stains, color very bright, unwashed; tiny appliqué stitches; 72 × 72 (price for the pair) $395

OHIO ROSE: 1920s; pinks, green, cream; top only, cream border, 16 blocks with roses and buds, tiny appliqué stitches; 82 × 100 $350

PALM TREE: 1930; light rose on pink; Hawaiian appliqué; top only, a few stains, some loose stitches; 88 × 91 $295

SAILBOATS: 1950s; pastels; top only, double border of pink and lavender, machine pieced, covered with embroidery; 77 × 96 $125

CHAPTER TWELVE

OTHER ANTIQUE QUILTS

The quilts included in this section simply defy classification into the previous two groups of quilts. These include trapunto, some reverse appliqué, whole-cloth, embroidered, and novelty quilts. Also included are blocks that are available for sale, so you can set them into a quilt top and create a new family heirloom while still using pieces of the past.

Refer to chapter 9 for an explanation of the terms used in the following price lists.

Embroidered Quilts

In the 1880s, a new kind of quilt was created with patterns thought to be copied from Kate Greenway's art depicting children, animals, toy clowns, and Noah's ark figures. In this variation, figures or simple scenes were embroidered on a ground fabric, most often in chain stitch using red thread. Some quiltmakers filled in the figures with more embroidery and detail. Soon quilts depicting nursery rhyme characters, the alphabet, and signature wheels appeared in the same style. Embroidered crib quilts were popular from the turn of the century through 1925.

Single-colored embroidered quilts, preferably in red on white, are sought after by knowledgeable collectors. Not only are they attractive and emotionally appealing, but they are examples of one of those quilt styles that represent a specific time period. More of their history and origins is known than for other quilts.

EMBROIDERY, BASKETS: 1920s; white, nine flower baskets in large squares with white sashing, embroidered on edges; feather quilting around baskets, curved and pointed quilting in sashing; 72 × 72   **$425**

EMBROIDERY, BIBLE SCENES: early 1900s; red on white; 24 blocks with scenes; red sashing, binding, border; some repair to binding, quilted overall; 55 × 66   **$225**

This classic 1910 coverlet is called Dreams of the Forest and features red embroidery on white muslin squares. This is a quilt top with the edges finished so it can be used for a bed cover.
Quilt courtesy of Florence Atwater

EMBROIDERY, CHILDREN'S: 1900; large black wool squares covered with children's multicolored; unique and simple embroidery in squares and on seams; dated; 66 × 70 **$500**

EMBROIDERY, FLOWERS: 1920; red on white; sampler, red border; few discolorations, unwashed, unused, quilting lines remain; cable quilting on border, grid quilting overall; 76 × 80 **$485**

EMBROIDERY, FLOWERS: 1930s; multicolored embroidery on white; blocks with embroidered flowers alternate with plain white blocks, good-to-excellent condition, few tiny stains, minimal use; very good to excellent embroidery, feather ring quilting in white blocks; 77 x 77 **$325**

EMBROIDERY, FLOWERS IN BASKETS: 1930s; rose-pink on white; pink sashing and border, blocks embroidered with flowers in baskets, doves with ribbons, baby in center block; from Pennsylvania; good-to-excellent condition, few stains, unused, unwashed, very good assembly and embroidery, small even stitches, cable and leaf quilting on border, grid quilting in blocks; 78 × 76 **$600**

Another block of the same coverlet shows the date it was made and the initials of the maker.
Quilt courtesy of Florence Atwater

EMBROIDERY, KITTENS: 1930s; pink kittens on large white squares; satin border; 24 × 24 $95

EMBROIDERY, MOTHER GOOSE TALES: early 1900s; red on white; red binding, borders, sashing, corners; minimal use, diagonal straight-line quilting, 20 blocks with scenes; 50 × 63 $225

EMBROIDERY, STORYBOOK TALES: 1900; red embroidery on white; tied, no quilting; one small stain; 72 × 82 $365

FRIENDSHIP BLOCKS: 1903; light indigo blocks with red embroidered names in wheel pattern; 16 names per wheel, one wheel on each block; all from Oregon, Washington, Alaska; dated; embroidery skill varies from name to name; very narrow sashing with straight-line quilting; unused, washed once; 78 × 80 $575

Trapunto

Trapunto is a form of quilting developed in Italy and dating from the fourteenth century. The word is derived from *trapugere*, to embroider, which is derived from the Latin *trans-*, meaning through, and *pungere*, meaning to prick or pierce. It is one of the most aptly named of quilt methods.

In trapunto, two layers of cloth are stitched together with a design that might include straight lines, leaves, cherries, grapes, petals, stems, and vines. Larger areas of stitched space—the petals and flowers, for example—are stuffed with batting by making a small slit in the backing fabric. When the space was properly stuffed, the slit would be slipstitched closed. The lines of stems and vines would be stuffed with cording using a needle to pull the cord or threads through the double lines of stitching that formed the stem. When the stuffing was completed, another layer of cloth was added to the back and then quilting was done to hold the three layers together and to hide the slits and cording holes. The effect of trapunto gives a quilt a heightened, raised effect not possible with any other type of quilting, except perhaps stipple quilting.

Some trapunto makers didn't slit their backing cloth, preferring to use a loosely woven fabric for the back. Pushing the fabric threads aside, they'd stuff batting through the hole. When the space was filled, they simply pushed the threads back into place. This eliminated the need for the second backing fabric and the additional quilting. The photograph below illustrates this style.

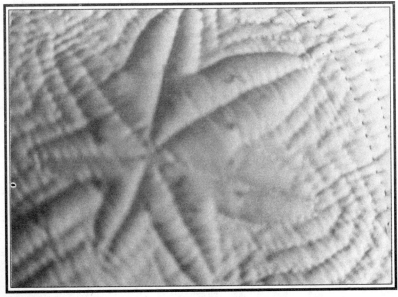

In close-up, the puffiness of the trapunto on this 1830s Grapes and Leaves whitework quilt can be seen. The little tufts in the center of the leaf are the sewed-up slits through which the quilter put the stuffing.

The trapunto method was popular from 1800 through the Civil War. Some historians attribute its popularity to the plentiful and inexpensive supply of cotton thread at the time. Trapunto is a whole-cloth method of quilting but can be seen in block-style quilts as well. It is sometimes erroneously referred to as whitework or all-white. Although both trapunto and whitework are both whole-cloth methods, and both were predominantly of white cloth with white stitching, whitework or all-white quilts usually refers to whole-cloth quilts covered with fancy quilting designs. Trapunto is indeed a fancy design, but technically, it is not quilting but stuffing.

The popularity of trapunto dropped off dramatically after the Civil War. Trapunto on an antique quilt is strong evidence that it was made before 1865. Naturally, these quilts are rare and expensive.

LEAVES AND GRAPES: 1860s; white on white; trapunto in leaves, grapes, elsewhere; from Wisconsin; excellent condition; never used; heavily quilted in close lines; 80 × 78 $10,000

LEAVES AND GRAPES: 1830; white on white; trapunto in leaves, grapes, central wreath, elsewhere; quilted central wreath; very good condition; 83 × 84 $6,200

ROSE WREATH: 1850; white on white; trapunto in wreath and elsewhere, excellent condition; unused; extensive quilting; 78 × 100 $4,500

64 BLOCKS: 1700s; white blocks containing teal, red, and brown hexagons surrounded by trapunto hearts, vines, baskets, and flowers; white and copper-plate-method brown chintz sash and border; plantation made; from Charleston, S.C.; unused, some minor fabric disintegration, some bleeding in brown chintz; 110 × 110 $7,500

TURKEY TRACKS (VARIATION): 1851; white with red, gold, and green leaves; grapes and pomegranates; trapunto in leaves, grapes, pomegranates, elsewhere; overall fade, replacement binding, one old homespun patch; signed; 71 × 83 $3,500

Whole-Cloth Quilts

Whole-cloth quilts are the original quilts, made from one whole piece of cloth for the top, another for the backing, with filling in between. Quilts started this way, and the style carries through to today. Although originally just the basic way to make a quilt, this style progressed to a way of showcasing superior quilting. The Amish make many whole-cloth quilts, a solid color on top, with excellent quilting as the primary focus of the quilt. Some antique whole-cloth quilts can still be found—many in poor condition, some in better. Many of those you will find are whitework bride's quilts, as this style was popular for the betrothed. If you want something unusual for your collection, you might consider one of these.

CHINTZ PRINT: 1875; brown, tan, teal chintz one side; Victorian cotton on other side; minimal straight-line quilting; unused; from Massachusetts; 73 × 80 $495

CRIB QUILT: 1910; white on white; overall feather quilting, few tiny spots; 44 × 48 $425

FLORAL CHINTZ: 1930; beige with blue flowers; fair condition, few tears in back, faded in spots, overall soiling, surface wear; very good quilting, small stitches, scalloped quilting on sides, grid quilting in center; 100 × 100 $250

PLAIN AMISH: 1930; solid blue; minimal use, very small stitches; 60 × 73
                                                                                                                                        $1,295

SIX-POINT STAR: 1925; white on white; star central; oak leaves, feather, vine, and wreath quilting; excellent condition, excellent work; from Ohio; 74 × 74 $880

WOOLSEY-WOOLSEY: 1830; brown, possibly walnut-shell-dyed; striped homespun-type back; poor condition, much fabric loss and deterioration, many tears, split seams; round, four-poster cutouts; black linen thread quilting in chevron stripe, feather, and clamshell designs; 100 × 100 $145

WHITEWORK: early 1900s; white on white; slight overall soiling, some stains; very good, very small quilting stitches, cable quilting on edge, fleur-de-lis and grid quilting overall; 68 × 78 $350

WHITEWORK BRIDE'S QUILT: early 1900s; white on white; scalloped edge, unwashed, unused, quilting lines remain; full-feathered peacock quilted as medallion in center, then band of quilted flowers, then wide section of grid quilting, more flower quilting in edge scallops, exquisite quilting; 80 × 82 $750

Uniques and Unusuals

Many and varied techniques have been tried in the making of quilts, and we found a few examples of these quilts. The Yo-yo quilt is a whimsical piece done with little circles of gathered fabric assembled together to make a quilt top—certainly not for the purpose of keeping anyone warm, but rarely purely as a decoration. Puff quilts were stuffed to exaggeration, and also were certainly

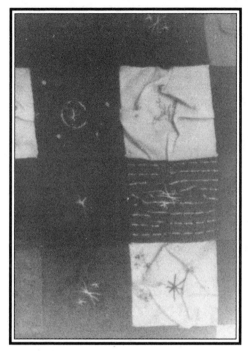

This close-up of a puff quilt, circa 1900, shows the individual embroidery on each puff. Made of wools, this quilt has suffered some moth holes and other fabric loss.

made as a decoration rather than for utility. We even found a variation on the penny rugs that were popular around the turn of the century.

If you are looking for something unique, keep your eyes open and let your quilt dealers know. There are not a lot of them, but unique examples of quiltmakers' creativity are there to be found.

PENNY QUILT: 1920s; blue-gray ground squares with colored felt pennies in six-point star design; appliqué similar to penny rug style, cotton chintz floral backing; tied, gold feather stitching on joints of squares; unique and rare design; 72 × 60   **$595**

PUFF QUILT: 1900; darks; cottons and wools with different embroidery on each puff, ruffle border; some stains, some small holes; 50 × 48   **$125**

PUFF QUILT: 1900; multicolors; top only, all satins with velvet binding, crib quilt; 24 × 44   **$65**

YO-YO: 1930s; multicolored yo-yos; green centers, purple sashing, assembled in blocks; 88 × 108   **$395**

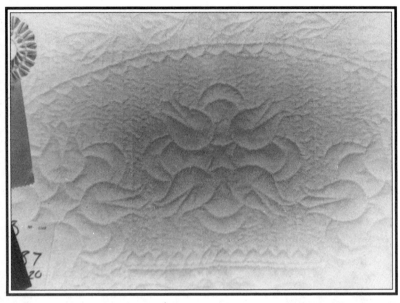

This white-on-white contemporary quilt is a good example of the style, where the quilting creates the design rather than the appliqué or piecework.

YO-YO: 1940s; pink yo-yos; pink sashing and border, excellent condition; 68 × 96 $245

Fabrics, Blocks, and Other Items

In searching for quilts, we also found many quilt-related items for sale. Quilt blocks are an interesting addition to a collection; they can be displayed in a small area, or can be assembled to produce your own finished quilt. Fabric is useful in repairing quilts, or for making whole ones. When you are searching through shops don't automatically pass on such items. Careful looking might find you a treasure.

BARN RAISING LOG CABIN WALL HANGINGS: 1910–1920; blues, red, multicolored; four blocks salvaged from larger damaged quilt; tied, no quilting, four 5-inch squares, side by side, mounted in 24-inch picture frame for hanging (price each) $75

BASKET BLOCKS: 1930s; red and white; salvaged from damaged top, excellent condition; seven blocks (price each) $10

This typical Yo-yo quilt has peach sashing and backing, which peeks through the spaces between the yo-yos. The decorative quilt was made in the 1940s.
Quilt courtesy of Joan Halla

BUTTERFLY BLOCKS: early 1900s; pastels; appliqué and embroidery; excellent assembly, appliqué and embroidery; four blocks (price each) $8

CROWN OF THORNS BLOCKS: early 1900s; pink on pink and white; fifteen blocks (price for the group) $45

DRESDEN PLATE BLOCKS: 1930s; multicolored; few stains overall; five blocks, 18 inches square each (price each) $5

DIAMOND GRANDMOTHER'S FLOWER GARDEN BLOCKS: early 1900s; solid brights and white; some slight stains; eight blocks (price each) $2

DRUNKARD'S PATH BLOCKS: 1930s; cranberry, tan; very good assembly, junctions match; thirty blocks, 12 inches square each (price each) $3

EIGHT-POINT STARS AND HEXAGONS CHEATER CLOTH: late 1800s; red, pink, brown; fabric very stiff; 1 1/2 yards by 24 inches $15

EMBROIDERED FLOWERS BLOCKS: 1930s; multicolored embroidery on white blocks; thirty-six blocks, 12 inches square each (price for the group) $65

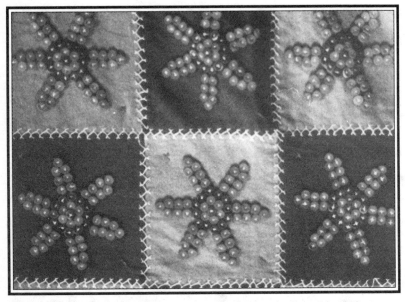

Made in the style of the penny rugs that were popular at the time, this 1920s quilt has various colored felt "pennies" stitched to gray and blue-gray squares, and gold feather topstitching over the seams. The fabrics are wool, but the backing is floral cotton chintz.

GRANDMOTHER'S FLOWER GARDEN BLOCKS: 1930s; various pastels and prints; fair assembly, not all junctions match; nine pieces, 9 inches square each, to make 12-inch blocks (price for the group) $16

HARVEST SUN WALL HANGING: 1890s; reds, browns; overall fade, salvaged from larger damaged quilt, straight-line quilting in outlines; 10-inch square mounted in 12-inch picture frame for hanging $45

HOLE IN THE BARN DOOR BLOCKS: 1920s–1930s; multicolored; eighteen 12-inch scrap bag squares (price for the group) $90

LEMOYNE STAR/DRESDEN PLATE COMBINATION BLOCKS: 1940s; browns; rounded points on plates, topstitching on appliqué edges, some stains, less-than-perfect assembly; ten 18-inch square blocks (price each) $3.50

NINE-PATCH WALL HANGING: 1910; red, white, blue; overall fade, salvaged from larger damaged quilt, blue sashing, excellent assembly, some straight-line quilting overall, 8-inch square mounted in 12-inch picture frame for hanging (price each) $50

These appliquéd Butterfly blocks sport black topstitching and 1930s print and solid fabrics. They would be lovely assembled and quilted into a wall hanging.

These 1930s red-and-white Basket blocks were salvaged from a damaged top, and could be assembled again to make a small quilt. Both the patch assembly and the appliqué handles are well done.

NINE-PATCH BLOCKS: 1940s; pastels; excellent assembly, forty 10-inch blocks (price each) **$1.25**

NINE-PATCH AND BOW TIE BLOCKS: 1920s; blue, burgundy, with various other colors; 6-inch square blocks (price each) **$1**

OHIO STAR WALL HANGING: 1940s; yellow; 4-inch square salvaged from damaged quilt, no quilting, set in 8-inch picture frame for hanging (price each) **$36**

SCHOOL HOUSE BLOCKS: 1920s; red, green, white; all solid colors; seven blocks (price each) **$5**

VARIABLE STAR BLOCKS: 1880s; pink on pink and white; fair-to-good assembly, most junctions match; twenty-four blocks, 10-inches square each (price for the group) **$70**

CHAPTER THIRTEEN

CONTEMPORARY QUILTS

As you start collecting quilts, you'll find yourself in the company of a diverse group of companies as well as individuals. The Esprit Corporation has a collection specializing in Amish quilts. Johnson & Johnson and Citibank bought contemporary art quilts to grace their walls instead of hanging paintings, photographs, or art posters. Former First Lady Nancy Reagan purchased a quilt from Julia Spidell and gave it to Raisa Gorbachev.

Interest in quilts has waxed and waned over the four centuries we've quilted, but the art never died out completely. The most recent wave of popularity began during the Bicentennial and shows no sign of stopping. Quilters subscribe to trade magazines in numbers over 100,000. The National Quilting Association, Inc. is the oldest quilting organization in the country and annually offers grants and scholarships "to promote and encourage quilters to further their knowledge of techniques, craftsmanship, and development of ideas." NQA also encourages the study of quilt history.

Quilters' Newsletter Magazine boasts 736 quilting guilds in the United States, Canada, Europe, Australia, and the Orient, with over 69,000 members worldwide. The opening of the new Museum of the American Quilter's Society drew over 11,000 quiltmakers, collectors, and quilt lovers to Paducah, Kentucky. MAQS is the brainchild of Bill and Meredith Schroeder, quilt collectors. In 1984, the Schroeders founded the American Quilter's Society, which now has 75,000 members.

Many of these quilters practice their art because their mothers or grandmothers were quilters. Some started quilting because none of their relatives did and they wanted to leave behind something of themselves for future generations. Some, like Jinny Beyer, never sell their quilts, preferring to keep them or give them away rather than deal with customers uneducated in the time and skill quilting requires. Some sell their quilts and earn a respectable living, while others do so on a part-time basis, quilting only for extra money because it's a hobby they enjoy.

Quilts are still made as political and social statements, just as quilts have always been made to comment on crucial events in our history. The Idaho Peace Quilt Group makes quilts that symbolize peace and sends them to leaders in foreign countries. AmeriCares, based in New Canaan, Connecticut, sent over 1,300 quilts to Romania for children there suffering with AIDS.

Perhaps the most widely known quilt today is the AIDS quilt. Now numbering over 2,600 panels, this quilt began in a storefront in the Castro District of San Francisco to commemorate and memorialize the victims of AIDS. At one point, Cleve Jones, who started the quilt, received anywhere from fifty to eighty new panels a day. Each piece of the quilt is a banner depicting the name of an AIDS victim. Surely this quilt, now estimated as larger than two football fields, as it combines the traditions of quiltmaking with the memories of the many lost to us, will remain a permanent testament to the universality and timelessness of quilts.

When we first started the research for this book we classified quilts into only two categories: antique and contemporary. Any quilt made before 1950 was an antique and any quilt made after 1950 was contemporary. Within the category of contemporary quilts, further distinctions rapidly became apparent. New quilts seem to fall into three categories even though the boundaries defining them are not always clear. In fact, the definitions get pretty fuzzy. There are the traditional contemporary quilts, contemporary quilts, and art quilts.

Traditional contemporary quilts are made by hand but are of patterns so well known they can be turned out quicker and cheaper than the other two categories. They are in the lower price ranges, some selling for only a little over $100.

"With traditional patterns, we don't have to train our quiltmakers," explained Randy Silvers, quiltmaker and owner of the Country Peddler Shop in Burnsville, North Carolina. "These are patterns the quiltmakers are familiar with. They've been making them for years and know how to make them efficiently. When you make a new design, the work doesn't end with making the templates. There are procedures to figure out to find the quickest, simplest, and most accurate way to make that new design. That takes time."

What most quiltmakers today refer to as contemporary quilts are those in a higher price range that incorporate new designs and block patterns into the traditional quilt form. Their creators stop just short of calling themselves artists and prefer the title quiltmaker. These quilts take traditional quilting design one step further, adding innovative elements of color, geometry, and quilting patterns. There may also be innovative use of fabrics, incorporating nontraditional pieces such as furs or denim. But these are rare. The contemporary quiltmaker innovates primarily with design and color, preferring to stay with high-quality designer cottons.

Someday, if properly cared for, this contemporary appliqué quilt will be an antique collectible. Since you have to live with it in the meantime, look for one that you love. Even a prize-winner isn't worth the price if it doesn't make you happy.

When we tried to define the art quilt, the dividing line with contemporary quilts became fuzzy. We decided to distinguish art quilts from the contemporary quilts by their higher level of innovation, and will discuss them by themselves in chapter 14. Certainly some contemporary quilts qualify as art quilts. In those cases, we defined the quilt by how the quiltmaker defined it.

We must point out that some of the fuzziness between contemporary quilts and art quilts is the result of old attitudes about what is art and what's not. There is the belief that people without art training cannot produce art, therefore the quiltmaker with no art background is not an artist. There is also the uneasy feeling that art is something so special, so unique, that it is beyond the grasp of most people. As Michael James points out in chapter 14, some quiltmakers feel it's presumptuous to refer to themselves as artists, hence their quilts, no matter how spectacular or innovative, are not art. Throughout the history of quilting, the mostly anonymous quiltmaker rarely referred to her or his work as art. That attitude persists today with many talented quiltmakers preferring the term *contemporary* rather than *art*.

Economics can also play a part in defining a quilt as art or contemporary. There is a difference in price. Where contemporary quilts range from $1,500 to over $3,000, art quilts may start at $3,000 and go as high as $20,000, depending on the quilt's size, design, and the artist's reputation. Some contemporary quiltmakers may feel they'll price themselves out of the market by defining their work as art. As we've stated, we'll define art quilts as those with very innovative designs and cover them in chapter 14.

Purchasing a new traditional or contemporary quilt requires the same common sense as buying an antique. Naturally you shouldn't have to worry about stains, tears, or wear in a new quilt as you would in an antique, but there are other things to consider.

"You should look at the amount of piecing and quilting in the quilt," said Randy Silvers. "If you're looking at a Double Wedding Ring, queen size, with forty-eight rings, which is six by eight over the top, or one with less, you're not getting the piecing and quilting you would in one of ours with sixty-three rings." Silvers's traditional patterned quilts, made with good-quality country calicoes and muslin, start at $300.

"If it has a different binding, a pieced border, or a pieced back, that adds to the price," continued Silvers. "And color coordination. That's important to me. I don't like a pretty blue, green, and mauve quilt with purple in it. Or a nice purple quilt with orange." The Country Peddler Quilt Shop also offers a slightly higher-priced quilt, more contemporary but still with a country flair, in the $400-to-$700 price range. The Colorado Log Cabin, a traditional log cabin that incorporates a pieced star into the intersecting corners, is one of these more contemporary, yet traditional, quilts. Silvers, as do most traditional and contemporary quiltmakers and dealers, does a lot of custom orders.

"My business is about fifty-fifty," he said. Silvers keeps anywhere from fifty to one hundred finished quilts in the shop from which customers select their purchase. He also takes orders for quilts and specializes in a Christmas quilt each year.

"We make it in February and hang it in the shop until October, taking orders." The Christmas quilts, as well as the other quilts for sale, are made by Silvers and a group of women who work out of their homes.

Quilting is a growing cottage industry in the United States. Omar and Sylvia Petershiem operate a quilt shop out of the basement of their home in Bird-in-Hand, Pennsylvania, in the middle of Lancaster County, considered the best place in the country to find exceptional quilts. The Petershiems employ over one hundred quiltmakers, some of whom specialize. One woman does only Lone Star quilts; two other women do only Double Wedding Ring quilts.

So specialized is the Petershiems' work force that the tops are made by different women than those who do the quilting. Completed tops are sent to the Petershiems, marked for quilting by their sons, assembled into the quilt sandwich, and sent to other women for quilting. The entire family staffs the basement showroom, and a centrally placed platform holds a stack of quilts. By folding them back, a task only the Petershiems perform, each quilt is displayed as it would look on a bed. Prices were in the same range as other traditional quilts for either geometric or appliquéd designs.

There are sources for new traditional quilts other than quilt shops. Regional fairs may offer quilts for sale. One of these is the Kutztown Folk Festival, held yearly in Kutztown, Pennsylvania, always during the week that includes the Fourth of July. In 1991, the festival celebrated its Twenty-Seventh Annual Quilting Contest during its forty-second consecutive year. Quilts are judged in three categories: pieced, appliquéd, and all-quilted (formerly known as white-on-white or whitework). Over 1,700 quilts were entered and $5,800 in prize money was awarded. All the entries, including the ribbon winners, were then offered for sale.

Racks of quilts stand waiting for owners at the Kutztown Folk Festival, an annual event held in Pennsylvania. Regional fairs are often good sources for traditional contemporary quilts.

The Quilt Barn at the Kutztown Folk Festival is comprised of twelve sections of racks, six on each side of the building. Each side section, as well as a space across the back of the barn behind the sales table, is draped with approximately one hundred quilts. They range in size from twin to king, and when we were there last the prices ranged from $413 to $498, including Pennsylvania sales tax. The festival committee takes a percentage of the sale and quilts are snapped up quickly. We attended on the third day of the festival and by that time almost half of the quilts had already sold. Many of the quilts were excellent examples of Pennsylvania Dutch–style appliqué.

You can warm yourself twice with your quilt purchase by buying a new traditional from a Mennonite Relief Sale. These are held throughout the country. These sales aren't exclusively quilts; there are other things for sale as well. Many Mennonite churchwomen, as churchwomen have over the centuries, make and donate quilts to these auctions. The proceeds benefit the needy.

For the last seventeen years, Susan Harris of New Canaan, Connecticut, has acted as an agent selling commissioned quilts made by Indiana Amish quiltmakers. Harris will even choose the material for your quilt and prewash the fabric. Then she mails the washed fabric with your design and size requirements to one quilter to piece and another to quilt. Quilts take two to three months to complete and average $800 to $1,000, which is less than a contemporary quilt.

The Freedom Quilting Bee in Alberta, Alabama, was founded in 1966 out of the Civil Rights movement when more than sixty black women formed a co-op to make quilts, supplement their incomes, and create a local industry. The Mountain Artisans of West Virginia are a similar group. Checking with a local quilt guild will give you many sources for new traditional quilts, and some of those sources may be cottage-industry-style co-ops that will benefit people in your area.

Another source for traditional quilts is the advertisements in quilting magazines. We contacted many of these advertisers and learned a few things we'd like to pass on to you. First, many of these quilts are machine quilted. In our opinion, which is echoed by many others, machine quilting isn't as pretty, and certainly not as well done, as hand quilting. Always ask if the quilting will be done by machine or by hand.

Through these ads you can specify a pattern, size, and color scheme, and have the quilt made especially for you. Or you can ask for pictures of what the quiltmaker has available. Most of the photos we received were taken with instant cameras. You can see the quilt, but it's hard to determine workmanship from the pictures. Although it's an extra expense, it's a good idea to ask to have a quilt sent to you to view. Only then can you see the quality of work and accurately judge the colors and prints included in the quilt.

Prices for quilts from these ads were incredibly reasonable. This is because many of these quiltmakers work part-time and need the money so desperately they're willing to work cheaply. Some of them simply don't know how to price their work because they can't, or won't, figure a reasonable hourly rate for their time. When they do attempt a realistic figure for their time, they may find that their quilts are overpriced for the market. Many quilt buyers simply don't know how much work goes into even the simplest quilt. These buyers want the handwork but think they should pay the same low price they would pay for a machine-quilted, mass-produced spread available in a department store. Regional differences also affect price. You'd expect to pay more in New York City than you would in Selma, Alabama. The price shouldn't be different, perhaps, for the same level of expertise, but regional differences do exist. And, like many other of our businesses, the quiltmaking cottage industry has come under economic fire from foreign sources in recent years, contributing to the low prices of these quilts.

"Too many people are mixed up on quality," said Margaret Cavigga of Northridge, California, owner of the Margaret Cavigga Quilt Collection. "Dealers are putting Americans out of jobs buying quilts made in China. They're buying them for thirty dollars and selling them in the hundreds. Most of these are not of the high quality of our quiltmakers. It's killing the quilt cottage industry."

The quality of the competition aside, even some of the advertisers we contacted were not doing high-quality work. Explore all your options by contacting these advertisers, but make sure you're getting the best possible quilt for your money. Ask for references and follow up on them. Always ask to see the quilt, especially if you're dealing long-distance. It'll cost you return postage if you decide not to buy the quilt, but that's less expensive than paying for one you don't want when you finally get it.

Ask what kind of fabrics are in the quilt. They should be quality cottons, but some quiltmakers will use polyester blends because they might wear better and are more colorfast. If you want only 100 percent cotton, make sure you ask for it. Also ask if the fabrics are prewashed. Most quiltmakers do this to prevent the colors from running after the quilt is completed and to preshrink the fabric. It only takes one piece of red fabric to run and turn an entire quilt pink to ruin it, and your investment, forever. A quilt made from unwashed fabrics will look smooth and even, but the first wash may cause wrinkles and puckers in the top. Always require that your quilt be made of prewashed fabrics.

Ask if the top is assembled by machine or by hand. Machine piecing, except in appliqué, is not a detriment to a quilt or its price. What's important is the surface design. If the points match, the seams are flat and even, and the sashings line up, whether it's done by hand or machine doesn't matter except for your personal preference. But you should expect to pay more for a quilt with a hand-pieced top than one that's machine assembled. Machine assembly saves time, so hand-piecing costs extra.

The exception, of course, is appliqué. By today's standards, appliqué stitches should be invisible. Some quilters use the close zigzag stitch on their machines to do appliqué. This practice reduces the price of a quilt because it drastically reduces the time required to complete an appliqué quilt. It is not, however, considered quality workmanship. Zigzag appliqués are already available, mass-produced, in department stores. You want a quilt that's one of a kind even if it's a traditional appliqué pattern. Insist that appliqué be by hand or find another quiltmaker.

Determine the amount of quilting. Outline quilting is easy and fast. A quilt with just outline quilting should cost less than one with more elaborate quilting designs. As you increase the amount and complexity of the quilting, the price should increase. Again, whitework should be the most expensive because the design and surface texture of the top are solely due to the quilting stitches.

As was already noted, a quilt with a plain border is less expensive than one with a design worked into it. Be prepared to talk about borders when you commission any quilt. You can request more than one border or one that has a pieced design. Sawtooth and Prairie Point borders are rare in antique quilts and you might want one on your new quilt. Be prepared to pay extra for this. It takes considerably more time to create a pieced border than it does to add multiple strip borders. A border of more than one strip should cost a little more than one with only one strip.

Make sure you know, before you talk to a quiltmaker, exactly what you want. Discuss the project thoroughly. The quiltmaker will have questions, too, about what size, design, and color scheme you want. She may raise other questions or point out aspects of her work that you need to know. It will make the quiltmaker's job easier if you're prepared, and this kind of preparation ensures you won't be disappointed with the finished quilt.

Expect to pay more for a contemporary-style quilt. As was already noted, these prices can run from $1,500 to over $3,000. That's more than many antique quilts cost but you're buying a known quantity. There's no guesswork in buying a contemporary quilt. You know the artist, the materials, and will be told how to care for the pristine-condition quilt to get as many years' use out of it as possible. A quilt guild in your area can provide you with names of local quiltmakers and artists. The guild should have information on upcoming shows and sales and should also know national-reputation quiltmakers and how to contact them. You should ask the contemporary quiltmaker several questions.

"Ask if it's an original design," said Randy Silvers. "And if it is, ask when it was made. Ask if it's signed and numbered." The work of contemporary quiltmakers is often cumulative with later works showing a greater level of sophistication, detail, and workmanship. Quiltmakers often work in series, as do other artists, constantly expanding an original theme. The first in a series, or the early works, may not be as innovative, as creative, or as extensive as the later works.

"Ask the contents of the fabric. They should be cotton," continued Silvers. "You need to see the fabrics and colors that will be used in the quilt. Ask how much and what kind of batting is inside."

Silvers also had concerns about the quilting.

"The quilting stitches should be at least eight to ten to the inch," he said. "That's a running inch. Sometimes the stitching line gets measured on the diagonal of a square inch. Those stitches are too big. Eight to ten stitches per running inch should be the minimum requirement."

Silvers recommended requiring a scaled-down drawing of the commissioned work. The quiltmaker needs latitude to create, but you should be happy with the design. So ask to see it first. This will be a rough drawing and probably not in color, although the predominant colors of the quilt should be noted. If you request a color drawing, expect to pay for it over and above the cost of the quilt. Color drawings take precious time the professional quilter needs for other things.

"You need to ask for the finished, completed price," said Silvers. Some quiltmakers assemble the top and send it out to be quilted. Most do the entire job themselves, but just in case the quiltmaker you've contacted doesn't, make sure you ask if the price quoted includes everything or if there'll be an additional charge for quilting and finishing.

"You'll probably be asked to pay a fifty percent deposit," said Silvers. "Most designers ask for that. It will usually only cover the price of the fabric and some of their time."

Don't buy just on price. A cheap price might mean a cheap quilt, and in that case, any price is too high to pay. Take your time commissioning a quilt or selecting one in a shop. Know what to ask for, what to demand, and how that will affect the price of the work.

The rule of thumb for buying a new traditional, contemporary, or art quilt is the same as for buying an antique: If you don't love it, don't buy it!

CHAPTER FOURTEEN

ART QUILTS

We've included this chapter on art quilts because they can be as collectible as antiques. Their collectibility comes from the skill and reputation of the maker in the same way that paintings and sculpture become collectible. Actually, the only method of distinguishing art quilts from contemporary quilts is by their level of innovation. Many of the quiltmakers using traditional patterns and techniques are also making art. If the quilt is a Carolina Lily, Drunkard's Path, Log Cabin, or other traditional quilt block *and* is assembled and stitched using traditional methods, then, whether it's for a bed or a wall, we've made the distinction that it's a contemporary quilt and dealt with it in chapter 13. The use of innovative patterns, assembly or stitching techniques, or the use of mixed media classifies a quilt, for our purposes, as an art quilt. We also abide by the maker's definition. If the quiltmaker says it's art, then it's art.

It's been our contention since the beginning of this book that most antique quilts survived because they were considered art by their makers and the succeeding generations who carefully preserved, repaired, and enjoyed them.

It appears that there are as many different definitions of what makes a creation art as there are artists, collectors, and critics. Whether or not antique, contemporary, or innovative quilts fit those definitions, and therefore qualify as art, is a highly debated issue between quiltmakers and the art world. It's certainly not a debate that will be decided within this chapter, but we include a discussion of the issue to help you decide within which quilt category you want to specialize.

One of the definitions of art taken to task by quiltmakers is that art is only art when the creator knows she or he is making art—when art and only art is the primary objective.

"There's still the belief that common people didn't make art," said Michael James, who's been creating art quilts for twenty years. "But the Native Americans didn't know they were making art when they made their pottery and weavings, and those items are in galleries and museums classified as art."

"I think the creation of great art is a rare phenomenon," wrote James in his book *The Second Quiltmaker's Handbook* (Prentice-Hall, 1981). "It is something that may begin with an artist's idea, but is built as much on the passage

This art quilt, made by Ann Argenio, incorporates the techniques of appliqué, embroidery, and cutwork, and contains dozens of different materials, including velvet, metallic threads, fabric paint, chenille, calicoes, prints, satins, and many others. Ann does work that ranges from this complex and intricate to simple optical illusion patches and small quilts.

of time and the steady yet evolving appeal of the work. It transcends its medium and its craft to express something that can be universally felt and appreciated."

The art world's side of the argument splits art into fine art and applied arts or crafts. Fine arts, according to our closest-to-hand dictionary, the *American Heritage Dictionary of the English Language*, defines fine art as "art produced or intended primarily for beauty alone rather than utility…" including sculpture, painting, drawing, and often architecture, literature, drama, music, and the dance. The inclusion of architecture, when quilts are generally excluded, is a mystery, but traditionally fine arts have meant, in broad terms and including all media, painting, drawing, or sculpture. Applied arts or crafts include furniture making, needlework, pottery, weaving, quilting—everything, in fact, also categorized as folk art. That quilts have been excluded from the realm of fine art simply because they have some utility seems absurd and certainly diminishes the work being done by serious artists such as James.

"Regrettably, these artists face considerable resistance from the male-dominated art establishment, which, for the most part, continues to associate fabric with 'women's work,'" wrote Penny McMorris and Michael Kile in their book *The Art Quilt*. "This denial of the changing role of fabric in art is spurious.…"

McMorris and Kile maintain, as we do, that quilts were always art. "Although they may not have wanted to verbalize this fact, our great-grandmothers knew this, and so did those in the family and the neighborhood who delighted in quilts and enjoyed them."

"The object that traditionally functioned as bedcover is for all practical purposes obsolete," continued James in *The Second Quiltmaker's Handbook*. "It serves as art form because there is a unique quality about a stitched-fabric surface design that can be duplicated in no other medium. It survives also because it can be art, enriching our daily experience of ourselves and our world."

That quilts were once made as necessary items, there is no argument. That they quickly became art forms made more for their beauty than their utility is a belief held by many. There are, after all, easier ways to achieve weight and warmth than expending the time, expense, energy, and expertise that it takes to create even the simplest block-style quilt. And, paraphrasing *Star Trek's* Mr. Spock, there always were alternatives. Comforters, tied instead of quilted, probably made from whole pieces of cloth, would have been far more practical, easier to make, and less expensive even in Colonial days. What Colonial housewife, after spending countless hours raising sheep, shearing, cleaning, carding, spinning, and weaving—or raising and preparing flax for linen—would then take that precious cloth and cut it into little squares to make a bed covering when all she really had to do was place cotton or wool batting between two lengths of cloth and tie them together to make a blanket? To believe that all quilts were made purely for utilitarian purposes is to underestimate the efficiency and economy of the Colonial or pioneer woman. Utility certainly diminishes their obvious love affair with color, design, and beauty.

"A quilt is not something that one dreams up on a Saturday morning and completes by Sunday night, as one might a small painting or a simple piece of pottery," wrote Robert Bishop and Carter Houck in *All Flags Flying: American Patriotic Quilts as Expressions of Liberty* (E. P. Dutton, 1986). "In terms of hours expended it is more on the order of creating a marble statue or painting a fresco."

That most quilts, certainly those around today, were works of art to the maker and the maker's heirs we believe is a given. But, of course, not all quilts made can pass the tests of time and universal emotion that stamp a creation as art now and forever. For the viewer to see an example and know it's art, there must be that indefinable something that James calls "the clear imprint of originality." James, a strong proponent of quilts as art, admits to one bias of what makes a quilt a work of art.

"I'm guilty of advocating that an artist has to have art training," said

James, admitting that the definition is partially based on economics. "Unlike the doctor and medicine, or the accountant, or other professions that have to be certified to be practiced as a vocation, anybody can be an artist. Anyone can hang out a sign that says 'Artist Within.' No one questions it; no one challenges it. I'm making a living with my art, and I feel artists should have some training before they call themselves artists. I believe not much art is made by people who don't have art background.

"I tell people I'm an artist. When they ask what kind, I say I trained as a painter but I make quilts," continued James. "Some people change the subject right there and some people ask more questions. Some people feel calling yourself an artist is presumptuous. I think of myself as more than a quiltmaker. I don't think or work the same way now as I did when I first started quilts and was making bed quilts in Carolina Lily patterns. Then I felt I was not making art, I was decorating."

Jinny Beyer, who makes about one quilt a year and has been creating them since 1972, calls herself a quiltmaker and dislikes the is-it-art controversy.

"I don't like those terms," she said when asked why she doesn't refer to herself as a quilt artist. "Every quilt is art. I'm a contemporary quiltmaker working in a traditional style. I like the geometry, symmetry, and orderliness that leads me to do different things." When Beyer first started quilting, she tried selling some small quilted items.

"I found out that when you put a price tag on your work you compromise your integrity," she said. "People start becoming critical, questioning the price, commenting on the colors. If you're true to yourself and do what you feel, you will be much freer to be creative. I'm my own critic. My quilts are such a personal thing, there's so much of me in them I can't put a price tag on them." Beyer is an author, lecturer, and teacher of quiltmaking, but not a salesman. She has never sold any of her quilts, preferring to earmark them to give away to family and friends.

"I've had people say 'Name your price,'" said Beyer. "I don't want the money. I'd rather give a quilt away. I just like to create."

"This is a discussion that's been going on for many years," said Stacy Hollander, associate curator at the Museum of American Folk Art, about the quilts-as-art debate. "It's been going on since we started studying folk art! If you're looking at quilts as folk art, then you'll have trouble gaining acceptance in the fine art world. There are many serious fabric artists whose work is fine art.

"It's a slow, uphill battle," Hollander continued. "Sure, there's some prejudice, I should say hesitancy, in the fine art world in accepting anything in the folk art world. But I believe there is room for any kind of art. When you talk about the talent and success of the work itself, then we have no problem accepting a work in any art world."

Age is another definition of a quilt as art. The belief is that antique quilts are art simply because they're old. They must have that clear imprint of individuality that James refers to, but sometimes the mere fact that a quilt is old gives it art status. This belief downgrades the work done by James and his peers to a craft simply because it's new. James believes that what really keeps quilts as crafts is economics.

"If you're talking about the New York art world, they're protecting their market," he explained. "That world doesn't want more competition. There's a lot of competition in art for very few dollars. If you can exclude one group, such as folk art, like quilts, then there's less competition for those few dollars. It's very easy to dismiss quilts as 'women's work.'"

Even among themselves, there is controversy between traditional and innovative quiltmakers. James related a recent experience.

"I spoke at a conference in San Francisco of about three hundred people," he said. "When I was done, while the rest of the audience applauded, enthusiastically, there were several women in the front row with their hands in their laps, backs straight, faces stiff. Obviously, I didn't reach them. There is some tension between the two camps, the traditional and the innovative. It's a very small percentage, but the tension does exist.

"Their reaction is a symbol, representative on a larger scale, of the push to conservative values and viewpoints in the country today. There's a stronger push to tradition and returning to traditional notions about the quilt." James sees the tension as also the result of too few dollars in the marketplace, creating more competition between traditional and innovative quiltmakers.

"Even in the craft world artists are desperately struggling to protect their own interests. If you can diminish another craft, it means a bigger market for what's left."

It's interesting to note that just as there is history to the quilt, there is also a history of the quilt as art. The first view of quilts as art came with the camera. John Perreault, in the introduction to *The Art Quilt*, states that he believes the invention of photography in the 1890s was the first step in classifying quilts as art. Because quilts photographed better on a wall, a vertical surface, than they did on a bed, a horizontal surface, people got their first full-length views of the startling and pleasing combinations of pattern, color, and workmanship that is a quilt. The simple act of taking a quilt off the bed and hanging it on a wall did more to promote the quilt as art than any other event because it was only then that we recognized the strong visual impact of quilts.

It was in the early 1900s that fine artists began a move away from the traditional forms of fine art by working with useful objects. This was one of the periods of intense industrialization in our country. During these periods, the love affair with technology was so great that applied arts declined in favor of the produce of that technology. But in this time period, the products were considered so ugly and poorly made that fine artists turned to applied crafts in a quest to combine beauty with utility.

"This involvement of the fine artist in the applied arts raised the status of all the crafts, quilts among them, in the eyes of impressionable critics and collectors," wrote McMorris and Kile. They date the hanging of quilts on walls to the early 1920s, when traditional quilts of the 1800s became collectible. As collectibles, they were displayed rather than used, hung on a wall instead of spread over a bed, viewed on the vertical like paintings. At that time, only antique quilts were displayed on the vertical, reinforcing the theory that old quilts were art, new quilts were craft.

Cloth has been used in traditional forms of fine art since as early as 1958. Quilts, say McMorris and Kile, are the origin of collage. Once confined only to pasting, collage is now defined as "the piecing or placing together of various pre-existing two-dimensional elements." The new definition clearly includes quilting, and since the quilt "predates anything done by Picasso or Braque," these authors attribute the birth of collage to quilts.

In the 1950s, Pop Art creators did what quiltmakers had done for years— used common, everyday objects in their work. Artists in the 1970s borrowed liberally from folk art forms, using patterns from quilts, tapestries, needlework, baskets, carpets, mosaic tiles, and other utilitarian, but decorative, common objects. Still, though artists borrowed from, learned from, and were inspired by folk art such as quilts, quilts themselves were still not accepted as art.

The second greatest leap along the path to acceptance in the art world came in 1971 when the Whitney Museum of American Art opened its exhibit "Abstract Design in American Quilts." Once again quilts were hung vertically, as art. This time they were exhibited by a well-known, well-respected member of the art world. After it closed in New York, the exhibit traveled the United States and Europe for four years, serving as a startling reminder of the visual, emotional, and artistic qualities of the quilt.

Although the Whitney exhibit is credited with bringing quilts as art to the attention of the public and the press on a national and international scale, it wasn't the first exhibit to remind us that quilts are art. In 1965, the Newark Museum exhibited a show titled "Optical Quilts," marking the first time quilts were viewed purely for art instead of for their historical, technical, or nostalgic value.

The quilt shows of the 1960s and 1970s fanned a fire of interest in quilts, and in the 1970s the quilt finally stood as a truly unique American creation. Finally, it had garnered some of the respect it took centuries to earn. In 1976 the Museum of Contemporary Crafts showcased new quilts in an exhibit titled "The New American Quilt." In 1979 the first Quilt National was held, sponsored by the Ohio Cultural Arts Center. This was the first such show to spotlight contemporary, original designs instead of concentrating on traditional ones. Even the crafts world, late to recognize the importance of quilting, took another look. The quilt shows, whether featuring antique or modern designs, were attracting much attention. Sales of antique quilts hit a peak in the 1970s and contemporary quiltmakers busily designed, assembled, and quilted to meet the demand for more and more quilts. As in the 1920s, fine artists turned their attention to the quilt medium. Traditional and innovative quiltmakers alike surged into the quilt art scene, making new quilts designed as art, their only function to be displayed on walls, as well as making quilts for beds as decoration.

In the early 1970s, the coming Bicentennial promoted a burgeoning interest in quilts just as the Centennial had a hundred years before. Local quilt shows and fairs inspired a renewed interest in making quilts, and quilt groups and guilds formed that are still meeting today. Once again, their historic implications and close link to our national heritage created a quilt revival, bringing quiltmaking and the enjoyment of quilts out of the hands of a few and to the notice of many. Many of our current quilt artists learned their techniques in these groups. Most started as traditionalists, then began innovating.

"I'll be satisfied only if I feel that the works says something new," said Michael James, "about my involvement with the interaction of design, materials, and technique."

One other factor fueled the push to promote quilts to art status: the feminist movement of the 1970s. What the nostalgia of the Bicentennial began, the women's movement fostered and nurtured. Renewed interest in "women's work" uncovered the mysteries of antique quilts. Mostly unsigned and undated, they represented the most anonymous of traditional women's art. The feminist movement sent us scurrying to find the histories of these anonymous women, to make them known and therefore remembered. But even if they are never known, their quilts survive as a testament that they lived and created. People quilted to leave their mark on the world; to leave something behind to prove that they, too, lived, created, and mattered in the world.

McMorris and Kile quoted Bernice Steinbaum of the Bernice Steinbaum Gallery in New York as predicting that quilts will be the next medium to break through and achieve status in the art world. James doesn't agree.

"I don't think there's been any real acceptance of quilts as art in the 'art world,'" he said. "Quilts have brought people into galleries and museums who otherwise wouldn't walk through the door. Gallery owners and curators know that if they put a quilt show up, they'll get more people across the threshold. The bottom of the ladder in art is quilts."

Despite the reluctance of the recognized art critic and commentary world to embrace quilts, James knows his work is art. With a nonegotistical confidence born of accomplishment, he just *knows* his work will last.

"Getting visibility to promote and sell your work is difficult," said James. He sells his quilts direct to customers, occasionally showing at galleries. Most quilt artists don't have permanent relationships with galleries and James is no exception. "I know how to explain my work and how to display it. I think galleries are confused about that. But despite the problems, I feel strongly that my work, and the work of a few others, will survive. I really believe that a hundred years from now, my work will surface and increase in value. I won't be there, but I believe I've done such good work that my quilts will still be here." As proof of his confidence in his work, there have already been resales of James's earlier work.

As the controversy rages, traditionalists will continue to affect innovators and innovators will keep adding to the knowledge of quilt design and technique. Together they'll keep producing art for all of us to enjoy. Ultimately, the question of whether or not quilts are art will be decided by the people who view them as well as the people who make them.

"...art is what results when a person attempts to make something that he or she feels is beautiful and then, when completed, bears the unique fingerprint of the mind and hand that created it," wrote James. "To be art, an art activity and its product need simply be. Ultimately, the evidence is in the work itself."

Purchasing your art quilt involves a little more work than buying or commissioning a traditional or contemporary quilt. We covered those sources in the last chapter. This time, you'll have to educate yourself in the craft art world. Quilt guilds and associations frequently offer guest speakers and quilt artists are sought after for these groups. Join a guild, or get on a mailing list of local quilt groups so you'll be notified when, and where, guest speakers are coming to your area. Attend quilt shows and events, particularly those like Quilt National that tend to attract both innovative and traditional work. It is at these events that you'll see many quilt artists' work and can discover what you like, and more importantly, what you want to own. Keep reading those quilting magazines, too. Although most quilt artists don't advertise in them to the extent contemporary quiltmakers do, the magazines regularly profile quilt artists. It's one more way to "meet" the artists, see their work, and learn about their motivation and art process.

"I meet most of my customers at lectures, workshops, and conferences," said James. "That's where I come in contact with people who like my work." Although James shows at galleries, he has no exclusive relationship with any. It's not because he's not well known. James has sold work to IBM and the Newark Museum, as well as to individual collectors. Over his twenty-year career, James has completed over 140 quilts and has sold over 130—almost his entire lifetime production. The decision to sell direct was made more because galleries simply don't have the space to display quilts adequately and many are still not sure they're really art. Galleries specializing only in quilts are rare because the market can't, or hasn't, supported them.

Once you've been to several shows, or seen an artist's work in a magazine, and decided what you want to own, contact the artist.

"Most people call and say they saw my work and they're interested," explained James. "If I have pieces available, I'll tell them and then mail slides. If I don't have anything at the moment, I'll send a slide portfolio and a price list. I always follow up if I haven't heard from them in a week or so."

Commissioning an art quilt, as in all of the fine arts, requires knowing the space it will fill and what use the room or area serves in the structure. You can also discuss color combinations, but that's the creative side of commissioning a quilt and you should be prepared to not dictate too much of the creative process. You must remember that you are commissioning a work of art. After all, that's why you went to all the time and trouble to find an artist or quiltmaker whose work you particularly liked. When you commission a piece, let the artist do what he or she does best: innovate and create. You should tell the artist what, among the works you have seen, touched you. What piece caused in you the greatest emotional response? What was it about the work you viewed that made you call this quilt artist? That information doesn't interfere with the artist's creative freedom.

You should request a pencil design. Most artists will provide this automatically, but if the quiltmaker doesn't offer it, ask for it. If you really want a full-color design in order to make your decision, be prepared to pay extra for it. The time required for an exact color design is built into the price of the quilt after it's been commissioned. A full-color design created on speculation is costly and some artists may require payment for their time—it does, after all, take them away from paying work with no guarantee that you'll buy the quilt once the artist has designed it. Some artists don't charge for a color design, but you should be prepared to pay a fee if it's requested.

James's prices range from $3,000 for a small piece to $16,000 for the largest. As with all art, sometimes the price is negotiable.

"I'm more likely to negotiate with a previous customer because I know they're serious," said James. "I have negotiated prices. I like it best when I tell someone the price and they agree to take it, but it's not unreasonable to make an offer." James frankly admitted that how negotiable a price is depends on how much money he has at the time—another common theme among artists. James pointed out that, in the market for art quilts, his prices are reasonable.

"A corporate commission piece could be twelve to fifteen feet or one hundred inches square," he explained. "Paintings or low-relief sculpture in that same size by an artist with the same reputation would be ten times as much as I charge. Quilts are still a bargain."

"This is still a fairly new medium," said Hollander about the discrepancy between prices for art quilts and comparable fine art pieces. "So much of the art price structure deals with precedence. And there are people, like Nancy Crow and Faith Ringgold, who have reached the fine art level. We have absolutely no difficulty accepting them as fine art, but this is a slow, ongoing process."

You can also buy art quilts through galleries. But, just as the cream of the antique crop of quilts is sold before they ever reach a showroom, so are art quilts. To learn about the art quilt world, build a relationship with a quilt guild and contact the Studio Art Quilts Association or a local chapter of the American Quilter's Society or the National Quilting Association (check our sources listing for the addresses and phone numbers).

Ask your town's art society for information on local quilt artists. When you find them, you'll have access to a specialist. Like any member of a profession or specialized activity, most quilt artists will know the work of other quilt artists and therefore are valuable contacts. You can keep in touch with what's happening in the quilt art world through them.

Art quilts, however defined, are well worth the search. They range from small wall pieces to bigger-than-bed-size hangings. Innovation in quilting has produced spectacular results, and the fact that quilting has attracted design innovators proves that quilts, as a distinctly American art form, will be with us at least as far into the future as we have enjoyed them in the past.

CHAPTER FIFTEEN

AFRICAN-AMERICAN QUILTS

As we noted in chapter 8, "Trends in the Marketplace," we feel that African-American quilts will be the next most sought after style of collectible quilt. The research for this chapter provided us with the most interesting, intriguing, and captivating reading about quilts and quiltmakers available. The study of African-American quilt design provides the opportunity for a close focus on the evolutionary aspect of quilting that is not as easily available in traditional American quilt design. The link between African-American quilt design and the art of African cultures is not as easy to prove, but research continues in this field that is both fascinating and necessary to completing the lore of quiltmaking available to us. What *The Quilters* (Patricia Cooper and Norma Bradley Buferd, Doubleday & Co., 1977) reveals to us about how American traditional quiltmakers create and feel about their quilts, *Afro-American Folk Art and Crafts* (G. K. Hall & Co., 1983; edited by William Ferris) shows as the innate design sense and sensibilities of the African-American-style quiltmaker. Both profile quiltmakers whose stories warm and awe us. If you read nothing else contained in our bibliography, read these two books—they should be on the top of your required reading list.

We should make the distinction here between African-American quiltmakers and African-American-style quilts. African-American quiltmakers did, and do, work in traditional American quilt formats. The African-American-style quilt, on the other hand, is a type of quilt that is as different, in visual impact, from the traditional pieced and appliqué quilts as a Picasso is from a Rembrandt. Descendants of African cultures that none of them ever knew except in bits and pieces of lore handed down over generations, African-American-style quiltmakers still incorporate design and color principles and improvisations that echo the art and creative freedom of their unknown ancestors. This is the link being explored by historians: How is it that nineteenth-century African-American quiltmakers' work is so evocative of African cultures? To explore this studies continue in linguistics, African and African-American textile use, and even chemistry to develop a way to determine race from hairs found in the body of a quilt to authenticate African-American quilt creations.

Why do we think African-American-style quilts are going to be the hot collectible of the future? Because, until the last decade, their artistic qualities, not to mention their historical significance, have been underrated and misunderstood. African-American-style quilts show such distinctive design and color differences they were essentially written off as the work of novice quiltmakers.

"'Afro-Traditional' quilts have irregular patterns which have been misperceived, by people versed in the standard American quiltmaking tradition, as mistakes," wrote J. Weldon Smith in the foreword for the catalog of the show "Who'd a Thought It," held at the San Francisco Crafts and Folk Art Museum in 1987–88. "A deeper understanding allows us to see that something else is going on here—a distinctly different African-American aesthetic of improvisation."

We admit to first viewing, uneducated, African-American-style quilts and feeling that they were, indeed, amateurish, inept attempts at making the kind of quilts we knew. We were used to uniform pieces, harmonious color balance, and an overall, precisely pieced pattern. African-American-style quilts at first looked jarring, with their use of vibrant primary colors (which certainly wouldn't match our living rooms!) and the irregularity of the piecing, with sashings of several different colors or printed fabrics that didn't line up in the neat, precise rows we're accustomed to in traditional geometric quilts. A closer inspection, and with introspection and a little knowledge added, showed that there was, actually, great thought given to the design of these quilts. Further research into African and slave cultures gives a greater appreciation for the design heritage of the African-American-style quilt. In his foreword, Smith explained the heritage of improvisation within structure, using available materials, that is the legacy to the African-American-style quiltmaker from African culture.

One of those legacies is the ability of these quiltmakers to work from a "model in their minds" to produce quilts that utilize the block style of traditional quilts without precise measuring and cutting of the component pieces. Irregular pieces pose challenges for the quiltmaker because each block or strip, when completed, may be of different width and length than the rest. Yet the finished quilt will have the standard square or rectangular finished form as traditional quilts.

Smith wrote: "As she deals with irregularities, drawing on a body of Afro-traditional techniques, she has opportunities to explore and excel in improvisational possibilities not open to the standard-traditional quilter." It is irregular piecing that gives the African-American-style quilt one of its many layers of movement. "The enjoyment of the variation that inevitably results from approximation is one of the underlying parallel attitudes that suggest a continuity between African and African-American textile arts." Smith notes that approximate measurement of quilt pieces is the root of African aesthetics as applied to quilts. He also noted that approximate piecing is "antithetical to Anglo-American values" in quiltmaking.

"Afro-American quilts tend to emphasize design over craftsmanship, and they exhibit many design principles which are not emphasized in other American textiles," wrote Maude Southwell Wahlman and John Scully in their introduction to the chapter "Aesthetic Principles in Afro-American Quilts" (in *Afro-American Folk Art and Crafts*). "Some are self-conscious about the irregularities in their quilts and tend consciously to make more regular quilts for white people."

Another design difference between African-American-style quilts and traditional American patchwork is the use of color. Wahlman and Scully note that bright, contrasting colors are preferred and used close together to heighten not only the impact of each individual color but their combination as well. They noted that their research showed purple and green, purple and yellow, red and white, orange and green, and black and pink as frequently used combinations. Instead of making the color combinations uniform throughout the quilt, as is the tendency even in scrap bag traditional quilts, African-American-style quiltmakers use color to move the eye toward what the maker considers the important parts of the quilt.

Overall, the color placement adds multiple layers of movement within the quilt top. Viewed as a whole, the eye travels over the quilt, noting a jumbled, kaleidoscopic array of color. The placement of one color in one part of the quilt that is used no where else concentrates the eye on that particular section and reveals the pattern design used there and only there. While traditional-style quilts have a uniform pattern to color placement, African-American-style quiltmakers arrange color to draw us forever back to the quilt to discover yet something new within it every time we look at it.

African-American-style quilts utilize large-scale designs. They do not conform to the 10-, 12-, or 16-inch-size uniform blocks of traditional quilts. Between blocks, or as the design for the entire quilt, strips are preferred. Most often the strips don't line up from row to row, but that design technique only adds to the visually arresting quality of the quilts. Often the strips are pieced with fabrics of different colors or prints to make a strip long enough to use in the quilt. This is also a design choice and not just the result of the maker's running out of enough fabric to make a long-enough strip.

"They select colors and pattern designs which are easily distinguished from white traditions in Amish and Appalachian communities," wrote Ferris in the introduction to *Afro-American Folk Art and Crafts*. "Use of primary colors and their strip or 'string' patterns are particularly important in black quilts."

The earliest African-American-style quilts known today are the two pictorial Bible quilts made by Harriet Powers in 1886 and 1898. The first quilt, now owned by the Smithsonian Institution, was shown by Powers at the Cotton Fair of 1886 in Athens, Georgia. A white woman, Jennie Smith, saw the quilt and wanted to buy it. Powers refused. Four years later, after falling on hard times and needing money, she offered it to Smith, who bought it. Through Smith, Powers received a commission from women in Atlanta to create a second quilt, now owned by the Museum of Fine Arts in Boston. Both of these quilts illustrate the design differences between traditional and African-American-style quiltmaking. They also illustrate Powers's own artistic and creative intent in the selection of scenes.

"Judging by what she selected, I think she recorded fateful events concerning people in her society, cataclysmic natural occurrences, and biblical figures which demonstrated the Christian themes of her interest: threat, deliverance, and repose," wrote Marie Jeanne Adams, also in *Afro-American Folk Art and Crafts*. Both of these quilts are at once excellent examples of African-American-style quilts *and* pictorial quilts. The insights they offer into quilt design and artistic intent are many and varied. The Powers tradition in this quilt style is being ably carried on by contemporary quilt artists such as Faith Ringgold, who combines a multimedia approach using canvas, acrylics, cloth, and thread with the design principles of African-American heritage.

We also believe that the supply of African-American-style quilts, both antique and contemporary, has not yet been found or even sought out by dealers and collectors. But as appreciation for this style of quilt increases and the value rises, the forgotten and hoarded store of these quilts will be uncovered and placed on the market. The knowledgeable collector, and those collecting to preserve and increase our store of knowledge of women and their work, will recognize the historic importance of these quilts and the mystique of their makers.

"Our task as audience," wrote Ferris, "is to understand her eye and place it within the line of her hands, her region, and her history."

"We need to remember the women whose hands warmed, loved, protected, healed, and reassured," wrote Wahlman and Scully. "Quilting is an extension of those hands."

The African-American-style quiltmaker adds a richness to the body of work that is quilts and should not be forgotten. For that reason alone, these quilts are collectible.

References

SOURCES AND RESOURCES

Whether you are just starting the search for your first quilt or are continuing the search for your next one, it is always helpful to have people to whom you can go for information, advice, and for *quilts*! In scouring the countryside for just those three things we came up with many names, in all categories. We've listed those sources below so you will have a place to start. Happy quilt hunting.

Antique Quilts

There are many, many sources of antique quilts across the country; you can find them just by looking under "Quilts" in the yellow pages, contacting a local quilt guild or museum, or checking with local antiques shops. The sources we list below are just a few of those to be found, and in many cases they are where we found the nearly 750 quilts listed in the price list chapters. These are not the only places we found our quilts; many came from tiny to medium-size antiques shops, auctions, flea markets, and estate sales.

But the people and shops listed below all have extensive knowledge of quilts, not just of antiques in general. Many of them have been collectors and/or dealers for ten to thirty years, and many specialize just in quilts. We have found them to be reputable, knowledgeable, and willing to help collectors, beginners and experienced, to find the quilts they seek.

Often, antiques dealers will pick up a quilt or two in their travels looking for Americana, antique furniture, household items, and the like. Although they mean well, they may guess at the date and price of a quilt, and you may get taken for a ride. Of course, you can also find some incredible bargains. The former is more likely than the latter, though.

As we have noted, you are much safer sticking with knowledgeable dealers, at least until you are educated enough yourself to date and price reasonably well. And even if you find a prize in a little out-of-the-way antiques shop or barn sale, it is great to have a knowledgeable friend to help you evaluate your find.

As you might expect, we found many more dealers in larger cities than in small towns. You, of course, will have a much easier time locating dealers in your area, not having to work long-distance and being more familiar with the area. As you begin to look you will be amazed, as were we, how many sources you can find just based on referrals from other dealers, collectors, and such. If you are having difficulty, call one or more of the people listed below; they may just know someone in your area—or be willing to help you themselves.

Ames Gallery of American Folk Art
2661 Cedar Berkley
San Francisco, CA 94102
415-845-4949
Although a dealer in all sorts of folk art items, the owner of this shop is very knowledgeable about quilts, having been a collector for many years. She usually has forty to fifty on hand.

Black Mountain Antiques
100 Sutton Avenue
Black Mountain, NC 28711
704-669-6218
Aly Goodwin has some very high-quality quilts in her collection, and seems to have a knack for finding the unusual. She also collects the stories that go with the quilts, dealing directly with the families from whence they come.

Calico Country: Antique Quilts and Country Furnishings
79 Washington Street
Marblehead, MA 01945
Lynne Wynne has a lovely little shop in this marvelous New England seacoast town, and some great quilts, too. She can arrange for quilt cleaning and restoration, and also sells some nifty wall hangers for quilts.

Margaret Cavigga Quilt Collection
8648 Melrose Avenue
Los Angeles, CA 90069
213-659-3020
An acknowledged leader in the field, Margaret has one of the largest quilt collections in the world. She has written books on the subject of quilts, and has had her quilts featured on Hallmark calendars.

Ginnie Christie Quilts
38996 NE Scravel Hill Road
Albany, OR 97321
503-327-1473

    Ginnie does a lot of quilt shows, and sells her quilts out of a shop in her home, so she has no set hours but works primarily by appointment. She has a lovely collection with many very reasonably priced quilts from all over the country.

The Connecticut Quilt Collection at Main Street Cellars Antiques
120 Main Street
New Canaan, CT 06840
203-966-8348

    This quilt cooperative, in an upscale suburb near New York City, is a new venture for Sandra Wright and several quilt dealers. They have pulled together a great collection, including some in very affordable price ranges.

The Cooperage
South Street and Route 119
P.O. Box 998
Townsend, MA 01469-0998
508-597-3042

    This small shop is next to the Townsend Historical Society, which features some impressive quilt shows. Susan Bates, who runs this store, usually has a dozen or so attractive and attractively priced quilts available.

The Down Quilt Shop
518 Columbus Avenue
New York, NY 10024
212-496-8980

    This country store in New York City handles mostly contemporary Amish and other quilts, but also has some antique quilts at reasonable prices.

M. Finkel & Daughter
936 Pine Street
Philadelphia, PA 19107
215-627-7797

    Although this father/daughter team's association with quilts is primarily in the role of fabric restorers and cleaners, they also have antique quilts for sale.

Laura Fisher/Antique Quilts & Americana
Gallery #57
1050 Second Avenue at 55th Street
New York, NY 10022

Laura is one of the premier quilt dealers in the country, having hundreds available at any given time. For the long-distance buyer, she has a well-organized program for finding, photographing, and shipping just the quilt to meet the needs of any collector.

Golyesther
7957 Melrose Avenue
Los Angeles, CA 90046
213-655-3393

The name of this store is a play on the name of the owner rather than some exotic future fabric. But that would be appropriate, too, for Esther Ginsberg also deals in antique fabrics and linens. In business for over fifteen years, she is a good source for quilt tops.

The Great American Collective
1736 Lombard Street
San Francisco, CA 94123
415-922-2660

Although this shop deals with all sorts of Americana, it always has a dozen or more quilts on hand.

Hearts and Hands Galleries
c/o Creekside Antiques Collective
241 Sir Francis Drake Boulevard
San Anselmo, CA 94960
415-457-1266

San Anselmo bills itself as the antiques capital of California, and Linda Reutter is its premier quilt dealer. She has been in the quilt business for twenty-five years, has a great collection, and is very knowledgeable and helpful.

Hilltop Antiques
RD 2, Mekeel Street
Katonah, NY 10536
914-962-7272

Marion North was a quilt collector for many years before becoming a quilt dealer. She works by appointment only and offers nearly 100 quilts, many quite reasonably priced.

Oh, Susannah
18 South Broadway
Lebanon, OH 45036
513-932-8246

Joan Townsend is a very busy woman, dealing with quilt tours and shows as well as this well-known Midwest store.

Susan Parrish Antiques
390 Bleecker Street
New York, NY 10014
212-645-5020

This marvelous shop in the heart of Greenwich Village houses hundreds of quilts and is run by a wonderful and knowledgeable woman. Susan has an extensive collection, an eye for the unusual, and many reasonably priced quilts.

Pieces of the Heart
158 Shawnee Avenue
Easton, PA 18042
215-252-3673

Gina Kramer is a quilter, collector, and dealer who also collects antique fabric. Pennsylvania Dutch and Mennonite quilts make up a large part of her collection.

P.S. Country Stuff
513-236-5873

Pat Schuman, of Dayton, Ohio, does mostly shows and appointments, so she travels a lot. She sells whole antique quilts but also takes cutters and makes interesting items such as wall hangings, clock faces, hair clips, vests, lamp shades, and Christmas tree ornaments.

The Quilt Loft at Jos. Kilbridge Antiques
134 Main Street
Groton, MA 01450

Connie Sprong, C. J. Sprong & Company, 413-586-5853
James Carroll, James Carroll Quilts, 603-823-8446
Diane Reese, Just Quilts, 508-597-5149
Lezlie Colburn, Windmill Horse, 617-341-1359
Lynne Weaver, Lynne Weaver Antiques, 508-468-3841

Together and individually, these five collectors have the most diverse, extensive, and inclusive group of quilts we have seen. They have many reasonably priced quilts, quilt tops, and quilt blocks available, and are quite adept at finding particular pieces for collectors.

Quilts of the Past
415-334-4534

Gaby Burket, of San Francisco, California, has one of the largest quilt collections in the world. She is extensively involved in quilt shows as well as selling quilts, doing two to three every year abroad as well as in this country, so she works by appointment only.

Regent Street Antique Center
153 Regent Street
Saratoga Springs, NY 12866
518-584-0107

Although this thirty-dealer cooperative does not have someone dealing exclusively in quilts, several of its members are quite knowledgeable and always have plenty of quilts available.

Rocky Mountain Quilts

248 East Main Street	3847 Alt. 6 & 24
Gloucester, MA 01930	Palisade, CO 81526
508-281-3686	303-464-7294

Gloria White in Massachusetts and Betsey Telford in Colorado have teamed up to put together one of the most unique and interesting collections we have seen. Betsey does a large part of the finding of quilts and works very hard at getting the history of the quilts she finds. They are both quite knowledgeable, helpful, and very willing to work with beginners.

Star and Cross Quilts
400 East 59th Street
New York, NY 10022
212-593-5189

Alexandra Davis, a third-generation quilt collector, does shows and works by appointment out of her home. Her knowledge is extensive, and almost genetic—her family founded the Shelburne Museum in Vermont.

Warwick Valley Antiques
65 Main Street
Warwick, NY 10990
914-986-5535

Larry Zingale, who also happens to be a talented oil painter, has a wonderful quilt collection featuring some of the most interesting appliqué quilts we have seen. He also offers a descriptive videotape, *How to Buy an Antique Quilt* (available for $34.95), that is well worth the investment.

Wild Goose Chase Quilt Gallery
1511 Chicago Avenue
Evanston, IL 60210
708-328-1808

Also a painter and a sculptor, Gail Struve has been collecting quilts for twenty years. She deals primarily in antique quilts but also has a selection of traditional contemporary quilts available.

The Woodin Wheel
515 "B" Avenue
Kalona, IA 52247
319-656-2240

Marilyn Woodin started a quilt museum, has an extensive private collection, does many quilt shows, and is an expert on Amish quilts. She usually has over 200 quilts on hand, often more.

Yankee Doodle Dandy
1974 Union Street
San Francisco, CA 94123
415-346-0346

This store deals only in quilts and is one of the most extensive on the West Coast, if not in the country. It is overseen by Judith Koch, who has been involved with quilts for some twenty-two years and who carefully chooses all of the quilts found here herself.

Traditional and Innovative Contemporary Quilts

If you have decided to add a contemporary quilt to your collection, or perhaps are starting your collection that way, you will find many talented quilters in the marketplace. Some are listed on the following pages; there are many others. As we noted in chapter 13, traditional contemporary quilts are those made in the traditional styles and patterns. They generally are in the lower price ranges and are often intended to be used in the traditional way: as bed coverings. However, in many cases the quality and the price are such that you may restrict their use to special rooms or occasions, or to just hanging them on the wall.

The increased interest in quilts has brought forth many and varied sellers, and you will find "handmade" quilts in department stores, catalogs, and gift shops. Many are made out of the country, some with U.S. fabrics. Some of these are of good quality, but in terms of collectibility, you should look at all such quilts very carefully. The prices are quite low, and most are imported and may be of questionable quality and value. If you are looking for utility, they may be fine, but they are probably not what you want to leave as an heirloom to your grandchildren. If you want something that will be valuable in the future, consider the quiltmakers we list here, and others who do authentic, handmade, American quilts.

Innovative contemporary quilts may incorporate traditional patterns but show some amount of uniqueness, variation, and inventiveness. Many of the sources of traditional contemporary quilts also offer innovative ones, and we have so noted.

Arkansas Country Quilts
Route 2, Box 31CC
Lexa, AR 72355
501-572-5820

Fifteen quilters provide quilts for Arkansas Country Quilts in traditional patterns, combining quality materials with extensive hand quilting. Most of their work is custom ordered, with the customer choosing colors, fabrics, and quilting patterns. The store can also arrange for the application of batting, backing, and binding, and the hand quilting of one's own pieced top. Patterns include Double Wedding Ring, Drunkard's Path, Basket, Triple Irish Chain, Grandmother's Fan, Ohio Star, Giant Dahlia, Lone Star, Dresden Plate, and their signature quilt, Delta Log Cabin. Prices: King, $586; Queen, $535; Standard double, $453; Twin, $309; Crib, $217.

Betsy Brower
P.O. Box 831, Route 17M
Goshen, NY 10924
914-294-9420

The most exquisite quilting imaginable comes from the hands of Betsy Brower, along with impeccable assembly and color balance. Her innovative pieces are technical and visual masterpieces, contemporary interpretations of traditional designs. Unfortunately, she makes only a few pieces every year. She recently offered a unique variation of a Mariner's Compass in richly printed fabrics of maroon, hunter green, and desert tan, with exquisite and extensive quilting. The quilt price was $4,000; it should have been twice that much.

The Country Peddler
West Main Street
Burnsville, NC 28714
704-682-7810

The Country Peddler's quilts are all made and quilted by the owner, Randy Silver, and his mother, sister, aunt, and various other relatives and friends. They produce quilts of heirloom quality, made with top-notch materials, in both traditional and innovative styles.

Randy does most of the color matching, and his instinct for pleasing and striking color coordination is remarkable. The fabrics are 100 percent cotton, the filler Mountain Mist polyester, the piecework machine done, and the quilting and appliqué all by hand. The prices below are a small representation of what is usually on hand. They also do many other patterns, and will work with a client to meet nearly any request.

	Queen	King
Double Wedding Ring	$400–$450	$500
Lone Star or Trip Around the World	$300	$400
Log Cabin	$300–$400	$400
Colorado Log Cabin	$400	$500
Medallion Quilts: Grandmother's Fan	$850	
Bouquet of Peonies	$550	

Also: 3-Dimensional Dahlia, Log Cabin/Dresden Plate combination, and
various appliqués, up to $1,200.
Whole-cloth, off-white, queen-size, completely covered with quilting,
for $1,200.

Down Quilt Shop
518 Columbus Avenue
New York, NY 10024
212-496-8980

Right in New York City, this small country store offers both antique and
traditional contemporary quilts. It carries a line of quilts from India, made from
Indian fabric, which cost between $350 and $400 and must be dry cleaned due
to bleeding of the fabric colors. It also has more utilitarian quilts available that
are made from American fabrics and are assembled and hand-quilted in China.
Prices for twin size are about $100, while queen size costs about $160.

For the serious collector, it works with several Amish women who will do
custom traditional quilts in the $800–$1,000 price range. Here are the prices
for some Amish quilts, already made and recently available:

Giant Dahlia Patchwork	Purple, lavender, green	108 × 89	$1,200
Shadows	Primary colors, multi	108 × 82	$850
Log Cabin Variation	Black, gray, burgundy	100 × 90	$1,250
Grandmother's Flower Garden	Blue on off-white	108 × 92	$875

Dora B. Hamlin
Quilts of America
202-362-2220

Dora works out of her home as an agent for many talented quilters,
dealing primarily in appliqués, selling quilts all over the world. She handles
mostly traditional quilts but often has innovative work available as well, and
will work with a client to match space, color, and pattern desires. She insists on
only the best materials, assembly, and hand-quilting. Her stock varies, as most
of her work is commissioned, selling between $600 and $4,000 or more.

Susan Harris Amish Quilts
South Bald Hill Road
New Canaan, CT 06840
203-972-1424

For many years Susan Harris has worked with groups of Amish women to produce quilts custom-made to a customer's needs. She first works with the customer to pick a design and colors and to choose fabrics, which she then prewashes herself. The chosen fabric is assembled and quilted in Indiana, taking about two to three months to become a gorgeous, one-of-a-kind quilt. Prices run around $1,000, although the cost is actually calculated on the cost of the material, the complexity of the pattern and the time needed to produce it, and the amount of quilting on the finished piece.

The Gazebo
660 Madison Avenue
New York, NY 10021
212-832-7077

The Gazebo deals in antique quilts as well as handling traditional contemporary quilts made of all-cotton American fabrics, assembled and quilted in Haiti. It maintains control over the quality of its quilts by planning patterns and colors in New York before the quilts are made. The New York store and extensive color catalog also offer quilted pillows, wall hangings, and other items.

		Twin	Queen	King
Barn Raising Log Cabin	Browns	$395	$495	$595
Broken Star	Bright pastels	$775	$875	$975
Bows and Flowers Appliqué	Blues and pastels	$795	$895	$995
Rose Cross Appliqué	Blues	$495	$595	$695
Prairie Rose Appliqué	Blues	$495	$595	$695
Ohio Star with sashing	Pink, lavender	$395	$495	$595
Mariner's Compass	Reds, blues	$395	$495	$595
Sunburst	Solid blues		$895	$995
Crib Quilts				
Appliqué Animals	$325			
Four Hearts	$75			
Kitten Dresden Plate	$135			

Keepsake Quilting
Dover Street, P.O. Box 1459
Centre Harbor, NH 03253
603-279-3351

This store is a quiltmaker's delight, doing a booming business in quilting supplies, fabrics, and quilt kits both in-store and via an extensive catalog. It also handles finished quilts in traditional styles, handmade by various quilters. It often has some innovative pieces, too.

Hidden Wells	Full	$600
Double Wedding Ring	King	$725
Trip Around the World	Queen, tied	$350
Snowball	Queen	$720
Anvil Chorus	Queen	$550
Feathered Hearts	Queen, white, all quilting	$625
Flying Geese	Full	$725
Lone Star	King, Pineapple corners	$550
Biscuit	101 × 114, puff quilt	$475
Broken Star	King, flower quilting	$675
Boston Common	King	$960
Country Bride Appliqué	Queen, doves	$850
Storm at Sea	Queen	$600
Spider Web and Sunflower	King, Amish, all quilting	$600
Tranquillity	84 × 84, Log Cabin variation	$975
Encircled Tulips	Queen, Drunkard's Path variation	$650
Floral Appliqué	Queen	$725
Hearts Appliqué	King, lots of quilting	$675

Mercer & Bratt Amish Quilts
P.O. Box 883601
San Francisco, CA 94188-3601
414-334-2729

Mercer & Bratt are quilt brokers who sell traditional Amish quilts made to a customer's specific size, color, and pattern desires. With close ties to an Old

Order Amish community, they arrange to have each quilt handmade by an Amish woman and her family and friends. Colors can vary, but in true Amish patterns blues predominate. Fabrics are cottons or cotton blends.

Some popular patterns: Jacob's Ladder, Brick Work, Tumbling Blocks, Ohio Star, Trip Around the World, Rail Fence, Zigzag, Sunshine and Shadow, Love Rings, Irish Chain, Double Irish Chain, Grandmother's Flower Garden, Lone Star, Star of Bluegrass, Log Cabin, Rolling Star, Turkey Tracks, Flower Baskets, Dutch Rose, and "plain" quilts. Pick any of these patterns because these quilts are priced by size.

Doll	(16 × 24)	$175
Crib	(40 × 50)	$375
Twin	(66 × 100)	$775
Double	(84 × 100)	$875
Queen	(90 × 108)	$975
King	(100 × 120)	$1,075

Omar & Sylvia Petershiem Quilts & Crafts
2544 Old Philadelphia Pike
Bird-in-Hand, PA 17505
717-392-6404

This couple work and sell out of a showroom in their home. They employ over 100 talented quiltmakers who machine-piece and hand-quilt the traditional items they offer. Some recent examples:

Piecework

Trip Around the World	Rose, blue	96 × 106	$395
Diamond Star Log Cabin	Blue; heart/feather quilting	92 × 106	$550
Dahlia (Diamond Log Cabin)	Rose, blue; fan borders	95 × 111	$425
Dahlia Star (small)	Blue, white; fan border	94 × 113	$420
Lone Star	Green; circle/feather quilting	92 × 109	$385
Broken Diamond (Log Cabin)	Rose, green; wave border	95 × 111	$585
Ocean Waves/Dresden Plate	Orange, tan	Queen	$425
Pineapple	Blue; fan/leaves quilting	96 × 108	$450
Double Wedding Ring	Green, rose; flower quilted rings	94 × 107	$375

Sampler (20 blocks) (includes Basket, Bear's Paw, Ohio Star, School House, Rail Fence, others)	Red, beige, blue; heart quilted	96 × 107	$520

Appliqué

Country Love	Green, rose; medallion center	95 × 105	$895
Distlefink & Hearts	Blue, rose; heavily quilted	95 × 110	$525
Bridal Wreath	Rose, green; scalloped edge, embroidery	93 × 109	$495

Made-to-Order

Log Cabin (all variations)	Customer's choice of colors	Full, Queen	$375

Pinney Street Antiques
50 Pinney Street
Ellington, CT 06029
203-871-1406

At this shop, Ed Silva arranges for traditional Amish quilts to be made to a customer's specifications concerning size, color, and pattern. Prices will vary with size, colors, pattern, and so on, with a 78 x 105 double costing about $425. Production may take up to six months.

Some popular patterns: Lone Star, Dahlia, Log Cabin, Double Wedding Ring, and crazy quilts.

He also often has some already-made Amish quilts on hand.

Sunshine	Multi blues	41 × 41	$180
Granny's Favorite	Navy, burgundy, green	41 × 41	$265
Lone Star	Pastels	41 × 41	$180

Josephine Schepere
8057 East State Road 164
Celestina, IN 47521
812-389-2679

This quilter does traditional piecework and appliqué quilts and quilt tops in various patterns and colors.

Quilts

Double Irish Chain	Lavender	$225
Indian Hatchet	Blue, black, maroon	$150

Trip Around the World	Reds	$225
Rail Fence	Rusts	$200
Broken Diamond	Dark green	$200
Ohio Rose Appliqué	Yellow	$195
Ring of Roses Appliqué	Red	$215
Forget-me-nots Appliqué	Blues	$200
Dresden Plate	Orchid	$190

Tops

Turkey Tracks	Blues	$200
Shoo Fly	Mauve	$195
Double Wedding Ring	Peach	$200
Clay's Choice	Browns	$190
Trip Around the World	Rust and orange	$225
Double Irish Chain	Rose	$215

Letha Sheppard
Route 1, Box 326
Wedowee, AL 36278

This quilter does traditional piecework and appliqué quilt tops in various patterns and colors.

Some patterns: Rose Appliqué, Fan, Butterfly, Maple Leaf, Dresden Plate, Sunbonnet Sue/Overall Bill, Tulip, Dogwood, Monkey Wrench, Churn Dash, Double Irish Chain, Pansy, Bow Tie, Strawberry, Morning Glory, Southland Rose, and Oakleaf Cluster.

	Tops only	Completed quilts
Twin (64 × 100)	$35	$105
Double (74 × 100)	$35	$110
Queen (84 × 100)	$45	$130
King (94 × 100)	$55	$140

Betty Upchurch
HC86, Box 25E
Monticello, KY 42633
606-348-9698

This quilter has many traditional piecework quilts available for sale, or will work with you to choose colors and pattern for a custom-made quilt.

School House	Red on white	83 × 94	$250
Flower Garden	Multicolored	77 × 98	$285
Friendship Ring	Pink and blue	97 × 109	$250
Log Cabin	Peach and green	90 × 103	$200
Dresden Plate	Pastels	88 × 105	$250
Broken Star	Light blue	91 × 106	$265
Double Wedding Ring	Blue, pastels	90 × 103	$225
Love Ring	Peach	90 × 103	$250
Fans	Brights	78 × 97	$225
Lone Star	Peach, green	98 × 109	$250
Lone Star	Pink and rose	92 × 104	$250
Bull's Eye	Light blue	92 × 118	$250
Friendship Star	Cranberry and pink	80 × 95	$185

The Woodin Wheel
515 "B" Avenue
Kalona, IA 52247
319-656-2240

Marilyn Woodin has been in the quilt business for many years, primarily with antique quilts, but also as an agent for over 200 Mennonite women who make lovely traditional quilts. Each quilt is individually made, machine-pieced and hand-quilted, by one woman. Marilyn always has a large selection in her inventory so she generally avoids custom work. Prices are set by the maker, with Marilyn's advice on market condition and pattern desirability, and range from $395 to $950. Some patterns recently available: Carpenter's Wheel, Lancaster Rose, Mariner's Compass, Amish Star, Lone Star, Double Wedding Ring, Sampler, Ohio Rose, and Broken Star.

Art Quilts

Across the country dozens of excellent artists are working in the quilt media. Some turn out many pieces of work in a year, some do only a few. If you decide you want an art quilt, contact the artists—these and others you may find through quilt guilds, museums, and the like—and talk about what you want. Since you will likely be spending a good amount of money for this piece of artwork, take your time and look carefully. Ask for photos or a drawing for a planned piece, discuss prices, consider colors and materials. Be prepared, however, to give the artist much leeway in doing your quilt, for it's his or her creativity and uniqueness of style for which you will be paying.

Ann Spagnola Argenio
2341 Eleventh Avenue
Cayahoga Falls, OH 44221
216-945-9052

Although she lives in the middle of Amish country, Ann finds her work to be more influenced by the old European artists than her surroundings. Her first quilted piece was an original interpretation of Monet's *The Gleaners;* many of her other pieces were also inspired by the work of the Impressionists. She does commissioned pieces but also has some already completed work available, including a remarkable quilt-size wall hanging of an Oriental garden priced at $5,800. The prices for her more traditional quilts and wall hangings are from $200 on up.

Virginia Avery
731 King Street
Port Chester, NY 10573
914-939-3605

Active in the quilt world for over twenty-two years, Virginia has recently expanded her interest into patchwork clothing. Exhibiting at conferences and galleries, she once did a series of appliqué quilts based on Matisse's cut-paper work. Her prices, averaging between $350 and thousands of dollars, depend on the complexity of the design and how long it takes to execute the piece.

Nancy Crow
P.O. Box 37
Baltimore, OH 43105
614-862-6554

Well known as a contemporary quilt artist, Nancy's original designs have been featured on postcards and elsewhere, and are popular in this country and abroad. Her work is shown at galleries and exhibits, and runs in the thousands of dollars to own.

Michael James
258 Old Colony Avenue
Somerset Village, MA 02726
508-672-1370

Michael is one of the best known and most popular quilt artists in the country today. Since he started in 1974, Michael has produced award-winning pieces of stunning and innovative design. His work has been shown in Europe and Japan, and his lectures and quilt design and construction courses are taken by hundreds of people around the world. He often has pieces available or will do custom work. His prices start in the low thousands and go upward.

Paula Lederkramer
25 Swing Lane
Levittown, NY 11756
516-735-7870

Paula, in over twenty years of quilting, has collected a whole room full of fabrics, which works out well, for some of her quilts contain over two hundred different fabrics. She started with bed-size quilts, but finds that there is much more interest in smaller pieces, since people are more apt to be looking for wall art these days. She says that people seem to love the tactile nature of quilts, and that makes the medium even more interesting. Her work starts at $450 and goes into the thousands.

Yvonne Porcella
3619 Shoemake Avenue
Modesto, CA 95351

Yvonne believes so much in quilts as art that she helped found a national organization to educate the public about this art form. Her quilts show a strong geometric block base and even have some traditional components. She works in two palettes: one with bold, dramatic colors; the other with pastels hand-painted on silk. Her median price is $4,500, and she makes large pieces and smaller, down to about 50 by 50 inches.

Bets Ramsey
P.O. Box 4146
Chattanooga, TN 37405
615-265-4300

Bets, with a background in traditional art, wants to bridge the gap between quilts and the art world. She has recently been involved in showcasing the quilts of Southern artists and curating quilt shows. Her quilts often show abstract designs that conceptualize ideas, such as a textural piece all done in black fabrics. Prices for her finished pieces start in the hundreds and go into the thousands of dollars, depending on the complexity and the time involved. She does commissioned work but has other pieces available.

Elaine Stonebraker
Via de Mañana
Scottsdale, AZ 85258
602-991-4144

The quilts made by Elaine are heavily influenced by the things around her in her Southwest home—the brilliant colors of the desert, Indian pueblos, the warmth of the sun. She puts a little of herself into each quilt as well, so she doesn't do commission work. Each piece must come from the inner creative part of her heart. Priced around $2,500 to $3,000, her quilts are full-size or close, and are truly visual and tactile delights.

Museums, Societies, and Historical Associations

Many museums that feature American historical items, Americana, or other related items have the odd quilt or two as part of their permanent collection. Many others have temporary displays featuring quilts. Others are dedicated primarily to quilts. While you generally won't go to a museum to purchase a quilt, you will go there to enhance your own knowledge, and for various kinds of help. A museum, if it deals in any sort of textiles, may often have on staff a textile conservator who can be invaluable to you. And museums dedicated just to quilts are tremendous vats of knowledge. First, check around your area for museums, historical associations, and quilt guilds. Make contact and ask questions. Find out if they have printed materials or informational bulletins. Who knows? When your knowledge increases, they may even ask you to become involved as an expert.

The following museums are dedicated totally to quilts or have large quilt collections that they often display.

The Rocky Mountain Quilt Museum
1111 Washington Street
Golden, CO 80401
303-277-0377

The Kalona Quilt and Textile Museum
413 1/2 "B" Avenue
Kalona, IA 52247
319-656-2240

The New England Quilt Museum
Lowell, MA 01852
505-452-4207
   Note: As we went to press, the New England Quilt Museum, which was most recently housed at 246 Market Street in the Lowell National Historic Park, was looking for a new home after a flood forced it out of that location. The phone number remains the same; call before you go to find out where it is located.

Museum of American Folk Art
2 Lincoln Square
New York, NY 10023
212-595-9533

American Quilter's Society Quilt Museum
214 Jefferson Street
Paducah, KY 42001
502-442-8856

Esprit
900 Minnesota Street
San Francisco, CA 94105
415-648-6900

These museums have small to large numbers of quilts in their collections, may have quilt shows or displays, or are resources for finding shows, displays, or information. Call for what's available. The Cooper-Hewitt Museum and the Smithsonian offer abstracts on textile care and conservation; others offer other information.

Arizona Historical Society Headquarters
949 East Second Street
Tucson, AZ 85719
602-628-5774

The Oakland Museum
1000 Oak Street
Oakland, CA 94607
415-273-3401

The Denver Art Museum
Fourteenth and Bannock
Denver, CO 80204
303-640-2793

Connecticut Historical Society
1 Elizabeth Street
Hartford, CT 06105
203-236-5621

The Wadsworth Atheneum
600 Main Street
Hartford, CT 06103
203-278-2670

The Lyman Allyn Museum
625 Williams Street
New London, CT 06320
203-443-2545

The Mattatuck Historical Society Museum
144 West Main Street
Waterbury, CT 06702
203-753-0381

The National Museum of American History of the Smithsonian Institution
Fourteenth Street and Constitution Avenue, Northwest
Washington, DC 20560
202-357-1300

The Atlanta Historical Society
3103 Andrews Drive, Northwest
Atlanta, GA 30305
404-261-1937

The Art Institute of Chicago
Michigan Avenue and Adams Street
Chicago, IL 60603
312-443-3600

The Louisiana State Museum
751 Chartres Street
New Orleans, LA 70176
504-568-6968

The Museum of Fine Arts
465 Huntington Avenue
Boston, MA 02115
617-267-9300

Cape Ann Historical Association
27 Pleasant Street
Gloucester, MA 01930
617-283-0455

Museum of American Textile History
800 Massachusetts Avenue
North Andover, MA 01845
508-686-0191

Old Sturbridge Village
Sturbridge, MA 01566
617-347-3362

The Henry Ford Museum and Greenwich Village
20900 Oakwood Boulevard
Dearborn, MI 48121
313-271-1620

The Detroit Institute of Arts
5200 Woodward Avenue
Detroit, MI 48202
313-833-7900

Hennepin County Historical Society Museum
2303 Third Avenue South
Minneapolis, MN 55404
612-870-1329

The Cooper Hewitt Museum
2 East 92nd Street
New York, NY 10128
212-860-6868

The Witte Museum
3801 Broadway
San Antonio, TX 78209
512-829-7262

The Shelburne Museum
Route 7
Shelburne, VT 05482
802-985-3346

The Mount Vernon Ladies Association
Mount Vernon, VA 22121
703-780-2000

The Milwaukee Public Museum
800 West Wells Street
Milwaukee, WI 53233
414-278-2720

You will find many quilt study groups and quilt guilds around the country. These two groups are strong promoters and supporters of quilt projects.

The Studio Art Quilt Association
P.O. Box 287
Salida, CA 95368

American Quilt Study Group
669 Mission Street, Suite 400
San Francisco, CA 94105
415-495-0163

Care and Repair Materials

Museums, quilt guilds, and historical societies may be of help in finding materials for the cleaning and repair of quilts. You can also try the companies listed here.

University Products, Inc.
South Canal Street
Holyoke, MA 01041
413-532-9431

Process Materials
30 Veterans Boulevard
Rutherford, NJ 07070
201-935-2900

TALAS, Division of Technical Library Services
213 West 35th Street
New York, NY 10001
212-736-7744

Conservation Materials
240 Freeport Boulevard
Sparks, NV 89431
702-331-0582

Cleaners and Repairers

Most quilt dealers are themselves or have contact with qualified repairers of quilts, and will help you with cleaning as well. We happened, in our travels, on a few specific textile repairers.

Robin Greeson Textile Restoration
Box 276, Snydertown Road
Craryville, NY 12521
518-851-7979

K & K Quilted
Box 23, Route 23
Hillsdale, NY 12529
518-325-4502

M. Finkel and Daughter
936 Pine Street
Philadelphia, PA 19107
215-627-7797

GLOSSARY

Allover set: when a One-patch pattern is used for an entire quilt.

Aniline dyes: synthetic dyes created using coal tar.

Appliqué: the process of sewing a piece of cloth to a ground fabric.

Asymmetrical: also called split blocks; the optical effect changes when the blocks are turned.

Autograph Quilt: a quilt in which each block is signed by a friend, usually with a poem, picture, or Bible verse.

Batting: the middle of the quilt sandwich; usually cotton, wool, or polyester.

Bees: gatherings of quiltmakers to stitch finished tops; at first families were involved, later only quiltmakers.

Binding: fabric used to finish the raw outside edges of the quilt sandwich.

Bleeding: color loss from washing.

Block: the unit of a quilt that, when assembled, or set, form the quilt top; either appliqué or pieced.

Border: the fabric frame added around the outside of the patchwork top. Can be plain strips of fabric, pieced or appliqué.

Bridal quilt: the thirteenth in a Colonial girl's baker's dozen of quilts she took with her in marriage; not started until she was betrothed.

Broadcloth: so named because it was woven wider than other fabrics, anywhere from 54 to 63 inches.

Broderie-Perse: the method of cutting large-scale designs out of fabric and appliquéing them to whole-cloth tops.

Buyer's premium: the additional charge an auction house adds to the highest bid for an item. This fee pays the house's expenses and leaves the entire bid amount to go to the seller.

Calender: a process using heat and rollers to glaze wool.

Challis: a soft wool or wool-and-cotton cloth; plain, printed, or figured, and unglazed; twill weave.

Chambray: a gingham-type fabric, plain weave, often with a colored warp and a white weft.

Cheater cloth: fabric printed with patchwork designs that look like completed blocks.

Cherryderrys: a fabric with silk warp and cotton weft from the 1750s.

Color balance: the effect of colors placed next to or across from each other, or in patterns that are most pleasing to the eye.

Colorfastness: when a dye doesn't bleed, or fade, when it's washed.

Color loss: when fabrics fade or change color from washing, inferior dyes, exposure to light, crocking.

Comforter: three layers—a fabric top, usually whole-cloth, sometimes pieced; a batting; and a backing—held together by knots tied with thread or yarn.

Commemorative quilts: made to record a special event in history.

Compactness: how tightly a fabric is woven; the more threads per square inch, the more compact the weave.

Copper cylinder: a design is cut into copper, but instead of pressing the cylinder on a fabric, the fabric is rolled under the cylinder to print it.

Copperplate printing: designs are cut into copper plates, which are then inked and pressed onto fabric.

Crocking: when a fabric loses color from its surface. Check for crocking by rubbing a white cloth or paper over the fabric.

Dozens: refers to the practice of selling a cheap wool in lengths of about twelve yards.

Dresden: silk and worsted fabric; fancy.

Four-square: a quilt whose top is comprised of four large blocks; thought to be the precursor of the block style.

Friendship quilts or blocks: quilts of blocks made by more than one quiltmaker or, if made by one quiltmaker, given to memorialize a friendship.

Geometric: refers to squares, triangles, diamonds, and other straight-lined shapes; usually refers to pieced quilts, especially those with optical illusion effects.

Glaze: an additive to make fabric stiffer and appear shiny.

Grogrinetts: a worsted with watermarks.

Ground: the fabric smaller pieces of cloth are appliquéd to.

Homespun: cloth hand-woven from home-grown wool, cotton, or flax by Colonial and pioneer households.

Linsey-woolsey: a fabric made using two threads, one from wool and one from linen.

Loft: the puffiness on a quilt top from the batting beneath.

Madder browns: a term used to describe the reddish, deep browns used in quilts in the middle 1800s.

Medallion style: used with Broderie-Perse, this refers to a large intricate design filling the center of a quilt top.

Microwaving: a method of artificially aging fabric.

Mordant: an agent used to fix dyes in fabric.

Multigenerational quilt: any quilt worked on by different quiltmakers of different generations.

Muslin: a fine cotton fabric first made in India.

Nine-patch: the most frequently used division in geometric pieced blocks. The basic block is broken into three rows of three squares each, making nine segments that could be further divided.

One-patch: when the same single shape—such as hexagons, tumblers, and triangles—is used to create an entire quilt top.

Patchwork: the process of assembling smaller pieces of cloth together to make a quilt top.

This Nine-patch is from the 1830s and has the blocks set on point with zigzag sashing. The scrap bag colors include pinks, grays, browns, and just about every other.
Quilt courtesy of Helen Warner

Percale: a fine white cloth; used as a ground in India for painted chintz.

Picker: a person who locates quilts to sell to dealers.

Piecing: when patchwork is done by seaming two smaller pieces of cloth together instead of sewing them to a ground fabric.

Plain weave: where each warp or weft thread runs over and under the other in an even pattern.

Presentation quilt: a quilt made in any style that was then given to a respected member of the community, usually a minister or his wife.

A close-up of the same Nine-patch reveals the striped material of the sashing and some very interesting prints as well. *Quilt courtesy of Helen Warner*

Preview: the time offered before an auction at which you can closely inspect the offered merchandise.

Quilt: a sandwich of three layers: a top, usually of patchwork but sometimes whole-cloth; a batting; and a backing fabric.

Quilt dealer: specializes in finding, buying, and selling antique quilts.

Quilt frame: four long boards with clamps used to hold the quilt sandwich tight while stitching.

Quilt kits: packaged, pre-cut, pre-designed quilt materials and directions.

Quilt shop: usually offers materials and patterns to make quilts; may also sell new quilts on consignment.

Quilting: the stitching that holds the quilt sandwich together.

Resist: an agent to keep cloth from taking a dye.

Reverse appliqué: the method of placing two fabrics together, cutting out the top fabric so the back fabric shows through, and then turning under and stitching down the raw edges.

Sampler quilt: comprised of blocks of different patterns; used to learn quilting techniques.

Sashings: fabric strips that frame the blocks in the quilt top.

Satin weave: where each weft yarn passes over several warps and "floats," producing a surface sheen.

Scrap bag: the accumulation of pieces of fabric saved from other needlework or other quilts that are too small to use for clothing but too big to be thrown out.

Set: the way the blocks are assembled in the top. Straight set puts the blocks in horizontal and vertical rows. Blocks set on point appear as diamond shapes in a quilt top.

Signature quilt: usually a fund-raiser; people paid to have their names embroidered on a quilt top.

Staple: the fibers, of animal or vegetable origin, used to make thread.

Stipple quilting: when tiny stitches are sewed in close rows to create a higher loft in unquilted areas.

Stuff: a general term for worsted cloth; includes merino, shalloons, lastings, tammers, calimancoes, moreens, camblets, and plaids.

Symmetrical blocks: those geometric pieced patterns that always form the same design no matter how they're assembled.

Tea-dyeing: an artificial method of aging fabric; sometimes used to make new fabrics blend in with old, sometimes used to make a new quilt appear as an antique. Hard on the fabrics.

Tendering: when fabric wears out. Many times caused by the harsh mordant and resist chemicals used to fix dyes.

Tied and tying: holding the three layers of the fabric sandwich together with knotted thread or yarn.

Trapunto: sometimes called stuffed quilting, developed in Italy; used in whitework, in which two pieces of cloth are stitched together and stuffing is inserted in the unquilted areas.

Twill weave: like the satin weave, but the fibers that "float" don't all pass over the same warp threads, producing diagonal lines across the surface of the fabric.

Velvet: a pile fabric made of silk, wool, or cotton fibers.

Warp: the lengthwise threads in a fabric.

Weft: the fabric threads that run side to side.

Whitework: the design of these quilts is solely from the quilting pattern; usually done with whole-cloth although newer quilts may use plain colored fabric.

Whole-cloth: quilts in which the tops are not patchwork but a single piece of fabric.

Wood-block printing: a method in which patterns are added to cloth by using wood blocks cut into designs. Either dye or mordants were pressed onto the cloth.

Worsted: a lightweight cloth made from long-staple, combed yarn.

BIBLIOGRAPHY

Books

Adrosko, Rita J. *Natural Dyes and Home Dyeing.* New York: Dover Publications, Inc., 1971.

Affleck, Diane L. Fagan. *Just New from the Mills.* North Andover, Mass.: Museum of American Textile History, 1987.

Better Homes and Gardens. *Friendship Quilting.* Des Moines, Iowa: Meredith Corp., 1990.

Beyer, Jinny. *Patchwork Patterns.* McClean, Va.: EPM Publications, Inc., 1979.

Bishop, Robert, and Houck, Carter. *All Flags Flying:* American Patriotic Quilts as Expressions of Liberty. New York: E. P. Dutton in association with the Museum of American Folk Art, 1986.

Bogdonoff, Nancy D. *Handwoven Textiles of Early New England.* Harrisburg, Pa.: Stackpole Books, 1975.

Brackman, Barbara. *Clues in the Calico:* A Guide to Identifying and Dating Antique Quilts. McClean, Va.: EPM Publications, Inc., 1987.

Burnham, Dorothy K. *Warp & Weft:* A Dictionary of Textile Terms. New York: Charles Scribner's Sons, 1980.

Cooper, Patricia, and Buferd, Norma Bradley. *The Quilters.* New York: Doubleday & Co., 1977.

Dee, Anne Patterson. *Quilter's Sourcebook.* Lombard, Ill.: Wallace-Homestead Book Co., 1987.

Fennelly, Catherine. *Textiles in New England, 1790–1840.* Sturbridge, Mass.: Old Sturbridge Village, 1961.

Ferris, William. *Afro-American Folk Art and Crafts*. Boston: G. K. Hall & Co., 1983.

Finley, Ruth E. *Old Patchwork Quilts and the Women Who Make Them*. Newton Centre, Mass.: Charles T. Branford Co., 1929, 1957, 1970.

Fisher, Laura. *Quilts of Illusion*. Pittstown, N.J.: The Main Street Press, 1988.

Florence, Cathy Gaines. *Collecting Quilts:* Investments in America's Heritage. Paducah, Ky.: American Quilter's Society, 1985.

Fons, Marianne. *Fine Feathers:* A Quilter's Guide to Customizing Traditional Feather Quilting Designs. Lafayette, Calif.: C & T Publishing, 1988.

Hardingham, Martin. *The Fabric Catalog*. New York: Pocket Books, 1978.

Hechtinger, Adelaide. *American Quilts, Quilting, and Patchwork*. Harrisburg, Pa.: Stackpole Books, 1974.

Hoffman, Victoria. *Quilts:* A Window to the Past. North Andover, Mass.: Museum of American Textile History, 1991.

Holstein, Jonathan. *The Pieced Quilt:* An American Design Tradition. New York: Galahad Books, 1973.

Ickis, Marguerite. *The Standard Book of Quilt Making and Collecting*. New York: Dover Publications, Inc., 1949.

James, Michael. *The Second Quiltmaker's Handbook:* Creative Approaches to Contemporary Quilt Design. Englewood Cliffs, N.J.: Prentice-Hall, Inc., 1981.

Kentucky Quilt Project. *Kentucky Quilts: 1800–1900*. Louisville, Ky.: The Kentucky Quilt Project, 1982.

Khin, Yvonne. *The Collector's Dictionary of Quilt Names and Patterns*. Washington, D.C.: Acropolis Books, 1980.

Kile, Michael. "On the Road." In *The Quilt Digest*, pp. 76–85. San Francisco: The Quilt Digest Press, 1986.

Laury, Jean Ray, and the California Heritage Quilt Project. *Ho for California! Pioneer Women and Their Quilts*. New York: E. P. Dutton, 1990.

Leman, Bonnie, and Martin, Judy. *Log Cabin Quilts.* Denver, Colo.: Moon Over the Mountain Publishing Co., 1980.

Leon, Eli. *Who'd a Thought It:* Improvisation in African-American Quiltmaking. San Francisco: San Francisco Craft and Folk Art Museum, 1987.

Lipsett, Linda Otto. *Remember Me:* Women and Their Friendship Quilts. San Francisco: The Quilt Digest Press, 1985.

Lithgow, Marilyn. *Quiltmaking and Quiltmakers.* Photographs by Peter Kiar. New York: Funk & Wagnalls, 1974.

McMorris, Penny, and Kile, Michael. *The Art Quilt.* San Francisco: The Quilt Digest Press, 1986.

"Quilts in Art." In *The Quilt Digest,* pp. 66–75. San Francisco: The Quilt Digest Press, 1986.

Montgomery, Florence M. *Textiles in America 1650–1870.* New York: W. W. Norton & Co., 1984.

Peto, Florence. *Historic Quilts.* New York: The American Historical Co., 1939.

Pfeffer, Susanna. *Quilt Masterpieces.* New York: Hugh Lauter Levin Associates, Inc., distributed by MacMillan Publishing Co., 1988.

Pottinger, David. *Quilts from the Indiana Amish:* A Regional Collection. New York: E. P. Dutton in association with the Museum of American Folk Art, 1983.

Puentes, Nancy O'Bryant. *First Aid for Family Quilts.* Wheatridge, Colo.: Moon Over the Mountain Publishing Co., 1986.

Selsam, Millicent E. *Cotton.* Photographs by Jerome Wexler. New York: William Morrow and Company, 1982.

Spears, Jeannie M. *Pricing Your Work.* Profitable Quilting Series. Self-published.

Spencer, Audrey. *Spinning and Weaving at Upper Canada Village.* Toronto: The Ryerson Press, 1964.

Webster, Marie D. *Quilts:* Their Story and How to Make Them. New York: Doubleday, Page, and Company, 1915.

Weigle, Palmy. *Ancient Dyes for Modern Weavers.* New York: Watson-Guptill Publications, 1974.

Articles

Brackman, Barbara. "Patterns from Oregon and the Oregon Trail." *Quilter's Newsletter Magazine,* April 1991, pp. 22–26.

Braunstein, Jack. "Dixie McBride's Rags to Riches Stories." *Traditional Quiltworks,* no. 14, pp. 5–8.

Bray, Pamela. "Faith Ringgold: Artist-Storyteller." *School Arts,* May 1989, pp. 23–26.

Brown, Linda J. "Guide to Buying a Quilt." *Good Housekeeping,* October 1988, p. 227.

Callahan, Nancy. "Hard Times for Freedom Quilters." *The Christian Century,* March 22, 1989, pp. 317–318.

Carter, Catherine. "Stars—The Most Favored of Patterns." *Traditional Quiltworks,* no. 3, pp. 34–35.

"A Century of Progress." *Quilt Craft,* Spring 1991, pp. 28–31.

Cozart, Dorothy. "A Century of Fundraising Quilts 1860–1960." *Uncoverings—research papers of the American Quilt Study Group,* vol. 5, 1984, pp. 41–54.

"Crescendo of Quilts." *Americana,* May–June 1990, pp. 35–39.

Davala, Carol. "The Quilt Lady." (On Faith Ringgold.) *Quilt World,* February/March 1991, pp. 22–24.

"Designing with Scrap." *Quilt Craft,* Summer 1991, pp. 20–23.

Donegan, Frank. "Quiet Time for Quilts." *Americana,* December 1988, pp. 64–66.

Fisher, Laura. "Quilt Care and Storage." Self-published.

Fox, Sandi. "Comments from the Quilt." *Modern Maturity,* August–September 1990, pp. 58–63.

Freeman, Roland. "Quilts: From the Mississippi Heartland." *American Visions,* June 1986, pp. 28–32.

Gately, Rosemary Connolly. "Crazy Quilts in the Collection of the Maryland Historical Society." *Antiques,* September 1988, pp. 558–573.

Gleason, Jeanne. "Sue Rodgers: Quilter, Teacher, Trapunto Maestro." *Traditional Quiltworks,* no. 13, pp. 5–7.

Gordon, Meryl. "Bold Appeal of 20th-Century Quilts." *Architectural Digest,* June 1990, pp. 48–60.

Gutcheon, Jeffrey. "Not for Shopkeepers Only: The Dyestuffs." *Quilter's Newsletter Magazine,* April 1991, pp. 58, 70.

Halpin, Linda. "Hanging Quilts." *Traditional Quiltworks,* no. 13, pp. 65–66.

Hargrave, Harriet. "Quiltsense: Care of Today's Quilts." *Traditional Quiltworks,* no. 3, pp. 47–48.

Harrington, Gail. "Lancaster Color." *Trailer Life,* March 1987, pp. 76–77.

Harriss, Joseph. "The Newest Quilt Fad Seems to Be Going Like Crazy." *Smithsonian,* May 1987, pp. 114–124.

"Homage to the Quilt." The story of the exhibition at the American Craft Museum. *American Craft,* December 1987–January 1988, pp. 42–48.

Houck, Carter. "A View of the 1920s and 1930s." *Quilt Craft,* Spring 1991, pp. 6–9.

Jones, Lila Lee. "Something Old . . . Something New." *Quilt Craft,* Summer 1991, pp. 56–59.

Keck, Viola. "The Sunbonnet Alphabet Quilt." *Quilt World,* October/November 1991, p. 17.

Lipshultz, Sandra Lawall. "Blanket Approval." *Minneapolis–St. Paul Magazine,* February 1987, pp. 15–17, 54.

Marshall, Diane P. "Sewing Traditions in Lancaster County." *Travel-Holiday,* July 1988, pp. 85–88.

McBride, Dixie. "Repair and Restoration of Old Quilts." *Traditional Quiltworks,* no. 14, pp. 9–10.

Meyer, Jon. "Faith Ringgold." *ARTnews,* February 1989, pp. 139–140.

Mori, Joyce. "How Quilters Can Help Their Local Historical Society." *Quilt World,* December 1991/January 1992, pp. 30, 37.

Morris, Pat. "Quilters' Queries & Quotes." *Quilt World,* December 1991/January 1992, pp. 28–29.

Nadelstern, Paula. "Citiquilts: A Show of Diversity." *Quilter's Newsletter Magazine,* April 1991, pp. 35–39.

Rubin, Cynthia E. "Amish Needlework: Tradition and Change." *Early American Life,* June 1988, pp. 30–33, 74.

Ruskin, Cindy. "Taking Up Needles and Thread to Honor the Dead Helps AIDS Survivors Patch Up Their Lives." *People Weekly,* October 12, 1987, pp. 42–49.

Satterfield, Archie. "Hawaii's Prized Quilts." *Travel-Holiday,* January 1987, pp. 12–13.

Scheinman, Pamela. "Faith Ringgold—Bernice Steinbaum Gallery." *American Craft,* February/March 1989, pp. 72–73.

Simons, Scott. "Quilts as a New Art Form." *Quilt World,* October/November 1991, pp. 24–25.

"A Summit Gift from Nancy to Raisa." *People Weekly,* June 20, 1988, p. 51.

"Talk of the Town: Notes and Comment." *The New Yorker,* October 5, 1987, pp. 31–32.

INDEX

Italicized page numbers indicate illustrations.

ABOUT THE AUTHORS

This is LIZ GREENBACKER's fourth book. She is the author of *Private Lives of Ministers' Wives*, released in November 1991; *Bugs: Suckers, Stingers, Sweeties, Swingers*, a 1992 release; and *Christmas and Chanukah*, scheduled for 1993.

Greenbacker is a traditional quiltmaker who has completed over a dozen quilts and numerous quilted wall hangings, including three family heirlooms that she repaired and finished. For Greenbacker it all started with her great-grandmother's Dresden Plate quilt.

"I will be forever grateful to my mother, who somehow managed to keep that quilt," she said. "Mom was separated from her beloved grandmother because her parents divorced when she was twelve. It's ripped and ragged and badly worn, but there's care and creativity in every inch of it!"

Greenbacker lives in Meriden, Connecticut, with her husband and son.

KATHLEEN BARACH, a registered nurse turned journalist, has written for such diverse publications as *RN Magazine* and *The Carousel News & Trader*. Her first book, *The Last Carousel*, the history of one of the few remaining carousels in the country, was published in 1991.

"I collected just about anything but quilts until I fell in love with an 1870s rust and black on white Tree of Life with perfect assembly and quilting," she said. "I still won't quilt on anything but red fabric—it doesn't show the blood!"

Barach and her husband, Donald, live in Cheshire, Connecticut, with two cats, an exotic aquarium, and their carousel horse collection.

Liz Greenbacker

Photo by Kathleen Barach

Kathleen Barach

Photo by Donald Barach